AMC GUIDE TO

Freshwater
Fishing
IN
New England

How and Where to Fish in all six New England States

Brian R. Kologe

APPALACHIAN MOUNTAIN CLUB
BOSTON, MASSACHUSETTS

Cover Photograph: Hanson Carroll
Cover and text design: Carol Bast Tyler
Drawings: Brian R. Kologe

Published by the Appalachian Mountain Club
Distributed by The Globe Pequot Press, Inc., Old Saybrook, CT

"Table Talk," "The Smelt," and "The Eel" from *Verses from 1929 On* by Ogden Nash. Copyright 1942 © 1957 by Ogden Nash. "The Eel" first appeared in the *New Yorker*. "The Smelt" first appeared in the *Saturday Evening Post*. By permission of Little, Brown and Company.

Excerpt from "The 'Sunny' always Shines" by Peter G. Mirick. Copyright © *Massachusetts Wildlife*, 1986. Reprinted with permission.

Excerpt from "Tracking the Wild Trout" by Ted Williams. Copyright © *Massachusetts Wildlife*, 1973. Reprinted with permission.

Excerpt from "Those Weird Little Fishes" by Joseph Bergin. Copyright © *Massachusetts Wildlife*, 1974. Reprinted with permission.

Excerpt from *Trout Fishing in America* by Richard Brautigan. Copyright © by Richard Brautigan. Reprinted by permission of The Helen Brann Agency, Inc.

Library of Congress Cataloging-in-Publication Data

Kologe, Brian R., 1947–
    AMC guide to freshwater fishing in New England/Brian R. Kologe.
        p.   cm.
    ISBN 1-878239-07-4
    1. Fishing—New England—Guide-books. 2. Freshwater fishes—New England.
I. Appalachian Mountain Club.   II. Title
SH464.N48K65   1991
799.1'1'02574—dc20   91–9522
                                                             CIP

The paper used in this publication meets the minimum requirements for the American National Standard for Information Sciences—Permanence of Paper for Printed Library Materials, ANSI Z39.48-1984.∞

Printed on recycled paper.

**Due to changes in conditions, use of the
information in this book
is at the sole risk of the user.**

Printed in the United States of America
10 9 8 7 6 5 4 3   95 96

To Anne and Noah, my angling companions,
and to the memory of Robert Kologe, who taught me to fish
and Vincent Mulligan, who encouraged me to draw.

Contents

Fishing destinations for each species are listed at the ends of the chapters.

Introduction

The water's surface, mirror-smooth or rippling like muscle, divides us from a world of phantoms. Beneath that film, creatures slip through a heavier medium, appearing and disappearing in bright flashes. Fishing has been described as a kind of dreaming, but unlike an ordinary sleeper, the angler awakens with a piece of his or her dream.

I was not raised freshwater fishing, and my introduction began one warm spring afternoon when I adopted an orphaned fishing rod at a yard sale. Armed with a tin of worms and the notion that the only worthy quarry were the trouts and basses, I made my way to a sprawling pond not a mile from New England's busiest interstate.

A tribe of young anglers took pity on me. There were few if any trout, they told me; the state stocked trout in April, but the water was too warm for them to survive long. Nor were there many bass. Nevertheless, these resident experts were catching a variety of fish that they held up one by one and identified for me. Toward sunset, they lent me a small balsa minnow, and I watched the lure send out concentric ripples of distress with every tug on the line. The splash took me by surprise, but even with the keenest attention, there is no suddenness like the strike of a fish. Life itself was telegraphed up the thin line and into my hands. It was a handsome speckled creature that everyone admired but no one recognized. Trundling off to the library, I identified it as a calico bass. Before being asked to remove my trophy from the reference section, I learned that this native of the Mississippi watershed made, as I confirmed that evening, a respectable meal.

As the season unfolded, my fortune seemed boundless. The chain pickerel and yellow perch of May mornings gave way to the bluegill and pumpkinseed of June afternoons and the horned pout of July evenings. On a moonlit August night I even came face to face with the bass that haunted an ancient log in the shallows.

Fishing became a part of a day's picnicking, canoeing, hiking, camping, or bicycling, and a respite from indoor work or a long drive. In winter, ice fishing was added to my snowshoeing, cross-country skiing, and skating. I kept a diary, recording all the conditions that attended a particular catch, or a fishless day, hoping to summarize a bewildering spectrum of variables, and it paid dividends in following years. Despite its arcane vocabulary, elaborate strategies, and curious equipment, I found that freshwater fishing required little more than patience, a license, and some variation on a stick, a string, and a hook. You catch fish by doing something right, by being in the right place at the right time, by knowing the species, the season, even the weather. As skills sharpen with practice, the role of luck diminishes.

But fish or no fish, fishing became my excuse to watch dozens of sunrises and sunsets. Giant snapping turtles, furtive as submarines, watched my every move. Acrobatic bats dodged my line late at night. I witnessed owl attacks and mating blacksnakes, conventions of muskrats and gatherings of migratory geese. In summer the water was carpeted with yellow lilies, in fall its edges were bracketed with purple loosestrife. Even in winter, when life seemed remote, I hammered at the pond's armor and jigged its depths for perch.

As I ranged farther afield, it became apparent that one could fish the region a lifetime and never exhaust the possibilities. There were Cape Cod's sandy lakes, Connecticut's lowland ponds, the Green Mountains' icy streams, the Allagash wilderness, the freshwater oceans of Champlain and Winnipausaukee. Visiting some New England waters was like making a pilgrimage: the Batten Kill or Narraguagus Rivers, Moosehead or the Belgrade Lakes. Despite adventures on distant waters, fishing did not necessarily improve in proportion to how far I drove. There was good fishing within the beltways of Boston, in the suburbs of Hartford, fifteen minutes from downtown Brattleboro, Providence, Portland, and Portsmouth. Over a lifetime, the places one may enjoy most are the more familiar settings.

Throughout these wanderings, I sought a guide to the region's fish and its fishing, some work that would combine natural history and angling history, that would suggest likely places to look for particular fish and likely seasons and strategies for catching them. I examined recent publications and blew the dust off a number of earlier volumes, but since no single work existed, my scholarship began in earnest.

It was among the older works that I discovered the somewhat archaic term "angler," which I use on these pages to bypass the otherwise inevitable fisher*man*. The oldest fishing book in English—

Dame Juliana Berners's *Treatyse on Fysshynge wyth an Angle*, a lovely introduction to the art—reminds us that fishing transcends differences in age, race, class, and sex.

From earlier authors I also discovered that the notion of "sports" fishing, a contest in which fish are regarded as trophies and success is measured by the weight, species, and number of fish brought to the net, is of relatively recent vintage. Dame Juliana, Izaak Walton, and others not only preached restraint, they valued variety. Today, though many anglers concentrate fishing pressure on a few "game fish," New England's waters harbor over thirty fascinating and edible species. To limit fishing to the well-known species is like taking up birding and ignoring all but the bald eagle or the red-tailed hawk.

So, I set out to gather the lore of New England's freshwater fishes, to praise not only the sportsman's trout and bass but to give equal status to the perch and the pumpkinseed, the burbot and the calico, and all those other worthies ordinarily herded into a last ignominious chapter entitled "panfish." I've gone so far as to pursue the angling that dare not speak its name—fishing for what the American sporting press rejects as "coarse"—the massive but subtle carp, the homely sucker, and the nearly indestructible bullhead.

It will come as no surprise that Native Americans took for granted a bounty inconceivable today. Seasonal runs of shad, salmon, eel, and smelt filled the rivers; brook trout and yellow perch swam in the streams and lakes year-round; pickerel, bullhead, and sunfish flourished in warm lakes; and, togue, whitefish, and landlocked salmon lived in deeper, colder waters.

In 1624, Captain John Smith noted that Native Americans fished with spears, nets, hand lines, and bone hooks. Because it was "their ordinary exercise from their infancy," Smith wrote, "they esteeme it a pleasure and are very proud to be expert therein."

Captain Smith beheld an angler's paradise. "What exercise should more delight them than ranging daily these unknown parts, using fowling and fishing," he wrote of prospective colonists, "may they not make this a pretty recreation, though they fish but an houre in a day, to take more than they can eat in a week...and what sport doth yeeld a more pleasing content, and lesse hurt and charge than angling with a hooke."

Only eighteen years later, Miantonomo, a Narragansett sachem, feared that fishing was being destroyed, that soon his people would want for sustenance. Overfishing was not to blame so much as European clear-cutting. As ancient forests fell, the streams silted;

without a canopy of branches overhead, the streams warmed. Brook trout—once common even in Boston's city limits, and a staple of the Indian diet—were an early casualty.

As colonial life became less precarious, cane fishing rods, those symbols of leisure as opposed to commerce, were imported from England. The earliest arrived in 1689, and a few years later Cotton Mather raised his eyebrow at the newfangled gear. "Alas!" he wrote, "the Ministers of the Gospel now *fish,* not with *Nets,* but with *Rods;* and after long *angling,* and *baiting,* and *waiting,* how few are taken!" Mather regarded fishing as "an opportunity for many useful Reflections," but after his boat overturned in Arlington's Spy Pond and he nearly drowned, he was given to morbid speculations about "Satanic Baits" and "the *Hooks* with which the Destroyer proposes to take me." I rather suspect that Mr. Mather could spoil even a very good day's fishing.

A cheerier perspective survives in the form of an anonymous grocery list dated 1757, a wonderful inventory entitled "List for a Fishing Frolick," which includes: "Boat, Rum, Sugar, Lemons, Port, Onions, Pepper, Salt, Meal Bisket, Match, Pipes, Tobacco, Cyder, Water, Iron Pot, Drinking pot, Dish or Bowl, Tinderbox, Hatchet, Frying pan, Hogs fat, Knives & Forks, Spoons, Vinagar, Cucumbers, Bate, Saltfish, Bear, Canoo, Twine, Hooks, Charcoal." This list of bare albeit occasionally cryptic essentials suggests, as many have ventured before and since, that there's more to fishing than catching fish.

By the end of the American Revolution the new republic was already seriously depleting the fisheries. At the beginning of the nineteenth century, dams, overfishing, and pollution had put an end to salmon and shad in many rivers and seriously imperiled the ubiquitous brook trout. With the rising popularity of angling, its practitioners sought to control the excesses of commercial fishing. Pickerel, whitefish, trout, and smelt were netted in such extraordinary numbers that places were fished out. In 1822, Daniel Webster, an avid flyfisher, and newly elected Massachusetts legislator, introduced a bill entitled "An Act to prevent the destruction of Pickerel and Trout, in the rivers, streams, and ponds, within the Commonwealth," which sought to limit freshwater fishing to hook and line. The following year, Dr. Jerome V. C. Smith made an earnest plea for conservation in his *A Natural History of the Fishes of Massachusetts,* the first substantial work on American fish and fishing.

In the nineteenth century, partly as a result of diminishing cold-water species, many self-appointed fisheries managers began introducing exotic species, transforming local waters into cauldrons of experimentation. Thus entered the European carp and the German brown trout from across the Atlantic; the large- and smallmouth bass, the bluegill, and the crappie from below the Mason-Dixon line; and the rainbow trout from west of the Rockies. Some of the new species perished, others competed successfully with native species already stressed by an altered environment. The prolific white perch, originally one of the region's saltwater fishes, was persuaded to extend its territory into fresh water, often with disastrous effects upon neighboring species.

New England's waters are both richer and poorer than they were, and they are still changing. There are arrivistes, usurpers, venerable natives, and those like the Atlantic salmon and American shad that are struggling, with our help, to regain a place in waters they were forced to abandon two centuries ago.

Broadly speaking, New England's waters can be divided into warm and cold. Some species, like landlocked salmon or trout, seldom prosper where water temperatures exceed sixty degrees Fahrenheit. These fish thrive in the infertile, oxygen-rich lakes and streams at higher elevations or in waters fed by cold springs. In contrast, most species—including largemouth bass, pickerel, and catfish—thrive in warmer water, farther downstream or in still lakes and ponds at lower elevations. From the estuaries, an environment alternately fresh and salinated by the turning of the tides, anadromous fish migrate upstream into fresh water to spawn in spring and fall.

This book's chapters are arranged so the reader swims upstream from the estuaries, over the dams and into warm water, and finally up the icy tributaries and lakes of the high country. To help anglers find species near them, the waters are listed by proximity to nearby towns. In northern Maine, ponds and lakes are arranged by county as well.

One final point. While few activities connect us as quickly with primitive food gathering, fishing is not of necessity a blood sport. Today many anglers subscribe to a catch-and-release philosophy, turning loose all they land or whatever is beyond their needs. Closing hook barbs with a pair of pliers makes it much easier to back the hook out and set a fish free. Treble hooks hold fish better but do far more damage.

Fishing with bait usually guarantees better catches than fishing with lures, but because fish take bait with less reservation, they are hooked deeper. Lures, whether balsa minnows, insects fashioned from hair and feather, or plastic worms, demand greater skill and faster reflexes but hook fish superficially and are easily removed. An invaluable accessory is the hemostat, a surgical clamp that locks onto a hook shank and allows you to remove deeply stuck hooks with a gentle twist.

Return your catch gently. Cradle the fish upright until it regains equilibrium and swims off. Avoid penetrating gills or mouth with your fingers, and try not to damage the mucuslike film that coats the fish's scales.

Whether a means to solitude or companionship, fishing should rise above winning and losing, success and failure. It is a skill learned over a lifetime, an exercise that puts one in intimate contact not only with a complex aquatic environment but with oneself. As Thoreau wrote of a neighbor, "his fishing was not a sport, nor solely a means of subsistence, but a sort of solemn sacrament and withdrawal from the world, just as the aged read their bibles."

Part 1

Estuarial Species

1.
Atlantic Salmon

And because the salmon is the grandest fish that any man can go after in fresh water, I intend to start with him...the salmon does not bite at the bottom of the pool or stream, but at the float. Also you may catch him, although he is seldom seen with a fly, at that time when he is leaping, and in the same way that you catch a trout...

—Dame Juliana Berners
Treatyse on Fysshynge wyth an Angle, 1496

The Atlantic salmon, *salmo salar*, is one of the few species of fishes, along with the eel, burbot, pike, and members of the yellow perch and smelt family, that Europeans would have recognized immediately in the New World. At that time its range extended in an arc across the North Atlantic from Spain, Britain, Scandinavia, Iceland, Greenland, and the Canadian Maritimes down through Maine, Massachusetts, and Connecticut as far south as the Delaware River.

In the Old World, the salmon had long been an object of awe, and fishing for it represented the pinnacle of angling. Izaak Walton affirmed Dame Juliana's high opinion by annointing it "king of the fresh-water fishes." (Incidentally, while Walton was assigning fishes a place in the Great Chain of Being, he also crowned the carp "Queen of Rivers.") However, not long after sending their notice and last month's rent to George III, citizens of the new republic did worse than de-throne the salmon, they nearly drove it to extinction on these shores.

When John Cabot explored the coast in 1497, he reported the natives spearing salmon by torchlight. In seventeenth-century New England, schools of Atlantic salmon ascending to spawn were so abundant they had been observed knocking individual salmon ashore in their race upstream. Some were harvested with pitchforks, and many were used as fertilizer. Fishmongers pressured customers to take one salmon for so many shad, just so they could unload their surplus. Dr. Jerome V. C. Smith—physician, mayor of Boston, and early American ichthyologist—reported in 1833 that when farm help negotiated their board, they made it clear they would eat salmon no more than twice a week.

Even then, the salmon's life had been so carefully observed and documented in Europe that it had its own vocabulary. Though they spend their adult lives in salt water, salmon spawn in fresh water, laying their eggs in *redds*, twenty-foot-long nests the female digs with her caudal, or tail, fin. Eggs are laid between mid-October and mid-November, covered with gravel, and hatch in May. Females produce about 800 eggs per pound, which translates to between 4,000 and 19,000 eggs. The hatchlings, or *alevins*, remain near where they were hatched for six weeks, supported by the yolk of their eggs.

When they begin to feed—and only a fraction make it to even this stage—they are known as *parr*. For two years parr live locally and grow into silvery *smolts*, which are a little over six inches long. Smolts leave for the sea between two and four years after birth. In 1963 the submarine USS *Nautilus* discovered that the smolts migrate to the

Davis Straits between Greenland and Labrador. There they batten on herring, capelin, sand launce, smelt, alewives, and the like and return to repeat the cycle one to three years later. (Using this intelligence, the Danish fishing fleet concentrated their efforts there with devastating results for the salmon population. Eventually, the U.S. negotiated a treaty establishing quotas.)

It is commonly held that salmon find their native streams by smell, either of the water itself, or of a pheromone they had left behind as smolts. The early arrivals, those reappearing after only a single season at sea, are known as *grilse;* the older fish are called *bright salmon.* Grilse will weigh three to six pounds, bright salmon slightly more than twice that.

During spawning season the fish cease eating, living off fat acquired at sea. In the fall, after spawning, or in the following spring, a handful of these weary, vulnerable, and depleted specimens, known as black salmon, or *kelt,* find their way back to the ocean. I found one of these struggling in a shallow, muddy channel one fall. The tide was falling, the fish was disoriented, and several gulls had gathered for the end. The pitiful brown creature, mottled with red, fins in tatters, scales abraded from its flanks in patches, still commanded respect.

Unlike the Pacific species, the Atlantic salmon may return to the sea and spawn again, though it is estimated that only a tenth of those that spawn once will endure the adventure a second or third time.

This cycle, which had been repeated in New England since at least the last ice age, depended mostly on clean oxygenated water. Rapids, waterfalls, rocks, and other obstructions were no problem for a fish whose Latin name means "the leaper." At least not until the dams.

"Probably the Connecticut has been more distinguished for this fish," Dr. Smith wrote, "than any other river in Massachusetts, but they are becoming more and more scarce, from year to year. Locks, steamboats, the common business of navigation, and above all, increasing settlements, conspire to interrupt the progress of the salmon towards the headwaters. Still, however, they overcome great artificial obstacles, such as dams, etc. by their muscular dexterity."

Even in Dr. Smith's time, however, the dams were putting an end to the salmon in southern New England. Two Massachusetts dams, one built at Turners Falls in 1798 and the other at Lawrence in 1847, destroyed spawning in the Connecticut and Merrimack rivers. In 1872, when an isolated specimen was netted in Saybrook, Connecticut, local fishermen had no idea what it was.

A little over a hundred years later, in a Newburyport tackle store, I saw an angler enter with a fish he couldn't identify. He had been casting in the surf near the Merrimack's mouth for striped bass. The tackle store owner recognized the fish immediately. She asked wistfully if it had jumped, and the angler nodded, beginning to comprehend what we were all staring at. The fish, with a dark blue dorsal area and flanks like hammered steel, was marked at intervals on the upper half by small black X's. The fish had the characteristic *kype*, or hooked jaw, of the mature male. At fifteen pounds, it was a little above average for our region but small in the scheme of things; the world record, from Norway, had weighed seventy-nine pounds.

In northern New England, conditions went from bad to worse, mostly from overfishing and pulp mill pollution in the nineteenth century. In 1948, prompted by angling interest, Maine began an effort to bring the Atlantic salmon back, and the federal government began matching funds in 1965. Since then Maine has succeeded on at least seven rivers, and nearly a dozen more show promise. In southern New England the effort began over 120 years ago, but because of the greater distances involved (the Connecticut River is over 400 miles long), the water quality, and the number and size of the dams, progress is slow, though promising.

The history of salmon in New England—the neglect, indifference, and greed—can lead a person to despair; on the other hand, the saga of restoration—the millions of dollars and decades of effort, despite very small return—can inspire admiration for the perseverence of both *homo sapiens* and *salmo salar*. Reestablishing the salmon amounts to taking eggs from Canada and elsewhere and convincing the hatchlings that New England is their home, then getting the fish to reproduce here themselves. It means overcoming herbicides, pesticides, dams, hydroelectric turbines, natural predation, and bacterial infection. To achieve this, the government has launched millions of smolts down-stream only to see hundreds, dozens, or fewer return, depending on the year. In 1979 for example, after releasing eighty thousand fish into the Merrimack over a three-year period, a single female returned to the Lawrence Dam.

To further stack the odds in the salmon's favor, healthy specimens are netted, the eggs stripped and fertilized, and once the fish have a good head start, they are returned to the river. (In nature, under the best of circumstances, only 5 percent of the eggs make it to the parr stage.)

In the Connecticut and Merrimack watersheds, fish elevators have long been installed at the Holyoke and Lawrence dams, but it wasn't until 1987 that fish could make it past the dams in both Bellows Falls and Wilder, Vermont, giving them access to their original spawning grounds for the first time since the eighteenth century.

At present the problem is not only getting the parents upstream to spawn but getting the smolts back down through the dam's turbines. Thus far, there is no such thing as a fish elevator that takes its charges back downstream. In high-water years, the smolts, who stay near the surface, simply go over the dam; in low water, they need to be led around the turbines to a safer exit.

At this writing, Atlantic salmon fishing in New England is confined to Maine. Some of the rivers enjoy two distinct runs, one in spring, the other in fall. Salmon begin gathering in the rivers in mid-May though they do not spawn until mid-October to mid-November. Few come up during the summer, but they begin ascending again in the fall.

Salmon fishing's mythology includes the notion that it is an exclusive pastime of the wealthy, but, unlike in Europe or in the Maritimes where one often needs to pay for a guide, a boat, or access to private land, Maine's fishing is public and its rivers relatively small. An angler needs patience and persistence more than arcane skill or equipment. First, you need a license, appended with a special salmon stamp. Because salmon in Maine can only be taken flyfishing, you will need equipment that will handle a fish about thirty inches long, weighing between seven and twelve pounds. This translates into a nine- to ten-foot flyrod, loaded with 150 yards of backing, system 8 to 10 weight-forward floating line, and eight, ten, or twelve feet of 10-pound-test leader.

Unlike flyfishing in the puckerbrush, the banks of most of those rivers resemble golf greens, giving you plenty of room to cast. Productive salmon lies or pools, however, are few, and throughout the season, especially on weekends, anglers queue up to fish them. The pools themselves are inconspicuous sections of water, seldom much deeper than four feet, where the fish pause to rest on their way upstream. Fishing in rotation is the rule. This means holding a place by leaving your rod in a numbered rack and taking your turn. Your turn consists of casting, retrieving, taking a few steps, casting again. In most places if you are a native, you can take twenty to thirty minutes to cover that section of water. If you are from out of state, especially on the smaller rivers, after about fifteen minutes you may begin to hear what impatience sounds like Down East. In the Narraguagus River's Cable Pool, or at Sheepscot's reversing falls, your fifteen minutes may come up only twice a day.

In any case, many flies are cast, few are chosen. One veteran told me that he estimated that an angler got one strike per hundred hours fishing; the Maine Department of Inland Fisheries and Wildlife's estimate is more generous—thirty-eight hours to catch one fish. In an average year only about a thousand salmon make it to the landing net in the whole state. In short, for the casual angler, salmon fishing can be like playing one of New England's lotteries a couple of times a year and praying for a long shot.

In high water, short leaders and wet flies are the rule, ranging from relatively conservative patterns like Jock Scott, Green Highlander, Silver Rat, Mickey Finn, and Black Dose to locally tied fuzzies in Day-Glo colors that would embarrass Peter Max. Sizes run from number 4 down to number 8. In low water, anglers switch to standard trout dry flies like the Rat-faced McDougall, Quill Gordon, or Cahill on slightly smaller hooks—down to a number 10—and longer, finer leaders, up to twelve feet long and down to 5-pound-test tippets.

The procedure is simple enough: if you arrive in spring, clear enough blackflies out of your field of vision to see the river; then cast across current or slightly downstream, mending your line to keep the fly from dragging; when your fly reaches the bottom of its arc, drop it a little and retrieve. For variation you might want to skitter it across the surface once before picking it up. Dig the blackflies out of your ears, collar, and cuffs. Take a few steps downstream. Repeat. Repeat. Repeat.

Whether salmon inhale the fly out of irritation or in response to appetite is still unsettled. One theory is that they are sampling the local forage to see if it tastes like what they remember—to confirm that they have the right address. Unlike trout, they are neither shy nor spooky and will rise through several feet of water to meet the angler's invitation. Salmon rarely strike hungrily at a fly; they may menace it without even making contact, slash at it, whack it with their tails like a striped bass, or just close their mouths around it and move away. After several hours of fruitless casting, the mere sight of an interested fish will provoke the steadiest angler's nerves. It takes the concentration of a Zen master to resist a yank on the line that will either remove the fly from the salmon's mouth, move it out of range, or otherwise alert the fish to something fishy. Anglers schooled in trout need to repress a number of reflexes, most importantly setting the hook as soon as the fish takes the fly. Let the fish send you the signal, then lift the rod firmly, and the salmon will usually hook itself.

A few more caveats. A strike does not a salmon make. One weekend, after countless hours on the Narraguagus, I saw only two salmon take the fly: one leapt dramatically for the benefit of the audience, and both wrapped their respective angler's lines around rocks within a minute and were gone. Once the salmon makes contact, the initial sensation of the hook will bring a violent run and possibly several leaps. Let the fish run and wear itself down a little before even attempting to apply any drag to your reel. If possible, get downstream of a hooked fish, otherwise it not only has its own strength but that of the current in its favor. Rather than stripping line, use your reel to bring fish in. Some anglers swear by those antireverse reels that keep the slack out, especially when the salmon charges the angler.

Though a salmon is certainly an impressive prize to show around the neighborhood—and you are entitled to keep your catch—you greatly increase the species' odds by returning it unharmed. As with trout, barbless hooks help. Try to keep the fish in the water, handle it gently, keep your fingers out of its gills, and if you can't easily remove the hook, cut the line. The hook will eventually dislodge or dissolve.

As a cautionary note, a brook trout can look a lot like an Atlantic salmon parr. The parr will have a forked rather than "square" tail fin, and on its back it will have dark spots on a light background as opposed to light spots on dark. The brookie will also have spots on its tail fin where a parr will have none. If in doubt, release your fish.

MAINE

Rivers and Streams

Bangor and Veazie
Penobscot River

Cherryfield
Narraguagus River

Dennysville
Dennys River

Hancock County
Union River

Lincoln County
Sheepscot River

Machias
East Machias River
Machias River

2.
American Shad

All in the merry month of May,
Where Turner's pouring waters play,
And lash, and dash, and roar, and bray,
Were wont to gather, there and then,
Fishers of shad and not of men.

A simple haul would bring ashore
Some forty, fifty, sixty score

* * *

A few hours toil, and you might heed
Shad piled like hay-cocks in a mead.

—J.D. Canning
"The Shad-fishers," 1854

In late April and early May, drooping white petals appear on New England's shadbushes, makeshift clocks that herald the courtship of the American shad. Birds do it and bees do it, and, as Cole Porter reminds us, shad do it, too. When the rivers warm to about fifty-six degrees, male shad leave the sea and enter fresh water, the females following shortly afterward. Swarming upstream by night, they rest by day in deep cuts near the bottom. Until the water temperature reaches sixty-six degrees, usually in early June, the fish continue to arrive. By mid-June their numbers diminish rapidly.

Though referred to as the "poor man's salmon," the American shad, *alossa sapidissima,* is actually the largest member of the herring family. Arrayed in wide, loosely affixed, iridescent silver scales, shad ordinarily weigh between two and six pounds, growing to two feet or longer. Large females reach ten pounds and more. They enjoy a well-earned reputation as dramatic fighters.

Like the Atlantic salmon, shad ascended our rivers in numbers that astonished early European settlers. In 1777, when Washington's army was starving at Valley Forge, a shad run, harvested by Continental troops armed with pitchforks, contributed to the nascent republic's survival. Into this century, shad were one of the most valuable commercial resources in eastern waters.

In 1896, a record 50 million pounds were landed on the East Coast. However, pollution, dams, overfishing, and habitat destruction severely decreased their numbers, until by 1976 the commercial catch on the Atlantic seaboard diminished to 2 million pounds. In 1849 Thoreau, observing their plight on the Merrimack, wrote "Still patiently, almost pathetically, with instinct not to be discouraged, not to be reasoned with, revisiting their old haunts, as if their stern fates would relent, and still met by the Corporation with its dam: Poor shad! Where is thy redress? When Nature gave thee instinct, gave she thee the heart to bear thy fate?"

Nevertheless, hardier than the Atlantic salmon that swam with them then, the shad can be reared in hatcheries and reestablished in rivers where they have fallen off or even disappeared. Males mature at five years and females at seven, and in our part of their range, the shad may spawn twice or more. Seth Green, known in some circles as the "father of American fish culture," went to Holyoke, Massachusetts, in 1867 and quadrupled the output of the shad in the Connecticut River using hatching boxes. He also introduced them to the Pacific Coast, where they continue to thrive today. Today fish ladders and fish elevators assist the shad's migration to the spawning grounds of its ancestors.

The arrival of the schools are a social as well as a biological event. Seeking a cure for cabin fever, pale anglers emerge from their doorways in April, squint into the spring sunshine, and make their way to the river. At first two or three, armed with heavy waders and thermoses of hot coffee, will tug at their suspenders and todder down to the banks. If they have any luck, more appear the following day until the banks are packed from dawn to dusk.

Although the shad run nearly the length of a river, anglers seem to prefer a handful of rips and channels, and the crowd, swelled a little each year by new blood, bellies up to the cold water in the same places. A carnival atmosphere takes hold as coffee gives way to Budweiser, but for the most part people are well behaved, and joviality, or at worst resignation, prevails. One can also fish from small boats, but inevitably the boats lie crowded at anchor just across from their shore-bound counterparts. Anyone who could discover new and dependable hot spots would do the fishery a great service.

During the year, the shad's diet consists mostly of invertebrate aquatic life, but, like the Atlantic salmon, when shad enter a river to spawn, they are no longer feeding. Why they hit a lure is a mystery, though some people believe it may be either out of reflex or irritation. Shad are most frequently taken on shad darts, small silver or gold hooks embedded in metal cones painted in a variety of colors. The darts are made in hook sizes from number 2 to number 6, with weights from a sixteenth to a half-ounce, the heavier darts intended for swifter current.

Tie your darts singly or in tandem spaced a foot to a foot-and-a-half apart and cast slightly upcurrent. The lower portions of rivers are tidal, so this will change twice a day. As the dart swings downstream it will bump bottom. Retrieve it along the bottom, and with any luck it will pass under the noses of the fish. It is common to snag and lose several darts in a few hours fishing; it is also common to snag and recover someone else's snagged dart. The trick is to skim the bottom slowly enough to get a strike but quickly enough to save the dart. Most anglers give their lines a light twitch, both to keep it free and to give it a little life.

Though anglers use line from 4- to 8-pound-test, give your line weight some thought. Using heavier line may save you a few darts if you are fishing a rugged bottom. If you need to, you can always add lead shot to extend your range. Looping your line through the dart's eye more than once may also allow you to yank it free without losing it. Before you put pressure on it, try wading above where you cast and tugging gently; often this reverses the hook from a sunken log or cleft between stones and frees the dart. If the example of the anglers I have observed is worth anything, profuse swearing helps.

Flyfishing is most effective in relatively shallow water. Anglers use sinking line and wet flies. The patterns are probably the models for the darts. They tend to be foil-wrapped hooks dressed in white feathers and red trim or yellow feathers with red trim. Red beads are also strung on the line to add weight, and a few old-timers add an inch or more of red chenille to the hooks of both flies and darts.

Initially, shad fishing can seem a lot more like roulette. Do not be disappointed if you go fishless while standing ten feet from someone who brings in ten or more fish. Popular wisdom maintains that novices go fishless for at least a season. You will receive copious free advice about time of day or changing lure color. Shad bite—when they bite—morning, noon, and evening. The one time dart color may matter is when the water is murky from rain or wind; on those days the brighter fluorescent colors, chartreuse or orange, may help the fish see the lure. The important thing, as mentioned, is keeping the lure near the bottom.

Because of their delicate mouths, when shad hit a lure anglers must repress the reflex to set the hook with a sharp backward pull. The fish must be played slowly and gently, with the drag free to run out when the fish bolts. Shad will usually jump clear out of the water once or twice on their way in, and the angler quickly discovers how little stress on a line it takes to tear the hook out. One should attempt to land the fish only after it has exhausted itself. Landing nets are an asset.

Despite the fact that the shad's species name, *sapidissima*, means "delicious," most anglers release their catch rather than face removing the more than one thousand tiny Y-bones bristling the shad's flanks. The Micmac Indians claim that shad descend from a discontented porcupine who was turned inside out by the Great Spirit for complaining. Rather than even attempt to fillet the fish, those interested usually wrap the cleaned fish in foil and bake it at 250 degrees for five or six hours, which dissolves the smaller bones. On the other hand, shad roe, a spring delicacy, can simply be fried in bacon fat or butter. The roe sacks contain about a quarter of a million eggs. No one said it better than Ogden Nash:

I'm sure that Europe never had
A fish as tasty as the shad.
Some people greet the shad with groans,
Complaining of its countless bones;
I claim the bones teach poise
And separate the men from boys.
The shad must be dissected subtle-y
Besides, the roe is boneless, utterly.

Given how few New England rivers still have shad runs, we can go into them in detail. In recent years hundreds of thousands of shad have migrated up the Connecticut, a handful making it as far as Vernon, Vermont. A favorite fishing spot used to be below the Enfield Dam near the Massachusetts-Connecticut border, but that dam has been breached, so farther upriver, the Holyoke Dam in Holyoke, Massachusetts, has become the new shad mecca. Anglers have yet to investigate the river between Holyoke and the Turners Falls Dam. One particularly good year, 300,000 shad ascended the Holyoke Dam while only 18,000 continued above Turners Falls. Simple arithmetic puts 280,000 shad milling between the dams. Fishing may be promising here, though it will probably be restricted to boats as there is little shore access.

In the Merrimack River, in a semirural setting, shad frequently congregate in an eddy of the river, just above the Rocks Village Bridge in West Newbury, Massachusetts. Shad, and two of its cousins, the tiny alewife and the larger bluebacked herring, also run at this time. One can often hook the latter on wet flies or darts, while the former swims in schools around your feet. Atlantic salmon, Coho salmon, and small striped bass also pass by this time of year, and all, when in the mood, will hit any small shiny lure dragged under their noses. However, the only legal catches are shad and Coho salmon.

Farther upstream shad pause at the Essex Dam in Lawrence, Massachusetts, under the huge red-brick mills, where anglers have easy access. Another popular spot is below the dam, under I-495, where the Shawsheen River once entered the Merrimack. The Merrimack migration presently ends at the dam in Manchester, New Hampshire (also a favorite spot), but there are plans to help them over, which may make Hooksett the top of their range.

Small, self-sustaining shad populations also run the North and Palmer rivers in southern Massachusetts. Unlike the Merrimack or Connecticut rivers, the North is shallow and best suited for wading and flyfishing. Fishing on the North is also nocturnal; anglers actually cast to spawning shad on their way upriver. Since the numbers of fish are few, it is better to return your catch. Here also, occasionally an angler is treated to a strike from a Coho salmon.

Rhode Island has a very small run on the Runnis River, and restoration is in progress on the Pawcatuck River. Fishing was opened briefly on the Pawcatuck, but at this writing it is closed until stocks grow stronger. Restoration is also underway on the Charles River, in metropolitan Boston, using adult shad from the Connecticut. Fish ladders have been installed in Watertown and Newton, but the population is still small.

In Maine, shad tend to be regarded as trash fish, especially by salmon enthusiasts, but for those who are interested, shad run into Merrymeeting Bay and then up the Cathance and Abagadasset rivers.

MAINE

Rivers and Streams

Abagadasset River

Cathance River

NEW HAMPSHIRE

Rivers and Streams

Merrimack River

VERMONT

Rivers and Streams

Connecticut River

MASSACHUSETTS

Rivers and Streams

Charles River (future)

Connecticut River

Indian Head River

North River

Palmer River

Westfield River

CONNECTICUT

Rivers and Streams

Connecticut River

East River

Eight Mile River

Salmon River

Scantic River

RHODE ISLAND

Rivers and Streams

Runnis River

Pawcatuck River (restoration in progress)

3.
American Eel

I don't mind eels
Except as meals.

—Ogden Nash

American Indians, seventeenth- and eighteenth- century British colonials, European immigrants of the nineteenth and twentieth centuries, all actively sought to make a meal of the sweet and wholesome flesh of the American eel. In Derryfield, a very modest New Hampshire hamlet on the Merrimack, eel were so prominent in the local diet that they came to be known as "Derryfield beef." In 1851 one Manchester native wrote:

> Our fathers treasured the slimy prize:
> They loved the eel as their very eyes;
> And of one 'tis said, with slander rife,
> For a string of eels he sold his wife!

Unlike their forebears, most contemporary New Englanders find the very thought of *anguilla rostrata* repellent in the extreme and consider the remarkable fish inedible. A pity. Izaak Walton noted that "it is agreed by most men, that the eel is a most dainty fish," and there are a few people, usually with Old World roots, who develop an occasional craving for eel, especially around Christmas. Appreciating its flavor and nutritional value, the Japanese began cultivating the eel in 1884 and have returned it to limited favor in New England sushi bars from Greenwich to Portland. On the other hand, the eel's resemblance to a serpent led one British author to describe it as the "least loved of fish." So despite all this culinary acclaim, most anglers still relegate it to the lowly status of live bait.

Though one may argue its value as a table fish, the eel's life cycle makes it one of the most fascinating creatures that swim in our waters. For centuries, people on both sides of the Atlantic puzzled over the creatures because no one had ever seen an eel egg nor seen eel breed. They appeared to completely lack the organs of procreation. Aristotle concluded that they were sexless, arising spontaneously from mud. Other explanations differed mostly in particulars: the eel, they posited, sprang from horsehair, slime, dead eels, and so forth. In 1862, one writer boldly proclaimed that he could hide the truth no longer: the progenitor of the eel was a certain small beetle that lived on the marsh. As late as the turn of this century, biologists confidently wrote, though without having witnessed the act, that the eel bred in our estuarial waters.

In 1922, after searching more than a dozen years, Dr. Johannes Schmidt, a Danish ichthyologist, turned up some surprising facts. Schmidt found that, unlike anadromous fishes like the shad or salmon that live most of their life in salt water and breed in fresh, the catadromous eel leaves fresh water to breed in the ocean. Schmidt discovered that eel, both the American and the European populations, migrate to an area near the Sargasso Sea, about a thousand miles off Florida, to spawn and lay their eggs. No one had ever seen the eel's sexual organs because the creature doesn't reach maturity until it is far out to sea and beyond human observation. We assume the adults die after spawning because they never return.

Despite Schmidt's contributions, there are still a few outstanding questions. For example, the jury is still out as to whether the American eel and the European eel belong to the same species. The American eel has one to nine more vertebrae than its Old World counterpart, but some believe that this may be environmentally determined. In the matter of eels, that ends up sounding beside the point, and we can at least be grateful that we know more now than the ancients.

While perhaps lacking the flutter and poetry of the monarch butterfly's journey southward, the eel's migration is no less spectacular. Mature eel move downstream in the fall, making their way to the ocean and a two- to three-month journey to the Sargasso Sea, hundreds of miles off Bermuda. There the female lays some 20 million eggs. After about a year riding the current northward, the transparent larvae, or *leptocephali* (small-headed ones), not yet four inches long, return to our coasts. They acquire pigmentation while living in estuarial waters and metamorphose into elvers. The male elvers mature, preferring to remain in the brackish water of estuaries their adult lives, while the females continue upstream and take up residence in warm-water lakes and ponds. Female elvers are determined creatures that will leave the water, travel over rock and grass, and even wriggle up dams on their way to their new homes.

Females leave fresh water to spawn after anywhere from four to twenty years in their lakes or ponds. Sexual maturity is believed to be linked to food supply. If they are cut off from the sea, these thwarted maidens are reported to live to a prodigious old age; some are believed to reach thirty or forty years, and one specimen is known to have lived twenty-five years in captivity. Males grow to between one and two feet, while females average about three feet in length. Hence, contrary to what one might suppose, the largest eels by far dwell in fresh water, often miles from the sea.

Adult eels have small conical heads, a single pair of pectoral fins, and most of what remains is tail. A single fin runs without a break from the dorsal, around the tail, and back along the bottom to the anus. Eel are yellowish brown to dark brown on the dorsal side, the ventral being much paler, usually white or yellowish. They should not be confused with the sea lamprey, another inhabitant of our waters, which it superficially resembles. Lampreys are equipped with a round disk of nasty teeth, which the parasitic adults fasten onto other fish.

Eel live in an unsuspected amount of our watershed, finding their way up innumerable small streams into unlikely habitats. While I am not surprised to find them in estuarial waters, I have caught them miles from the sea, while fishing for other species. The first one I caught—if I've correctly reconstructed its route—had made its way up the Piscataqua River, across Great Bay, and up the Lamprey River. From there it went up Pawtuckaway River—not much more than a stream—and ended up in the fresh water of Pawtuckaway Lake, a body of water noted for its annual largemouth bass tournaments. This journey, however, pales beside the migrations of those that come to rest in the Connecticut Lakes in northern New Hampshire. One forty-four-inch, eight-pound individual made its home in Crystal Lake, Gilmanton, New Hampshire, where it was caught by an angler in 1975.

I don't want to unsettle the squeamish, but eel have been known to leave the water at night, not only to migrate but to slither through marsh and low meadows hunting for mice, insects, or frogs.

Eel can be caught any time of year, except in winter when they bury themselves in mud and hibernate. In the fall, the migrating fish, known as silver eels because of their change in color to black and silver, are harvested commercially in nets. Like many other fish, eel cease to feed when overcome by the urge to spawn, so at that time of year, one will only catch immature eel on hook and line. Small wire traps are another means of harvesting eel, at least for bait. The Indians and the early colonials often resorted to spearing eel. In 1832, Jerome V. C. Smith fondly recalled one old revolutionary war pensioner on Cape Cod who hunted them by torchlight.

While I've never met anyone who willfully went after eel with a hook and line (or none who admitted to it), I've known quite a few eel to arrive on the end of a line uninvited. They are usually caught by anglers fishing muddy bottoms for horned pout, white perch, or some other species. They are nocturnal bottom feeders, and their aquatic diet includes shrimp, crayfish, insects, and small fish; they will also scavenge dead animal matter. Worms are the most available bait.

If you are trying to catch an eel, you will need a hook no larger than a number 2 and probably a little smaller. Like horned pout, eel tend to swallow the hook whole after a moment's investigation. If you feel small taps and keep pulling to set the hook without catching anything or losing your bait, you can eliminate perch and assume you are entertaining a horned pout or eel. Unless you hook eel through the mouth, it is almost impossible to disgorge the hook from one of these slippery creatures. While you are trying, it will be tying your line in knots. The quickest expedient is to cut your line and retrieve your hook later.

Even several hours out of water, eels are still full of life, and the only quick way to dispatch them is to put them into a large bowl or pot of coarse salt and cover it.

While the salt kills the eel and removes much of the slime, one still needs to resort to drastic measures to secure the eel for cleaning. Nail the head to a board, as you would a catfish, and tie a string tightly behind the gills. With a sharp knife, cut through the skin behind the string and along the string's circumference. Make other lateral cuts to loosen a flap of skin, then grasp the flap with a pair of pliers and pull the skin off toward the tail. After entirely skinning the eel, remove the head and entrails, and fillet the meat the same way you would any other fish. With the skin off, it becomes apparent that one is definitely dealing with an unusually conformed fish, not some species of vile serpent. At this point, if you cut the fillets into two or three inch chunks, you will have pretty well disguised the identity of your catch, and you may be able to convince yourself and others to try it.

Because the meat is very firm, some recommend, especially with larger specimens, that you may want to simmer the pieces in salt water fifteen minutes before frying them. They can be sautéed in butter; baked, smoked, or pickled in a brine solution; added to a chowder or bouillabaisse.

The American eel's full range in New England isn't documented but is assumed to be extensive. Any body of water with even remote access to a major river system, like the Connecticut, Merrimack, Androscoggin, or Penobscot, probably has a population of females; and estuarial waters, from Connecticut to Maine, have an abundance of males. They are found unexpectedly in large bodies of fresh water like Maine's Moosehead Lake or Meddybemps Lake or Vermont's Lake Champlain.

4.
White Perch

Perch-fishing in the month of May, in brisk water where the run of fish is from nine to twelve inches, is not a whit inferior to bait-fishing for trout...To a man of wholesome, unpampered appetite, it is hard to serve up a better dinner than fried Perch, with good bread and butter, and a little claret.

—Thaddeus Norris
The American Angler's Book, 1865

In Uncle Thad's day, as Norris was known to his contemporaries, the white perch's range was limited in New England to brackish estuarial waters. However, like the striped bass, its closest relative, it is a hardy and adaptable creature, and zealous fishery managers (and a few self-appointed enthusiasts without portfolio) transplanted it into many inland waters entirely cut off from the sea. In these new environs it not only survived but prospered, dominating and even extinguishing what many anglers regarded as more desirable game species. As the white perch population in New Hampshire's Winnisquam Lake grew, for example, there was a noticeable decline in lake trout and landlocked salmon.

The subject of this controversy is so nondescript in appearance that I once heard it described as "your average, generic fish." The great virtues of the white perch, *morone americana*, which is neither white nor closely related to the yellow perch, are that it is easy to hook, a determined fighter, and wonderful to eat. Silvery (though darker in fresh water), it has tough scales and may initially have been confused with the yellow perch because the two species present similar silhouettes and even share some habits. Both travel in extensive schools and can be taken in similar ways with similar baits. Unlike the yellow perch, however, schools of white perch include members of various age groups, so when you encounter a school you may catch fish in a variety of sizes and weights. A large freshwater specimen might weigh a pound and grow to about ten inches. The largest member of the species ever landed, four pounds, twelve ounces, was pulled out of Maine's Messalonskee Lake in 1949.

IN FRESH WATER

In fresh water, white perch spawn in the shallows when water temperatures reach about fifty-five degrees. They are prolific, releasing between one hundred thousand and two hundred thousand eggs and abandoning them on the gravel. Because they compete so favorably with other species in enclosed waters, there are no limits on the size or quantity of your catch.

The white perch's diet in fresh water consists of small fishes, fish eggs (including their own), and larval insects. They are very easy to hook, lacking the nibbling guile of the yellow perch. In lakes and ponds, using a worm or minnow for bait near the bottom will work well, provided you can find the school. On clear, high-pressure days they tend toward the deeper parts, but on overcast days, you will occasionally find them feeding near the surface in early morning or at twilight; at that point they will respond to dry flies or small surface lures such as spinners and spoons. The schools will also feed on hatching mayflies in the spring, just as trout would. On other occasions, when they round up bait fish and drive them into small coves, wet flies and streamer flies like the Mickey Finn or Grey Ghost are a good bet for the flyfisher, and spinners are a good bet for the spincasters.

IN SALT WATER

In estuarial waters, the white perch rises to spawn early in the spring—mid-March in southern New England and a month or more later in the north. The fish actually spawn in fresh water at the farthest point they can reach upstream, when the water reaches about forty-six degrees. In many places, white perch are the fishing season's ice-breaker, giving anglers just enough time to stow their ice fishing augers and find their warm-weather gear. If you don't often frequent the marshes at this time of year, you will want to overcompensate for the weather: it's probably colder and damper than you remember. Dress warmly, bring rubber boots, and pack a thermos of hot coffee or cocoa.

The perch remain a while after the weather warms, and if you crave solitude, perch fishing may also have a particular appeal. When it seems like nearly every other angler on the planet is loaded for trout and barreling north on the interstates, you can continue to fish in peace until at least May.

If you miss the white perch in the spring, it visits again in the fall and on both occasions affords the angler an excuse to visit coastal rivers and marshes that were frigid all winter and overrun by mosquitoes in summer. Bird migrations are in full swing, and there's always something appearing unexpectedly. One afternoon when I was convinced the fish were elsewhere, I was proven wrong by a fellow fisher of greater skill—a harbor seal who bobbed to the surface every few minutes with yet another mouthful of perch.

Though freshwater worms will work on these runs, one will do better to purchase sandworms from bait shops that specialize in saltwater fishing. Small grass shrimp, crabs, and mummichogs or killifish are also part of the white perch's diet and make great bait if you can find them and are willing to pay a little more. A good spot to fish is in eddies, downstream of an obstruction (a large rock, island, or bridge piling), as the tide is beginning to rise or to fall. Perch will often school in the eddies and wait for food to pass. At dead high tide and dead low you won't find much action—in the first case because the water isn't moving, in the second because it often isn't there.

Another strategy, useful in open water or from a boat, is to weight your line with split-shot, cast, allow your bait to touch bottom for a second, then reel it in slowly. This is especially helpful in locating schools in bays and channels devoid of conspicuous features.

On spring and fall evenings, white perch are also attracted by streetlights, and you may see them feeding near the surface in the vicinity of bridges and marinas. A baited hook floated by a bobber is effective under those conditions as are wet or dry flies cast on floating flyline.

Most often, however, white perch hold fairly near the bottom, and setting two hooks about a foot and a half apart, you can catch more than you need in only minutes if the fish are there. Anchor the line at the bottom with a sinker heavy enough to hold, or very slowly drift with the tidal current, and be sure your lowest hook is high enough not to tangle with weeds on the bottom. While hooks as small as numbers 6 through 10 have been recommended, perch will hit larger hooks, and unless you don't mind removing a lot of bluegills from your hook in fresh water or eels in brackish, you may want to go with a larger hook, up to a number 2.

For fishing in relatively still water, jigs dressed with yellow or white hair are effective. It is also possible to flyfish for them under such circumstances, but it requires a pretty fast sinking flyline and a deft sense of the bottom.

MAINE

—— Estuarial Waters ——

Androscoggin River

Eastern River

Kennebec River

Marsh River

Merrymeeting Bay Tributaries

Penobscot River

Piscataqua River

Saco River

—— Fresh Waters ——

Princeton
  Big Lake

Millinocket
  Pemadumcook Chain

Molunkus Township
  Molunkus Lake

Township 7, Range 14, Piscataquis County
  Caucomgomoc Lake
  North end of Chesuncook Lake
  Millinocket Lake

NEW HAMPSHIRE

—— Estuarial Waters ——

Bellamy River

Exeter River

Great Bay

Lamprey River

Swamscott River

Taylor River

—— Fresh Waters ——

Barnstead
  Halfmoon Lake

Barrington
  Swains Pond

Canaan
  Goose Pond

Chatham
  Kimball Pond

Conway
  Conway Lake

Enfield
  Mascoma Lake

Franklin
  Webster Lake

Gilmanton
  Crystal Lake

Hillsboro
  Pierce Lake

Holderness
  Squam Lake

Jaffrey
  Contoocook Lake

Laconia
  Winnisquam Lake

Manchester
  Massabesic Lake

Moultonboro
  Kanasatka Lake

New London
Little Sunapee Lake
Nottingham
Pawtuckaway Lake
Stoddard
Highland Lake

Wakefield
Great East Lake
Lovell Lake
Wolfeboro
Lake Wentworth

VERMONT
Fresh Waters

Burlington
Lake Champlain

MASSACHUSETTS
Estuarial Waters

Agawam River
Bass River
Coles River
Coonamesset River
Eel River
Essex River
Ipswich River
Lees River

Merrimack River
North River
Palmer River
Parker River
Rowley River
South River
Weeweanitic River

Fresh Waters-Rivers

Charles River

Connecticut River (Oxbow)

Fresh Waters-Lakes and Ponds

Arlington
Spy Pond
Auburn
Dark Brook Reservoir
Barnstable
Mystic Lake
Belchertown
Metacomet Lake
Boylston
Wachusett Reservoir
Braintree
Old Quincy Reservoir

Brewster
Long Pond
Lower Mill Pond
Walkers Pond
Bridgewater
Nippenicket Lake
Brimfield
East Brimfield Reservoir
Sherman Pond
Brookfield
Quaboag Pond

Charlton
Buffumville Lake
Clinton
Mossy Pond
Douglas
Manchaug Pond
Dracut
Long Pond
Dudley
Gore Pond
Fall River
South Wattupa Pond
Framingham
Waushacum Pond
Great Barrington
Mansfield Pond
Hadley
Warner Lake
Halifax
Monponset Reservoir
Holland
Hamilton Reservoir
Holland Pond
Hopkinton
North Pond
Whitehall Reservoir
Lakeville
Long Pond
Lee
Laurel Lake
Lunenburg
Massapoag Pond
Lynn
Flax Pond
Sluice Pond
Monterey
Garfield Lake

Natick
Cochituate Lake
Dug Pond
New Salem
Quabbin Reservoir
North Attleboro
Falls Pond
Norton
Norton Reservoir
Winnecunnet Pond
Otis
Benton Pond
Otis Reservoir
Palmer
Forest Lake
Petersham
Pottapaug Pond
Plymouth
Billington Sea
Little South Pond
Long Pond
Rutland
Long Pond
Whitehall Pond
Shrewsbury
Flint Pond (Quinsigamond)
Springfield
Loon Pond
Watershops Pond
Sturbridge
Cedar Lake
Leadmine Pond
Walker Pond
Sutton
Singletary Pond
Taunton
Sabbatia Lake
Wakefield
Quannapowitt Lake

Warwick
   Moore Pond
Webster
   Webster Lake
Westborough
   Chauncy Lake
Westford
   Long Sought For Pond
Weymouth
   Whitmans Pond

Wilbraham
   Nine Mile Pond
Winchendon
   Dennison Lake
   Monomonac Lake
Worcester
   Coes Reservoir
   Indian Lake
Wrentham
   Pearl Lake

CONNECTICUT

Estuarial Waters

Connecticut River
Eightmile River

Housatonic River
Thames River

Fresh Waters

Branford
   Lake Saltonstall
Brookfield

Lake Lillinonah
Danbury
   Candlewood Lake

RHODE ISLAND

Estuarial Waters

Narrow River
Pawcatuck River

Sakonnet River

Fresh Waters

Barrington
   Brickyard Pond
Charlestown
   Pasquiset Pond
Coventry
   Carbuncle Pond
   Quidnick Reservoir
   Tiogue Lake
Cranston
   Mashpaug Pond
   Meshanticut Pond

Print Works Pond
Randall Pond
Spectacle Pond
Tongue Pond
Glocester
   Waterman Reservoir
Johnston
   Oak Swamp Reservoir
Lincoln
   Olney Pond

Newport
Lily Pond
New Shoreham
Middle Pond
North Smithfield
Upper Slatersville Reservoir
Providence
Wenscott Reservoir
Smithfield
Georgiaville Pond
Woonasquatucket Reservoir

South Kingstown
Hundred Acre Pond
Indian Lake
Thirty Acre Pond
Tucker Pond
Worden Pond
Warwick
Gorton Pond
Westerly
Chapman Pond
West Greenwich
Mishnock Pond

5.
SEA-RUN TROUT
Brook Trout and Brown Trout

Old John Attaquin, then a patriarch among the few survivors of the Mashpee Indians, had often been Mr. (Daniel) Webster's guide and companion on his fishing trips and remembered clearly...how this great fisherman, after landing a large trout on the bank of the stream, "talked mighty strong and fine to that fish and told him what a mistake he had made, and what a fool he was to take that fly, and that he would have been all right if he had let it alone."

—Grover Cleveland
Fishing and Shooting Sketches, 1906

Surprising as it sounds today, at one time in estuarial streams from Long Island Sound to Labrador you could bait a hook with shrimp or minnow and catch wild sea-run brook trout. Until the mid-eighteenth century, the Plimoth Colony enjoyed such a fishery, and when Europeans first landed, sea-run trout, or "salters" as they were known, swam in over half of the brackish streams south of Marshfield, Massachusetts, and on Martha's Vineyard as well. In the nineteenth century, Daniel Webster was still practicing his orations on the unfortunate fish that fell to his casts on the Mashpee River.

Accounts of the sea-run's slaughter at the hands of anglers, even if exaggerated by a factor of three, are staggering. In the 1820s Dr. Jerome V. C. Smith reported catches yielding hundreds of fish on the Waquoit, Mashpee, and Quashnut (all Cape Cod rivers), as well as on the Dennys River in Maine.

"It would be well if some who are in the habit of angling here," he entreated his readers, "would remember the petition of the fish in the fable, and release all trout under the size of minnows, instead of basketing every one they catch merely to swell their number, without regard to weight. Beside the detriment to future sport—such conduct is a wanton sacrifice of life, which no true angler will countenance."

Angling was only the tip of the iceberg. It is sobering to realize that in 1833 Dr. Smith already comprehended the effects of sawmills, gill nets, and factories, long before the trout faced massive cranberry operations, pesticides, or the Cape Cod Canal.

"Alas! That the manufacturing interest should clash with the *fisheries*!" he wrote. The fish "are dispersed and degenerated, the waters are poisoned, and the legitimate current of the rivers, like the present course of politics, is forced into new and *untried* channels."

While some of those effects have been reversed, today only about twenty streams in Massachusetts contain wild sea-run brook trout—precarious populations at best. Fisheries personnel and anglers who know the streams usually decline to name them.

Long after the sea-run's numbers had painfully diminished, many anglers were still arguing over taxonomy: was this indeed a true brook trout or something else? Was it, in one writer's words, "a cadet of the noble salmon race, or merely the chief of the familiar brook-trout tribe?" Some anglers have an inexhaustible passion for class distinctions. Thaddeus Norris at first believed they were a distinct species. The Canadian sea-trout, as he referred to them:

fresh from the sea, as compared with the brook trout, has larger and more distinct scales; the form is not so much compressed; the markings on the back are lighter and not so vermiculated in form, but resemble more the broken segments of a circle; it has fewer red spots, which are also less distinct...in color, when fresh from the sea, this fish is a light, bluish green on the back, light silvery gray on the sides, and brilliant white on the belly...the tail is quite forked in the young fish, as in all salmonidae, but when fully grown is slightly lunate.

Others observed that the fishes arrived in fresh water silvery, as Norris describes them, but after a week or two working their way upstream, regained the familiar livery of the brook trout. Norris finally concluded, as did Dr. Henshall and others, that the mystery fish was indeed "the S. Fontinalis gone to sea."

In one respect, freshwater brookies and salters are different: feeding on small marine creatures, as well as insects, the sea-run fish reach considerable size. A healthy freshwater brookie reaches eight to nine inches as an adult, while its marine relative grows to twice that size, sometimes reaching one to three pounds.

It's refreshing to note that the salter continues to be an enigma. Most firsthand observations are more than a century old, and even the fish's seasons are obscure: they spend part of the year at sea, but which part? By one account they enter the estuary in February and March. By another, they arrive briefly in May chasing bait fish and then go back out to sea. A third observer contends that they chase alewives upstream in May, and if the water is cold, they drop back into bays and rise again in October, November, or December when they spawn in freshwater gravel. In some streams they rise to meet the alewife fry that descend in the fall and then continue to concentrate upstream. According to several sources, the committed angler will be bundled up and in his or her waders sampling the salt marsh's cold breath while the sane world is warming its hands on Yule logs.

As for how to catch them, one is also thrown back on old sources or forced to reinvent angling, which, in an age of flyfishing schools and video instruction, may be a very rewarding discipline. In the 1870s Fitz James Fitch, a nineteenth-century sea-run afficianado, noted that "the sea trout will take the same bait, rise at the same fly, and rest at the same hours of the day, as brook trout."

Fitch used freshwater trout flies, though he had them tied a little "more gaudy than the usual," at least for overcast days. His fishing companion A. R. Macdonough adds that "as to flies, the indifference of sea-trout about kind, when they are in the humor to take any, almost warrants the belief of some anglers that they leap in mere sport at whatever chances to be floating...they will take incredible combinations, as if color-blind and blind to form." He nevertheless recommends three general patterns: "the red-bodied fly with blue tip and wood-duck wings for ordinary use, a small all gray fly for low water in bright light, and a yellowish fly, green striped and winged with curlew feathers, for a fine cast under the alders for the patriarchs." To these have been added a number of streamers in number 6 and number 8 hooks including the Grey Ghost Maribou, Mickey Finn, Black Nose Dace, and the Muddler Minnow—or anything else that resembles a mummichog—and the grass shrimp pattern. Anglers fish the top with wet and dry flies or use sinking line to probe the bottom. With spin tackle, anglers use small spoons and spinners not longer than an inch.

Until recently, salters were all but forgotten, and they probably will never attract a large following. Few people have the perseverance to find them, a taste for the season when they run, nor the ingenuity to take a wild fish. Catching and releasing a few in a lifetime of angling will not endanger the breed—that's more likely to be done by development and pollution. And, if one never goes near them, it's comforting to know, nonetheless, that they are still there. While no one knows how many remain in southern New England, a healthy population persists in many small rivers in Maine.

But the "salter" is only half the story. In Scottish and Irish estuaries runs another sea trout, *salmo trutta*, the familiar brown trout that in its marine incarnation grows large enough to be confused with a salmon. In 1960 Connecticut quietly experimented with the brown and had good returns (fish reaching ten pounds) but decided to put their energies into restoring the Atlantic salmon.

More recently Massachusetts tried to establish self-sustaining sea-run brown trout populations. Though the obvious route would have been to import wild trout from Scotland, a quarantine led the Commonwealth to attempt to transform their domestic stocks into wild trout. After fourteen years of running back and forth between the hatchery and the estuary, they had made remarkable progress. Unfortunately, one year a bluefish population explosion—some say seal predation contributed—dramatically slashed returns, and the cost of the project convinced them to go back to stocking domestic browns.

The Massachusetts program was successful enough for Maine and New Hampshire to follow suit. New Hampshire began releasing two thousand brown trout annually into Berry Brook in Rye and later extended the program to some neighboring waters. In the fall of 1986, when their biologists netted a sampling to retrieve some breeding stock, they were momentarily disappointed to find that few fish had exceeded sixteen inches. Before the evening was over, however, an angler hooked, fought, and landed a six-pound specimen. Others report ten- and eleven-pound fish.

These brown trout go out to sea for a portion of their lives, but as with the salters, no one knows how far or for how long. In late September and October—as early as August on the Ipswich and as late as December on the Cape—they return to spawn.

On a clear October evening, with the tide ebbing, I went to Berry Brook in Rye, New Hampshire, to see for myself. At sunset the marsh grass bowed over the mirror-still water, and the smell of sea wrack rose from the mud. My breath hung visibly in the waning light. Not knowing any better, I tried a few random casts until I was interrupted by a series of splashes twenty yards farther upstream. There is some question as to how shy sea-runs are. Some say they are nearly as bold as salmon, others that they are as cautious as their freshwater cousins. The lack of cover was excruciating, but I got within casting range and put a streamer on the edge of the subsiding ripples. Nothing. I tried upstream for another half hour and gave up.

On a small bridge nearby, I met two anglers scanning the water downstream with binoculars. They said that on several occasions spectacular fights had erupted between male sea-runs competing for a female. That was probably what I had seen. They recommended casting to the loser after giving him a few moments to sulk, that a streamer or a wobbling spoon would often receive a vicious, vengeful strike. Overall, however, in all three states, anglers admit to just blindly feeling their way forward with these fish.

I learned later that sea-run browns are most visibly active in Berrys Brook at low water, when they are confined to a few pools, and can be seen herding bait fish into the shallows. Like ordinary brown trout, sea-runs tend to be nocturnal feeders, and anglers fish for them from two hours before to two hours after low tide. You need to husband your movements, keeping false casts to a minimum. Some anglers suggest long tippets tapered down as fine as 6**X**. Flies include Mummichog Muddlers, nymphs, Ghost Maribous, shrimp, and eel patterns. You can also take these fish on light spinning tackle and even on bait, but everyone I spoke to was flyfishing and committed to a catch-and-release policy.

The following year I arrived in time to see an angler running along the brook's edge, rod held high, trying to keep a hooked fish from snapping his leader. He failed.

The combination of tides matching dusk and the scarcity and elusiveness of the fish make sea-run fishing what industry would call a time-intensive project. One angler assured me that it took him a good sixty hours on the water before he caught one.

The most painful moment was a September evening on a remote section of the Parker River in Massachusetts, where I saw one or two fish making distinct rises beneath an undercut bank. They might have been white perch, but if they had been perch I probably would not have left my rod and reel home. I contented myself with watching them sip insects off the surface in the remaining light.

SEA-RUN BROWN TROUT

—— Maine ——

Brunswick
  Androscoggin River
Ogunquit
  Ogunquit River

Whitefield
  Sheepscot River
Yarmouth
  Royal River

SEA-RUN BROOK TROUT

—— Maine ——

Addison
  Pleasant River
Brunswick
  Androscoggin River
Gouldsboro
  Whitten Parritt Stream
Jonesboro
  Chandler River
Lincolnville
  Duck Trap
Machias
  Middle River
New Harbor
  Pemaquid River

Searsport
  Stowers Meadow Brook
Stuben
  Tunk Stream
Whitefield
  Sheepscot River
Whiting
  East Stream
Winterport
  Cove Brook
  Deer Meadow Brook
Yarmouth
  Cousins River

—— New Hampshire ——

Durham
  Oyster River
Hampton
  Taylor River

Newmarket
  Lamprey River
Rye
  Berrys Brook

—— Massachusetts ——

Falmouth
  Childs River
  Coonamessett River
  Quashnet
Ipswich
  Ipswich River

Kingston
  Jones River
Mashpee
  Santuit River
Mattapoisett
  Mattapoisett River

Newbury
Parker River

Sandwich
Scorton River

Saugus
Saugus River

6.
Rainbow Smelt

Oh, why does man pursue the smelt?
It has no valuable pelt,
It boasts of no escutcheon royal
It yields no ivory or oil,
Its life is dull, its death is tame,
A fish as humble as its name.
Yet—take this salmon somewhere else,
And bring me half a dozen smelts.

—Ogden Nash

The rainbow smelt, *osmerus mordax*, known in earlier times as the sparling or frostfish, has been a diminutive autumn and winter visitor to our estuaries for hundreds of centuries. Long before Europeans arrived, it was harvested in considerable numbers. Though the new immigrants would have been familiar with a European variety, *osmerus epurlanus*, which was occasionally eaten, at least by the Scots, this New World smelt was larger and far more readily available.

"Of smelts there is such abundance," wrote Captain John Smith in 1622, "that the Salvages doe take them up in the rivers with baskets and sives." A few decades later, another writer noted that "the frostfish is little bigger than a *Gudgeon*, and are taken in fresh brooks; when the waters are frozen they make a hole in the ice, about 1/2 yard or yard wide, to which the fish repair in great numbers, where, with small nets bound to a hoop about the bigness of a firkin-hoop, with a staff fastened to it, they take them out of the hole."

Just to bring this full circle, in our own time Leslie Thompson mentions a table of young New Englanders in Paris stricken with homesickness by a fragrant plate of *eperlans frites*. Unfortunately, Thompson also notes that Boston Harbor's pollution all but eliminated the smelt from his own neighborhood, though he did see one brave school spawning on the Charles River in 1953.

Pollution, however, was only part of the problem. By the late nineteenth century, the smelt had already been so overharvested commercially in the estuaries that fishing for it by net became illegal in some states. Even today, in Massachusetts, smelt fishing in the estuary is restricted to hook and line, which effectively limits the catch.

A long silver streak runs across the smelt's dark back just before the green dorsal color pales to iridescence along its flanks. The smelt has large scales and a distinctively forked tail, but its profile, the arrangement of its fins, especially the presence of an adipose fin, will look quite familiar to trout and salmon anglers. "They may be regarded as reduced *Salmonidae*," noted Jordan and Evermann, "smaller and in every way feebler than the trout, but similar to them in all respects except in the form of the stomach." One might further press the comparison by noting that smelt, like the more illustrious salmonids, come in both marine and landlocked varieties. Smelt are found in cold, fresh water not only where they were trapped after the last ice age but where they have been introduced as a forage fish to support lake trout and landlocked salmon populations.

A truly mighty smelt may grow to fourteen inches, but the majority never get to half that, seldom reaching a half pound soaking wet, so to speak. Because they are not very ambitious jumpers, they are slowed by the slightest obstructions and brought to a complete halt by the lowest dams. In short, fishing for smelt is for the angler unashamed of his catch's dimensions or athletic prowess. On the other hand, what smelt lack in size they often make up for in sheer numbers. "Given the proper time and place," wrote Dr. Henshall, "and with tackle and bait in readiness, it only remains to cast the baited hook, retrieve the fish, and so on *ad infinitum*."

The anadromous members of the smelt clan spend their summers schooling in the ocean or in bays. Beginning in October and continuing through February, they gather in the estuarial streams in preparation for spawning. It isn't clear what this preparation consists of, except that the male, the smaller of the two, grows tiny tubercules on his sides to help position himself against the female as she expels eggs. In any case, they don't actually get serious about one another until mid-March, after ice-out, when water temperatures rise above thirty-eight degrees. Then the female nocturnally broadcasts between eight thousand and sixty thousand eggs over a period of two to three weeks. Larval smelt pass the summer in the estuary, then enter the sea for two or more years before maturing and returning to repeat the cycle.

Freshwater smelt mimic their salty cousins by breeding in the tributary streams of their lakes. They tend to be smaller than salters— in many waters too small to bother with—and of a paler green hue. Their diet consists of insects, though in some lakes they turn to cannibalism. Most fishing for freshwater smelt is through the ice (see chapter 28, "Ice Fishing"). Keep in mind that although live smelt are often sold as bait, accidentally introducing them into waters where they are not welcome may threaten the fry of other species such as brook trout. See the state regulations issued with your fishing license.

In the estuary, smelt season offers anglers a cure from cabin fever and an opportunity to tour the salt marsh or the lake without the company of biting insects. Anglers fish for them from shore, bridges, floating docks, boats, and finally through the ice.

The plentitude or dearth of both fresh- and saltwater populations differ from state to state, as do rules and restrictions for anglers. In Massachusetts, for example, it is currently illegal to fish for spawning smelt in the estuaries between March 15 and June 15. In contrast, New Hampshire licenses commercial fishermen and allows dip nets as well. However, circumstances change from year to year, so be sure to read state regulations carefully.

Smelt fishing is simplicity itself. Some anglers prefer short stiff rods, others press old fiberglass flyrods into action. I definitely think there is greater virtue in a flexible, lightweight rod. In any case, using sufficient split-shot or a sinker to match the current, bait a small hook (number 10 or number 12) with scraps of worm, clam, grubs, shrimp, live mummichog, or pieces of smelt. A bobber may also help you register a bite. Try fishing a variety of depths until a school is located. Though they may be found anywhere from top to bottom, schools are seldom found in water deeper than twenty feet, and they generally favor areas less than a mile from shore. Be prepared, however, to meet an occasional school off their feed. I offered everything but candy to a huge school milling below a dam one year, yet not a single one was having any of it.

Thaddeus Norris, writing in *The American Angler's Book* in 1865, praises New England's smelt fishery and recommends, of all things, flyfishing. "There is not the least doubt that much sport may be had in angling for Smelts with fine tackle and a light pliant Trout-rod, and that they would take the fly on a favorable day, for they are caught...with hook and line in all the harbors." Norris didn't mention specific flies, but you might try one of the small saltwater shrimp patterns. Like trout, they orient themselves facing upstream but tend to congregate in large schools where the water is slow. They are most easily caught at night, and anglers usually bring a lantern to attract them and a bucket to collect them.

In fresh water anglers use worms, grubs, or snail flesh. Although ice fishing is the rule, they can be caught in very deep, cold water even in summer, at depths down to eighty feet and more.

On the table, smelt are a special treat, though many people prefer the saltwater variety to the fresh. Their sweet fragrance and flavor (*osmerus* translates as "smell" or "scent") has been compared by some to cucumbers and others to violets, but because they are a relatively oily fish, they are best eaten quickly or put on ice soon after catching them. Some people, very few, consume the diminutive fish whole, "everything but the wiggle," in the words of one writer, but cleaning them is hardly a chore. Scale the fish, then remove the head and entrails. Rinse the body in fresh cold water and dry it, then roll it in batter or flour, and fry it in cooking oil. The bones are very small and can be eaten like those of sardines or herring.

MAINE

——Lakes and Ponds——

Acton
    Great East Lake

Allens Mills
    Clearwater Pond

Attean Township
    Attean Pond
    Wood Pond

Auburn
    Auburn Lake

Belgrade
    Messalonskee Lake

Belgrade Lakes
    Long Pond

Chain of Ponds Township,
    Franklin County
    Chain of Ponds

China
    China Lake

Cooper
    Cathance Lake

Damariscotta
    Biscay Pond

Danforth
    East Grand Lake

Davis Township
    Kennebago Lake

Dedham
    Hatcase Pond
    Phillips Lake

Denmark
    Hancock Pond
    Moose Pond

Dexter
    Wassookeag Lake

East Orland
    Toddy Pond

East Otisfield
    Thompson Lake

East Palermo
    Sheepscot Pond

Ellsworth
    Branch Lake
    Green Lake

Embden
    Embden Pond

Enfield
    Cold Stream Lake

Fayette
    Echo Lake

Fayette Township
    Parker Pond

Frenchtown Township
    Roach Ponds

Fryeburg
    Kezar Pond

Grand Lake Stream
    West Grand Lake

Greeley
    Sebec Lake

Greenville
    Moosehead Lake
    Wilson Ponds

Hartland Township
    *Moose Pond (Great Moose
    Lake)*

Hobbstown Township
    Spencer Lake

Island Falls Township
    Pleasant Pond

Jacksonville
    Gardner Lake

Jefferson
 Damariscotta Lake
Liberty
 St. George Lake
Linneus
 Drews Lake (Meduxnekeag Lake)
Magalloway Township
 Richardson Lakes
Manchester
 Cobbosseecontee Lake
Mariaville
 Hopkins Pond
Meddybemps
 Meddybemps Lake
Millinocket
 Pemadumcook Chain of Lakes
Monmouth
 Cochnewagon Pond
New Vineyard
 Porter Lake
North Windham, Sebago Lake State Park
 Sebago Lake
Otis
 Beech Hill Pond
Parkertown Township
 Aziscohos Lake
 Lincoln Pond
Poland
 Range Ponds
Rangely
 Dodge Pond
 Quimby Pond
Rangeley, Rangeley Lake State Park
 Rangeley Lake
Rome
 Great Pond

Sandy River Plantation
 Beaver Mountain Lake
Sapling Township
 Indian Pond
Shapleigh
 Mousam Lake
South China
 Threemile Pond
Stetsontown Township
 Little Kennebago Lake
Sullivan
 Flanders Pond
Sullivan Township
 Tunk Lake
Tauton and Raynham Academy Grant
 Brassua Lake
Township 3, Range 12, WELS, Piscataquis County
 Chesuncook Lake
Township 3, Range 14, WELS, Piscataquis County
 Lobster Lake
Township 3, Range 4, BKP WKR, Somerset County
 Spring Lake
Township 6, Range 8, WELS, Piscataquis County
 Matagamon Lake
Township 7, Range 9, Piscataquis County
 Millinocket Lake
Township 7, Range 2, NBPP, Washington County
 Pleasant Lake
Township 15, Range 5, Aroostook County
 Square Lake

Township 17, Range 5, Aroostook
   County
      Cross Lake
Vassalboro
   Webber Pond
Waterboro
   Little Ossipee Lake
Wayne
   Androscoggin Lake

Wilton
   Wilson Pond
Winthrop
   Maranacook Lake
Woolwich
   Nequasset Pond

NEW HAMPSHIRE
—Estuarial Waters—

Exeter River
Great Bay

Lamprey River
Oyster River

—Lakes and Ponds—

Derry
   Island Pond
Dublin
   Dublin Pond
Enfield
   Crystal Lake
   Mascoma Lake
Errol
   Umbagog Lake
Hebron
   Newfound Lake
Holderness
   Squam Lake
Laconia
   Winnisquam Lake
Madison
   Silver Lake
Meredith
   Lake Winnipesaukee
Nelson
   Granite Lake
   Nubanusit Lake

New Durham
   Merrymeeting Lake
New London
   Pleasant Lake
Ossipee
   Dan Hole Ponds
   Ossipee Lake
Pittsburgh
   First Connecticut Lake
   Lake Francis
   Second Connecticut Lake
   Third Connecticut Lake
Rumney
   Stinson Lake
Stewartstown, Coleman State
   Park
      Diamond Ponds
Strafford
   Bow Lake
Sunapee
   Sunapee Lake
Wakefield
   Great East Lake

VERMONT

—— Rivers and Streams ——

Clyde River

—— Lakes and Ponds ——

Averill
  Great Averill Pond
  Little Averill Pond
Barnet
  Harveys Lake
Barton
  Crystal Lake
Benson
  Sunset Lake
Brighton
  Island Pond
Burlington
  Lake Champlain
Charleston
  Echo Lake
Chittenden
  Chittenden Reservoir
Concord
  Shadow Lake
Danville
  Joes Pond
Eden
  Long Pond
Greensboro
  Caspian Lake
  Lake Eligo
Holland
  Holland Pond
Leicester
  Silver Lake
Ludlow
  Lake Rescue

Marlboro
  South Pond
Morgan
  Seymour Lake
Newark
  Center Pond
Newport
  Lake Memphremagog
North Calais
  Lake Mirror
Peacham
  Peacham Pond
Plymouth
  Amherst Lake
  Woodward Reservoir
Salisbury, Salisbury Municipal
  Forest
  Lake Dunmore
South Poultney
  Lake Saint Catherine
Thetfords
  Lake Fairlee
Tyson
  Echo Lake
Westmore
  Lake Willoughby
Wilmington
  Harriman Reservoir (Lake Whitingham)
Woodbury
  East Long Pond

MASSACHUSETTS

Estuarial Waters

Acushnet
  Acushnet River
Beverly
  Beverly River
Gloucester
  Little River
Hingham
  Weir River
Ipswich
  Ipswich River (Town Wharf)
Kingston
  Jones River
Marshfield
  *Scituate Harbor and Green
    Harbor River*

Newbury, Thurlow's Landing and
  South Shore Bridge
  Parker River
Newburyport
  Merrimack River
Plymouth
  Eel River
  Plymouth Landing
Route 3A
  Hingham Shipyards
Rowley
  Rowley River
Rowley, Wood Island
  Mill River
Squantum
  Boston Harbor Marina

Lakes and Ponds

Ashland
  Ashland Reservoir
Becket
  Greenwater Pond
Concord
  Walden Pond
Huntington
  Littleville Reservoir
Orange
  Lake Mattawa
New Salem
  Quabbin Reservoir

Pittsfield
  Onota Lake
Plymouth
  Long Pond
Sturbridge
  Big Alum Pond
Tyringham
  Goose Pond
West Boylston
  Wachusett Reservoir
Worcester
  Lake Quinsigamond

RHODE ISLAND

Estuarial Waters

Pawcatuck River

Part II

Warm-Water Species

7.

European Carp

The Carp is the queen of rivers; a stately, a good, and a very subtle
fish...And my first direction is, that if you will fish for a carp, you
must put on a very large measure of patience.

—Izaak Walton
The Compleat Angler, 1676

From my diary—7th September 1935...again the float trembles, a
moment and the line slides away ten feet—twelve feet—fifteen feet; I
tighten and the hook sets into something that appears to be uncommonly
solid; then away goes the fish at lightning speed down and across the river
using up most of the hundred yards of line. He pauses under a canoe
occupied by two members of the Audubon Society innocently peering
through binoculars at a downy woodpecker...unaware of the monster held
in leash a few inches directly beneath them.

—Leslie P. Thompson
Fishing in New England, 1955

Leslie P. Thompson witnessed his first carp combat in a pond near Boston's Charles River. A bamboo rod seemed to be propelling itself across the water with a young urchin swimming behind it in earnest pursuit. After a heroic struggle the boy caught up with his tackle and beached his six-pound prize. Thompson confessed that his Yankee upbringing prejudiced him toward the likes of trout and salmon, but his resistance crumbled: the grand fish swept his imagination down the ancient streets of Cathay.

The German, European, or Common carp, *cyprinus carpio*, originally native to Asia, is celebrated in the Far East for its strength and courage. Known in Japan as *Koi*, its effigy, in the form of a kite, is flown on May 5, *Koi Noburi*, to honor the nation's male children; even in our neck of the woods you occasionally see these decorative wind socks swimming from flagpoles or suspended limply from porch eves.

A gargantuan member of the minnow family, the carp's flanks are covered with large overlapping scales. On the dorsal side, they look like anodized metal, from greenish to bronze in color, becoming paler as they progress down to the ventral. Around its relatively small mandarin mouth, it sports four barbels. Carp tolerate pollution, low oxygen levels, freezing winters, blistering summers, and survive twenty to fifty years. In our waters they grow to between three and fifteen pounds, though domesticated specimens occasionally reach up to fifty pounds, which puts them among our heftiest fish.

The carp enjoys a worldwide reputation for its extraordinary ability to rapidly transform fodder into edible flesh, making it an ideal food fish, a kind of swimming pig. In ideal conditions, carp can gain up to three pounds a year. Because it could also endure long journeys under less than ideal conditions, over the centuries the wandering carp has colonized the world. It arrived in Europe around A.D. 1200 and was well known and much praised in Walton's England. The world's angling record, eighty-three pounds, was caught in South Africa.

New Englanders began importing the carp in a haphazard way in the 1830s as an ornamental and table fish. It was an era when Americans seemed to think they could introduce whatever species of fish wherever they wanted with impunity. Dr. Jerome V. C. Smith praised the aesthetic qualities of the carp, writing, "there are basins of water in every direction, in the immediate vicinity of Boston, of no kind of use whatever, at present, that might be most valuable appendages to an estate, by stocking them with pickerel or carp. There is a pond in Brookline, in which beautiful specimens may be seen, coursing along the margin."

Alas, that was just the beginning. In 1876, the U.S. Fish Commission began a campaign of importing carp from Germany, breeding them in the capital, and allowing congressmen to graciously seed them into the waters of their unsuspecting constituency. For better or worse the carp came to New England—and stayed.

While American fishing sensibilities have been in some measure imitations of British tastes (certainly where the salmon and trout are concerned), the lengths to which some of Walton's descendants will go to catch a carp today would horrify most self-respecting American anglers. There are carp journals, carp fishing tournaments, and a devoted catch-and-release policy. Regardless of the reverence carp inspire across the sea, carp fishing in America is now perceived as less than socially acceptable. Bluntly put, it smacks of poverty and recent immigration; one might go so far as to describe carp fishing as the angling that dares not speak its name.

However, before you dismiss carp as rough or coarse, keep in mind that it is no pushover. An elusive quarry, it will put quite a bend in your rod before you bring it to bay—if you can get it to strike to begin with. Walton writes of a friend, "a very good fisher," who angled "diligently four or six hours in a day, for three or four days together, for a river carp, and [did] not have a bite..." Keen of sight and hearing, laboratory tests suggest that carp are relatively intelligent fish in possession of good memories—once hooked, twice shy. They also seldom want for food.

Carp inhabit a variety of fresh and brackish waters but seem most content in warm, slow-moving rivers. Unlike many of its fellows, the carp likes its salad: a large portion of its formidable diet is aquatic vegetation. Unfortunately, this appetite can make them extremely disruptive, if not outright fatal, to the ecology of enclosed waters like ponds and lakes. Carp remove oxygen-generating plant life from the water and stir up clouds of mud on the bottom; it is less clear whether they also eat other fishes' eggs. In short, what you do with any carp you catch is your business; it's unlikely anyone from Greenpeace will interfere. On the other hand, if we continue to pollute our waters and demolish what remains of our fisheries, the humble carp will very likely be the only fish we have left.

Come spring, carp spawn in the shallows, and one can witness their boisterous, enthusiastic coupling starting in May in southern New England and a month or more later in the north. The female, depending on her size, can broadcast over 2 million eggs. Spawning inspires an awesome appetite in carp, and in the week or two following they are reputed to eat nearly their weight. Their feeding soon moderates and they make their way into deeper waters, sometimes more than twenty feet, but continue to feed well into the fall.

Most carp fishing is attended in the evening, at night, or early morning, occasionally on overcast or rainy days. When fishing the surface, float your bait and add a light quill bobber above it. (Leslie Thompson favored porcupine quills for this.)

Despite their conspicuous appearances on hot still days, when they roll along the surface like indolent hippos, carp feed principally off the bottom, sucking up vegetation and whatever other provender comes with it. For bottom-fishing try a single very small split-shot above your hook; if you are fishing in current, anchor it with the smallest slip sinker that will hold the bottom. A better alternative is a sliding quill bobber or, if you need to get your bait out a ways, one of those bubble bobbers that can be partly filled with water.

Chumming, or as the English call it, ground-baiting, is commonly practiced to attract carp. Some anglers pour the juice from canned corn with a handful of kernels into the water and then bait their hooks with a couple of the remaining kernels. Walton recommends casting chewed bread on the waters to help attract and deliver the quarry to your hook.

Though carp feed largely by smell, they don't require the bullhead's catalogue of the long dead, ripe, or vile. Baits include peas, beans, berries, half-boiled potato, dough balls, corn kernels, worms, marshmallows, and small mollusks or crustaceans. Whatever you choose, it should no more than cover the tip and half the shank of a number 8 or 6 hook; carp, for all their bulk, have relatively tiny mouths and a very delicate bite. Line weight between 6- and 8-pound-test should be satisfactory, unless you think you will be engaging monsters, in which case you might go to 10 or 12.

To keep the fish from detecting untoward pressure on the bait, keep the tip of your rod pointed toward the bait. Some anglers keep the bailers on their reels open, closing them and setting the hook only when the fish moves off with the bait. In any case, when you see the bobber register contact, allow the fish to move off a ways before striking: carp have a habit of daintily carrying a morsel in their lips, even dropping it and picking it up again, before eating it.

There seems to be a tradition of ease associated with carp fishing. Essential equipment includes lawn chairs, picnic baskets, and forked sticks to prop up your rod. I think the principle here is fighting indolence with indolence. On the other hand, if you leave your rod unattended, you might find it absent when you return. Once hooked, carp make a beeline for deep water and are smart enough to look for something to wrap your line around if you're not paying attention. Their strength is not to be underestimated.

Those lacking the requisite patience, attention span, or light touch that this kind of still-fishing demands might be interested to know that several New England states permit hunting the carp with bow and arrow, even with spears. (You will be obliged, however, to draw the line at explosives.)

As with everything else involving carp, considerable controversy surrounds its appropriateness on American tables. For what it's worth, Euell Gibbons praises them in *Stalking the Wild Asparagus* but notes that out West where he grew up, the popular instructions for carp preparation were to bake it in cow manure, then discard the carp. Walton would have differed with this low estimation; he liked his simmered in claret and flavored with herbs, oysters, and anchovies.

In Europe, especially in Eastern Europe, and in Asia, the gustatory qualities of carp are widely recognized. Carp are cultivated commercially in European ponds and appear, along with whitefish, in gefilte fish. With the enduring popularity of Asian cooking in New England, it is surprising that anglers are not more interested in this massive creature. More than a few people have paid dearly to see them swimming in sweet-and-sour sauce in Chinese and Korean restaurants.

Before consuming your catch, first be sure that the water you took it from is reasonably clean. Fillet the fish, remove the skin and dark flesh, then either bake, broil, or smoke it. It can also be put into fish cakes or chowder.

MAINE

Kennebec River   Merrymeeting Bay

NEW HAMPSHIRE

Rivers and Streams

Merrimack River

Lakes and Ponds

Masconoma Lake

VERMONT

Rivers and Streams

Connecticut River   Winooski River

Lakes and Ponds

Burlington
  Lake Champlain

MASSACHUSETTS

Rivers and Streams

Charles River (esp. Silk Mill Pool,   Lower Ipswich River
  Needham, and Moody Pool,   Merrimack River
  Waltham)

Lakes and Ponds

Boston   Pittsfield
  Jamaica Pond   Onota Lake
Foxborough   Shrewsbury
  Sunset Lake   Flint Pond (Quinsigamond)
Lee   Springfield
  Laurel Lake   Watershops Pond
Methuen   Stow
  Forest Lake   Delaney Pond
Natick   Worcester
  Dug Pond   Indian Lake

CONNECTICUT

Rivers and Streams

Connecticut River

RHODE ISLAND

Lakes and Ponds

Cranston
  Fenner Pond
  Mashapaug Pond
  Spectacle Pond
  Tongue Pond

Providence
  Upper Canada Pond
  Wanskuck Pond
  Wenscott Reservoir

Smithfield
  Georgiaville Pond

8.
Horned Pout or Bullhead Catfish

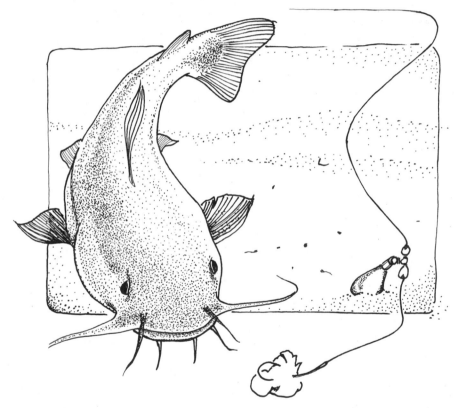

The Horned Pout, *Pimelodus nebulosus*, sometimes called Minister, from the peculiar squeaking noise it makes when drawn out of the water, is a dull and blundering fellow, and like the eel vespertinal in its habits, and fond of mud. It bites deliberately as if about its business.

—Henry David Thoreau
A Week on the Concord and Merrimack Rivers, 1849

Thoreau, seldom praised for sociability himself, further defames horned pout, calling them "a bloodthirsty and bullying race of rangers, inhabiting the fertile river bottom, with ever a lance in rest, and ready to do battle with their nearest neighbor." He seems to base this notion of the pout's belligerence on the long scars he observed on their backs, but after seeing several in the clutches of ospreys, eagles, and even gulls, I am inclined to believe that Thoreau's battered specimens may merely have been victims of attempted aerial predation.

Three species, collectively known as horned pout, reside in New England: the native brown bullhead, *ictalurus nebulosus*; the yellow bullhead, *ictalurus natalis*; and the black bullhead, *ictalurus melas*. The most common local variety by far is the brown bullhead. The brown is nearly indistinguishable from its much rarer black cousin, who arrived from the Midwest. The yellow bullhead (mostly concentrated in the Merrimack watershed) has white barbels and a longer anal fin than the brown. Anglers tend to ignore these distinctions, and so, while we will concentrate on the brown bullhead, what follows generally describes the behavior and habitat of all three species.

Horned pout are commonly found in warm, still, or slow-moving waters throughout New England all the way up to Maine. They thrive in eutrophic ponds that are on their way to becoming overgrown with aquatic weeds. Three words come up over and over in descriptions of horned pout: tenacious, omnivorous, and ubiquitous. New England fisheries and wildlife departments encourage taking them and waive catch limits; adult pout have few enemies and their large populations tend to be stunted and to compete with other species.

Horned pout are often dismissed as humble creatures: homely, plentiful, easily caught, indiscriminate bottom feeders, and by one description possessing all the ferocious game qualities of an "animated brick." Not exactly the sort of fish one pictures sportsmen such as Zane Grey wrestling to the boat, but then, somewhat less heroic figures like Grover Cleveland were not embarrassed to fish for pout in the Berkshire lakes. According to a pamphlet prepared by the Massachusetts Division of Fisheries and Wildlife, "Too many people overlook bullheads. They are not as flashy as pike nor do they have the press corps appeal of trout, but they're there. It's just that bullheads are not as visible as perch, pumpkinseeds or bass, perhaps because they are bottom dwellers, night feeders and basically solitary."

In any case, these creatures are one of late spring's unsung pleasures. Caught early in the season, dipped in batter and deep-fried, horned pout number among the sweetest meals one can take from the region's waters. Once the waters warm, pout are much easier to catch, but their firm beef-red flesh softens and acquires a weedy or muddy taste. Soaking the flesh overnight in water with two tablespoons of vinegar and one tablespoon of salt supposedly removes the muddy flavor, but I've yet to try it. This should be done in a refrigerator and the fish should be rinsed before cooking.

Since they remain fairly torpid when the water is below sixty degrees, the period in which they are both active and at the peak of their flavor is limited to a month or two at best. This ideal period is over in the pout's southern range—Massachusetts, Rhode Island, and Connecticut—by mid- to late-June, though it lasts well into August in northern Maine, New Hampshire, and Vermont.

In the spring and summer, bullheads approach the shore and deposit up to ten thousand sticky eggs in shallow nests that the females have excavated with their fins. During that season, the adults clean the eggs by taking them into their mouths and spewing them back out into the nest, then fan them with their fins to aerate them. Thoreau observed the adults shepherding their inch-long progeny around the shallows in great schools, "caring for them as a hen cares for her chickens." It is even said that when the fry are threatened, they hide in the parents' mouths until danger is past.

While their relations below the Mason-Dixon line may reach upwards of five pounds, New England specimens seldom weigh a fifth of that. Full grown at three or four years, native horned pout grow seven to twelve inches long. But the New England pout contends not only with very warm water in summer (up to ninety degrees) and low oxygen levels (down to one part per million) but with winterkill conditions that sometimes eliminate many of its supposedly nobler neighbors.

In 1833, Dr. Jerome Van Crowninshield Smith, once mayor of Boston, gave the following account of the horned pout's durability, along with a very curious view of goings-on at Boston City Hall:

> They are exceedingly tenacious of life—their vitality is so low, and their constitution so peculiar, that they may be partially frozen without destruction. The past winter the writer, by accident, left two pouts in a small tin pail, in an upper apartment of the City Hall, in the month of December, during a severely cold night; and in the morning they were found frozen closely in the ice. After being

exposed to the warmth of a stove with reference to emptying the vessel, to our utter amazement the fishes revived, and are now tenants of a cistern in Battery March Street.

Part of their tolerance for waters that would suffocate other species is due to their ability to absorb atmospheric oxygen through their skin and to gulp it from the surface and absorb it through the air bladders they use for buoyancy. Even if a pond dries up, they may survive by burying themselves in the mud, secreting a mucuslike substance to protect their skin, and lying in hibernation until water returns. Their tolerance for pollution has led medical researchers to use them as laboratory animals. As a result of their hardiness, it usually doesn't take long to fill a bucket or burlap bag with horned pout.

Although most active between dusk and midnight and again near dawn, horned pout will occasionally hit on overcast days. In most waters they will burrow into the mud during the day, but those that can find refuge in deep holes will continue to feed. One year the Commonwealth of Massachusetts noted that over seven thousand pout were taken from the Quabbin Reservoir during daylight hours. If you choose to go pout fishing at night, especially by boat, be sure you get the lay of the water beforehand, as darkness alters appearances to an unexpected degree.

In the spring, horned pout head into the shallows looking for snails, crustaceans, and other creatures among the weeds. Nevertheless, you need not go to any effort to match their natural diet. Recommended baits include worms, kernels of corn, chicken entrails, dough balls, ripe cheese, live or dead minnows, even brown laundry soap. In the horned pout the sense of smell, taste, and touch seem merged, at least from a human perspective. They locate food with some one hundred thousand taste receptors distributed over their skin. They also use the six barbels, or "whiskers," around their mouths, from whence the name "catfish," to investigate things closer up.

The stronger smelling the bait, the quicker they will strike. Bait and tackle stores sell "stink baits," strong-smelling substances that increase your bait's appeal. Some anglers sweeten their bait with drops of the anise flavoring used in baking and swear by the results. Others attract pout by lowering a punctured can of cat food to the bottom on a string—just be sure to leave with your can.

Your tackle need be no more sophisticated than your bait. Thoreau remembered catching them as a boy with a thread strung with worms—the thread would catch on their tiny teeth. If you are really intent on playing Huck Finn, you could probably manage with a sturdy branch or cane pole, a few yards of line, a number 4 or number 6 hook, and a small piece of split-shot secured a foot above to lend it weight. Otherwise any spinning or spincasting outfit will do. If you are ambitious, you may use a one-half-ounce bell sinker at the end of your line and space two or three hooks a foot and a half apart. Attaching a submerged bobber above the hooks will keep tension on the line.

Horned pout respond to bait rather than lures, and because their lips are bony, they tend to be hooked deeper down than most fish, so catching and releasing them unharmed is difficult. If you are fishing for horned pout, you are fishing for food. Don't strike immediately, but allow the fish to swallow the bait entirely. Exercise care in handling your catch. The dorsal and pectoral fins behind the head conceal sharp spines coated with an irritating venom—the horn, or "lance in rest," to which Thoreau refers. If you do get a puncture, a dab of clear household ammonia will relieve the sting.

Use a hook disgorger or needle-nose pliers to remove hooks, and keep in mind that those jaws are much stronger than they look. Though long-shanked hooks are easier to remove, you may be better off retrieving deeply lodged hooks later. Buying a package or two of inexpensive hooks and removing them when cleaning the fish saves you struggling in the dark. A flashlight and an old towel for grasping your catch are also useful accessories. Anglers intent on making a night of it bring lanterns, lawn chairs, picnic hampers, and a forked stick to support their rod. The really hard cases dangle a bell off the end of their rod tips to wake them when there's a strike.

The bullhead's smooth, slick, scaleless skin makes cleaning it a chore, but it's worth the trouble. Use a sharp knife and peel the skin off in strips with a pair of pliers. Some people nail the pout's head to a board to accomplish this. Since it is a small fish, you may choose not to fillet it but to fry the cleaned portion whole after removing the head, fins, guts, and skin. Cut into cubes, it also comes recommended as an ingredient in cream and corn chowders. Like bluegill, horned pout is a good species for children to catch, provided you are there to handle the fish itself.

MAINE

Lakes and Ponds

Allens Mills
Clearwater Pond

Attean
Wood Pond

Auburn
Auburn Lake

Belgrade
Messalonskee Lake
Salmon Lake

Belgrade Lakes
Long Pond

Bridgton
Highland Lake

China
China Lake

Crawford
Crawford Lake

Damariscotta
Biscay Pond

Danforth
East Grand Lake

Denmark
Hancock Pond
Moose Pond

Dexter
Wassookeag Lake

East Orland
Toddy Pond

East Otisfield
Thompson Lake

East Palermo
Sheepscot Pond

Ellsworth
Branch Lake
Green Lake

Embden
Embden Pond

Enfield
Cold Stream Lake

Fayette
Echo Lake

Fayette Township
Parker Pond

Frenchtown Township
Roach Ponds

Fryeburg
Kezar Pond
Lovewell Pond

Glenwood Plantation
Wytopitlock Lake

Grand Lake Stream
West Grand Lake

Greenville
Moosehead Lake
Wilson Ponds

Hartland Township
Moose Pond (Great Moose Lake)

Hermon
Hermon Pond

Island Falls Township
Pleasant Pond

Jacksonville
Gardner Lake

Jefferson
Damariscotta Lake

Lakeville
Junior Lake

Liberty
St. George Lake

Lincoln
Mattanawcook Pond

Magalloway Township
Lower Richardson Lake

Manchester
  Cobbosseecontee Lake
Millinocket
  Pemadumcook Chain of Lakes
Monmouth
  Cochnewagon Pond
New Vinyard
  Porter Lake
North Windham
  Little Sebago Lake
Orono
  Pushaw Lake
Orrington
  Brewer Pond
Poland
  Range Ponds
Princeton
  Pocomoonshine Lake
Rangeley, Rangeley Lake State
  Park
  Rangeley Lake
Readfield
  Torsey Pond
Rome
  Great Pond
Sapling Township
  Indian Pond
North Windham, Sebago Lake
  State Park
  Sebago Lake
Shapleigh
  Mousam Lake
Smithfield
  East Pond
  North Pond
South China
  Threemile Pond
Township 3, Range 12 WELS,
  Piscataquis County
  Chesuncook Lake

Township 3, Range 14, WELS,
  Piscataquis County
  Lobster Lake
Township 6, Range 1, NBPP,
  Penobscot County
  Scraggly Lake
Township 6, Range 8, WELS,
  Piscataquis County
  Matagamon Lake
Township 7, Range 2, NBPP,
  Washington County
  Pleasant Lake
Township 7, Range 9, Piscataquis
  County
  Millinocket Lake
Township 7, Range 13, WELS,
  Piscataquis County
  Chamberlain Lake
Township 7, Range 14,
  Piscataquis County
  Caucomgomoc Lake
Townships 11-12, Range 11,
  Aroostook County
  Musquacook Lake (4th)
Township 14, Range 8, WELS,
  Aroostook County
  Fish River Lake
Township 16, Range 5, WELS,
  Aroostook County
  Square Lake
Township 17, Range 5, Aroostook
  County
  Cross Lake
Township 27, ED BPP
  Big Lake
Township 40 MD, Hancock
  County
  Nicatous Lake
Township 43, MD BPP,
  Washington County
  Third Machias Lake

Vassalboro
Webber Pond

Waterboro
Little Ossipee Lake

Wayne
Androscoggin Lake

Wilton
Wilson Pond

Winthrop
Maranacook Lake

Woolwich
Nequasset Pond

NEW HAMPSHIRE

Rivers and Streams

Androscoggin River (Pontook Flowage)
Connecticut River

Exeter River
Lamprey River
Merrimack River

Lakes and Ponds

Amherst
Baboosic Lake

Barnstead
Halfmoon Lake
Lower Suncook Lake
Upper Suncook Lake

Barrington
Ayers Lake
Swains Pond

Chesterfield
Spofford Lake

Conway
Conway Lake

Deering
Deering Reservoir

Derry
Island Pond

Dublin
Dublin Pond
Thorndike Pond

Errol
Akers Pond
Umbagog Lake

Franklin
Webster Lake

Gilmanton
Crystal Lake
Manning Lake
Sunset Lake

Grafton
Grafton Pond

Harrisville
Silver Lake

Holderness
Little Squam Lake
Squam Lake
White Oak Pond

Jaffrey
Contoocook Lake

Kingston
Country Pond
Kingston Lake

Laconia
    Winnisquam Lake
    Paugus Bay
Madison
    Silver Lake
Manchester
    Massabesic Lake
Meredith
    Lake Waukewan
    Lake Winnipesaukee
    Pemigewasset Pond
    Wickwas Lake
Nelson
    Granite Lake
New Durham
    Merrymeeting Lake
New London
    Little Sunapee Lake
    Pleasant Lake
Northwood
    Jenness Pond
    Northwood Lake
Nottingham, Pawtuckaway State Park
    Pawtuckaway Lake
Ossipee
    Dan Hole Ponds
    Ossipee Lake
Pittsburgh
    Lake Francis
    Second Connecticut Lake

Rindge
    Lake Monomonac
Salem
    Arlington Mills Reservior
Stoddard
    Highland Lake
Strafford
    Bow Lake
Sunapee
    Sunapee Lake
Tamworth
    Chocorua Lake
Wakefield
    Great East Lake
    Lovell Lake
    Pine River Pond
    Province Lake
Warren
    Lake Tarleton
Washington
    Ashuelot Pond
    Island Pond
Weare
    Horace Lake
Webster
    Lake Winnepocket
Windham
    Canobie Lake
Wolfeboro
    Lake Wentworth
    Mirror Lake

VERMONT

—— Rivers and Streams ——

Barton River
Black River

Clyde River
Connecticut River

Hubbardton River
Lamoille River
Lemon Fair River
Lewis Creek

Missisquoi River
Otter Creek, Little Otter Creek
Rock River
Winooski River

—— Lakes and Ponds ——

Addison
    Dead Creek
Belmont
    Star Lake
Benson
    Sunrise Lake
    Sunset Lake
Brighton
    Island Pond
    McConnell Pond
    Spectacle Pond
Brimfield
    Sherman Pond
Bristol
    Winona Lake
Burlington
    Lake Champlain
Cabot
    Mollys Falls Pond
    Mollys Pond
Castleton, Lake Bomoseen State Park
    Lake Bomoseen
Charleston
    Pensioner Pond
Chittenden
    Chittenden Reservoir
Craftsbury
    Great Hosmer Pond
    Little Hosmer Pond
Danby
    Danby Pond

Danville
    Joes Pond
Derby
    Brownington Pond
Derby Center
    Lake Derby
East Brighton
    Nulhegan Pond
Eden
    Long Pond
Eden Mills
    Lake Eden
Elmore, Elmore State Park
    Lake Elmore
Essex
    Indian Brook Reservoir
Fairfield
    Fairfield Pond
Fernville
    Fern Lake
Fletcher
    Metcalf Pond
Franklin, Lake Carmi State Park
    Lake Carmi
Garfield, Morrisville Village Forest
    Green River Reservoir
Glover
    Daniels Pond
    Shadow Lake
Goshen
    Sugar Hill Reservoir

Greensboro
  Horse Pond
  Long Pond
Groton, Groton State Park
  Ricker Pond
Hardwick
  Hardwick Lake
Hinesburg
  Lake Iroquois
Holland
  Beaver Pond
Hortonville
  Lake Nineveh
Hubbardton
  Beebe Pond
  Halfmoon Pond
Leicester
  Silver Lake
Londonderry
  Lowell Lake
Lunenburg
  Neal Pond
Marlboro
  Sunset Lake
Marshfield
  Marshfield Pond
Milton
  Arrowhead Mountain Lake
Monkton Ridge
  Cedar Lake
Newport
  Clyde Pond
  Lake Memphremagog
North Montpelier
  North Montpelier Pond
Peacham
  Fosters Pond
Salisbury, Salisbury Municipal
  Forest
  Lake Dunmore

Shelburne
  Shelburne Pond
Shoreham
  Richville Pond
Somerset
  Somerset Reservoir
South Poultney
  Lake St. Catherine
South Ryegate
  Ticklenaked Pond
South Woodbury
  Sabin Pond
Stratton
  Grout Pond
  Stratton Pond
Sudbury
  Burr Pond
  Lake Hortonia
Tinmouth
  Chipman Lake
Walcott
  Walcott Pond
Walden
  Lyford Pond
Wallingford
  Wallingford Pond
Wells
  Little Pond
West Castleton
  Glen Lake
West Glover
  Lake Parker
West Milton
  Long Pond
Wheelock
  Flagg Pond
Whitingham
  Sadawga Pond

Winhall
  Gale Meadows Pond

Windsor
  Lake Runnemede

Woodbury
  Lake Greenwood

Worcester
  Worcester Pond

MASSACHUSETTS

—— Rivers and Streams ——

Merrimack River

—— Lakes and Ponds ——

Amesbury
  Lake Gardner

Amherst
  Factory Hollow Pond

Andover
  Foster's Pond

Arlington
  Spy Pond

Ashburnham
  Lower Naukeag Pond
  Stodge Meadow Pond
  Winnikeag Lake

Ashland State Park
  Ashland Reservoir

Auburn
  Dark Brook Reservoir
  Eddy Pond

Ayer
  Sandy Pond

Barnstable
  Chequaquet Lake

Beartown State Forest
  Benedict Pond

Becket
  Center Pond

Belchertown
  Metacomet Lake

Bellingham
  Lake Hiawatha

Boston
  Jamaica Pond

Brewster
  Long Pond

Bridgewater
  Lake Nippenicket

Brimfield
  Little Alum Pond

Brimfield State Forest
  Dean Pond
  Dearth Hill Pond
  Sherman Pond

Brookfield
  Quaboag Pond

Brookfield/Sturbridge
  Lake Quacumquasit

Carver
  Johns Pond

Charlton
  Buffumville Reservoir
  Gore Pond

Chelmsford
  Hart Pond

Cheshire
  Cheshire Reservoir

Chicopee
    Chicopee Reservoir
Clinton
    Coachlace Pond
    Lancaster Mill Pond
    Mossy Pond
Concord
    Walden Pond
Dracut
    Long Pond
Dudley
    Hayden Pond
    Pierpont Meadow Pond
Dunstable
    Massapoag Pond
East Brookfield
    Lake Lashaway
Easthampton
    Nashawannuck Pond
    Oxbow Pond
Erving State Forest
    Laurel Lake
Fall River
    Cooks Pond
Framingham
    Farm Pond
Gardner
    Dunn Pond
    Kendall Pond
Georgetown
    Pentucket Pond
    Rock Pond
Groton
    Duck Pond
    Knops Pond
Hadley
    Lake Warner
Halifax
    Monponsett Lakes

Hamilton
    Beck Pond
    Chebbaco Lake
Hanson
    Maquan Pond
Hardwick
    Hardwick Pond
Haverhill
    Lake Saltonstall
Hinsdale
    Ashmere Lake
    Plunket Reservoir
Holland
    Hamilton Reservoir
    Holland Pond
Hopedale
    Hopedale Pond
Hopkinton
    North Pond
    Whitehall Reservoir
Hubbardston
    Brigham Pond
    Moosehorn Pond
Hudson
    Lake Boone
Huntington
    Norwich Pond
Lakeville
    Long Pond
Lee
    Laurel Lake
Littleton
    Long Lake
Ludlow
    Chapin Pond
Lunenburg
    Shirley Reservoir
    Massapaug Pond
    Whalom Pond

Mashpee
> *Mashpee-Wakeby Pond*

Mendon
> *Nipmuc Pond*

Merrimac
> *Lake Attitash*

Middleborough
> *Tispaquin Pond*

Montague
> *West Pond*

Monterey
> *Lake Garfield*

Myles Standish State Forest
> *Fearing Pond*

Natick
> *Morse Pond*

Natick/Framingham
> *Lake Cochituate*

New Salem
> *Quabbin Reservoir*

Northborough
> *Bartlett Pond*
> *Little Chauncy*

North Reading
> *Martins Pond*

Norton
> *Norton Reservoir*

Orange
> *Lake Mattawa*

Orange/Athol
> *Lake Rohunta*

Otis
> *Little Benton Pond*
> *Shaw Pond*

Palmer
> *Forest Lake*

Pembroke
> *Furnace Pond*

Petersham
> *Connors Pond*

Pittsfield
> *Onota Lake*
> *Pontosuc Lake*

Phillipston
> *Queen Lake*

Plainfield
> *Crooked Pond*
> *Plainfield Pond*

Plainville
> *Lake Mirimichi*

Plymouth
> *Billington Sea*
> *Charge Pond*
> *College Pond*
> *Little Pond*

Randolph
> *Ponkapoag Pond*

Richmond
> *Richmond Pond*

Rochester
> *Marys Pond*
> *Snipatuit Pond*

Royalston
> *Tully Lake*

Rutland
> *Demond Pond*
> *Long Pond*

Rutland State Park
> *Whitehall Pond*

Sandwich
> *Lawrence Pond*

Sharon
> *Lake Massapoag*

Shutesbury
> *Lake Wyola*

Southwick
> *Congamond Lakes*

Spencer
Browning Pond
Howe Pond
Sugden Reservoir

Springfield
Five Mile Pond
Lake Lorraine
Watershops Pond

Sterling
East Waushaccum Pond

Stoughton
Ames Long Pond
Pinewood Pond

Sturbridge
Cedar Pond
East Brimfield Reservoir
Leadmine Pond
Walker Pond

Sutton
Manchaug Pond
Ramshorn Pond

Taunton
Lake Sabbatia
Prospect Hill Pond

Tolland State Forest
Otis Reservoir

Tyngsboro
Mascopic Lake

Upton
Pratt Pond
Wildwood Lake

Wakefield
Lake Quannapowitt

Ware
Peppermill Pond

Warwick
Moore Lake

Warwick State Forest
Sheomet Pond

Webster
Webster Lake

Wenham
Pleasant Pond

Westborough
Suasco Site

West Brookfield
Wickaboag Pond
Wickaboag Lake

Westfield
Buck Pond
Hampton Ponds
Pequot Pond

Westford
Forge Pond
Long Sought For Pond
Nabnasset Pond

Westminster
Wyman Pond Reservoir

Westport
Devol Pond
Sawdy Pond
South Watuppa Pond

Weymouth
Whitman Pond

Wilmington
Silver Lake

Winchendon
Lake Dennison
Lake Monononac

Winchester
Wedge Pond

Woburn
Horn Pond

Worcester
Coes Reservoir
Indian Lake
Lake Quinsigamond

Wrentham
Lake Pearl

CONNECTICUT

Lakes and Ponds

Andover
  Bishop Swamp
Bolton
  Bolton Lakes
Chester
  Cedar Lake
Coventry
  Eagleville Lake
Danbury
  Candlewood Lake
Deep River
  Messershmidts Pond
Eastford
  Halls Pond
East Lyme
  Powers Lake
Easton
  Saugatuck Reservoir
Enfield
  Saint Marthas Pond
Glastonbury
  Angus Park Pond
  Smut Pond
Griswold
  Glasgo Pond
  Pachaug Pond
Guilford
  Quonnipaug Lake
Hampton
  Hampton Reservoir
Hebron
  Gay City Park Pond
Kent
  Hatch Pond
  Leonard Pond
Killingly
  Alexander Lake

Lyme
  Norwich Pond
  Rogers Lake
Mansfield
  Bicentennial Pond
  *Mansfield Training School
    Ponds*
Middletown
  Crystal Lake
Morris
  Bantam Lake
North Stonington
  Andersons Pond
  Hewitt Flyfishing Pond
  Hewitt Pond
  Wyassup Lake
Norwich
  Bog Meadow Pond
  Mohegan Park Pond
Plainfield
  Moosup Pond
Portland
  Great Hill Pond
Ridgefield
  Mamanasco Lake
Salem
  Horse Pond
Salisbury
  East Twin Lake
  Wononscopomuc Lake
Somers
  Somersville Mill Pond
Stafford
  Bald Mountain Pond
  Whitney Flood Control Pond

Thompson
> *Keach Pond*
> *Perry Pond*
> *Quaddick Reservoir*

Torrington
> *Burr Pond*

Union
> *Hamilton Reservoir*
> *Morey Pond*

Vernon
> *Tankerhoosen Lakes*
> *Walkers Reservoir*

Voluntown
> *Beachdale Pond*
> *Hodge Pond*

Wallingford
> *North Farms Reservoir*

Windsor
> *Rainbow Reservoir*

Woodbury
> *Quassapaug Lake*

Woodstock
> *Black Pond*
> *Muddy Pond*
> *Roseland Lake*

RHODE ISLAND

—— Lakes and Ponds ——

Barrington
> *Brickyard Pond*

Burrillville
> *Herring Pond*
> *Pascoag Reservoir*
> *Peck Pond*
> *Sucker Pond*
> *Tarkiln Pond*
> *Wakefield Pond*
> *Wallum Lake*
> *Wilbur Pond*
> *Wilson Reservoir*

Charlestown
> *Deep Pond*
> *Pasquiset Pond*
> *Schoolhouse Pond*
> *Watchaug Pond*

Coventry
> *Flat River Reservoir*
> *Tiogue Lake*
> *Quidnick Reservoir*

Cranston
> *Dyer Pond*
> *Meshanticut Pond*
> *Print Works Pond*
> *West Warwick Reservoir*

Cumberland
> *Howard Pond*

East Providence
> *East Providence Reservoir*

Exeter
> *Breakheart Pond*
> *Browning Mill Pond*

Foster
> *Shippee Saw Mill Pond*

Glocester
> *Bowdish Reservoir*
> *Keech Pond*
> *Mowry Meadow Pond*
> *Ponagansett Reservoir*
> *Smith & Sayles Reservoir*
> *Waterman Reservoir*

Hopkinton
  Asheville Pond
  Long Pond
  Wincheck Pond
  Yawgoog Pond
Johnston
  Lower Simmons Reservoir
  Oak Swamp Reservoir
Lincoln
  Butterfly Pond
Newport
  Almy Pond
North Kingstown
  Belleville Pond
  Pausacaco Pond
  Silver Spring Lake
North Smithfield
  Upper Slatersville Reservoir
Providence
  Upper Canada Pond
  Wanskuck Pond
  Wenscott Reservoir
Richmond
  Canob Pond
  Sandy Pond

Smithfield
  Georgiaville Pond
  Slack's Reservoir
  Woonasquatucket Reservoir
South Kingstown
  Barber Pond
  Glen Rock Reservoir
  Hundred Acre Pond
  Indian Lake
  Thirty Acre Pond
  Tucker Pond
  Worden Pond
  Yawgoo Pond
Warwick
  Gorton Pond
  Warwick Pond
Westerly
  Chapman Pond
West Glocester
  Clarkville Pond
West Greenwich
  Carr Pond
  Mishnock Pond

9.
Channel Catfish

We catched fish, and talked, and we took a swim now and then to keep off sleepiness. It was kind of solemn, drifting down the big still river, laying on our backs looking up at the stars, and we didn't ever feel like talking out loud, and it warn't often that we laughed, only a little kind of a low chuckle.

—Mark Twain
The Adventures of Huckleberry Finn, 1885

New England acquired a real literary asset when Sam Clemens settled in Hartford in 1872. Though he would create Huckleberry Finn there, I've never discovered whether he fished the river that ran through his adopted city. But then the channel catfish he would have known from boyhood, that denizen of the Mississippi and points west, was not introduced into the Connecticut River until 1920.

The channel or spotted catfish, *ictalurus punctatus*, is one of the larger members of the catfish clan, bluish brown above with black spots on its silver-gray flanks that fade as the fish matures. Unlike the bullhead, it has a forked rather than rounded tail, vastly prefers gravel and sand to mud, and prefers moving water to still water. Today, it is mostly limited to southern New England's larger rivers: the Connecticut, Charles, and Merrimack.

New Englanders, accustomed to the bullhead or the diminutive madtom, find channel cats a proverbial whole new kettle of fish. Much larger than bullheads, channel cats average three to five pounds, and occasional specimens just over twenty pounds are not unheard of in our region. Regardless of size, they are noted for their stubborn resistance. Innumerable anglers who have hooked into one of these fish have confidently announced to all within earshot that they were on to an impressive pike, only to land fifteen pounds of bewhiskered catfish.

Catfish generally crave warmth, and the channel catfish is no different. Though occasionally caught in winter, it won't work up a serious appetite until water temperatures reach fifty-five degrees. This is even truer of their inclination to mate: they will not begin to feel par-ticularly amorous until the water reaches seventy degrees or more. Con-sequently, spawning takes place relatively late in the spring. The fish usually wander up feeder streams and seek out hollows in the bottom in which to deposit their eggs; special preference is given to protective structures like logs or the interiors of discarded buckets and tires.

Channel catfish get their name from their preference for deep holes or indentations in the bottom of a river, where they can lie beneath the current and pick off a river's provender as it passes. On the other hand, I've heard people in other parts of the country insist that catfish are not exclusively bottom feeders, that they form a stratified pecking order with the largest fish winning the surface and the smallest being relegated to the depths. If that is true, it would be worth floating a hefty lump of bait (A.J. McClane recommends fish entrails) near the surface, a foot or two under a large bobber, just to see what happens.

(On the Green River in Utah, I've seen trot lines set from bleach-bottle floats that arranged baits at a variety of depths.)

Be that as it may, most New England anglers keep their bait on or near bottom. By using a three-way swivel and a bell sinker, they float or bounce the bait from a half foot to a foot above the sand.

Bait includes many of the same wonderful items listed in a bullhead's catalog of dainties: ripe chicken livers, bad clams, marshmallows, and stinky cheese balls. But channel cats also have an appetite for crayfish, large minnows (living or dead), large strips or scraps of other fish, and, of course, worms. If you are fishing relatively slow water, you might want to keep your bailer open and let the catfish move off a little before setting the hook. In faster moving water, cast well upstream so the fish can smell the bait coming. If you prefer fishing even more actively, you can drift your bait downstream to the end of its arc, retrieve it a few feet, then let it drop back down before casting again. When you get a strike, try to keep the fish near the surface and away from anything it can use to tangle and break your line.

Since the fish themselves are strong, and you will also be contending with snags and submerged trees, use a heavy line, 10-pound-test or more. Many anglers prefer bait-holding hooks that run to the larger sizes, from number 1 on up to 2/0. Those powerful jaws can mangle a hook (not to mention a finger), so don't bother trying to re-move your hardware; just tie on a new hook. Like the bullhead, the channel cat also stores venom in its dorsal and pectoral fins, so watch your hands.

While conventional wisdom dictates that catfishing is a nocturnal occupation, many people report making catches during the day. Daytime fishing is reported to be particularly fruitful after a rain, when the rivers are swollen and turbulent.

The catfish you find in the frozen-food section of your supermarket are domestically farmed channel catfish, the very ones fried in batter south of the Mason-Dixon line or blackened by Louisiana chefs.

Now that I've whetted your appetite, let me note that at this writing, though the catfish in the Connecticut River have received the blessing of the U.S. Food and Drug Administration, their flesh occasionally contains sufficient PCBs (polychlorinated biphenyls) to warrant a health advisory. Children and expectant and nursing mothers are advised to abstain, and the remainder of the population should limit consumption to under two fish a month. One takes one's chances. I've had catfish in the South and out West, and I must say that until we get our rivers completely cleaned up, we're really missing something.

CONNECTICUT

Rivers and Streams

Connecticut River

MASSACHUSETTS

Rivers and Streams

Charles River
Connecticut River

Merrimack River
Quaboag River

NEW HAMPSHIRE

Rivers and Streams

Connecticut River

Merrimack River

VERMONT

Rivers and Streams

Connecticut River

Lakes and Ponds

Burlington
Lake Champlain

RHODE ISLAND

Lakes and Ponds

Hopkinton
Yawgoog Pond

10.
Chain Pickerel

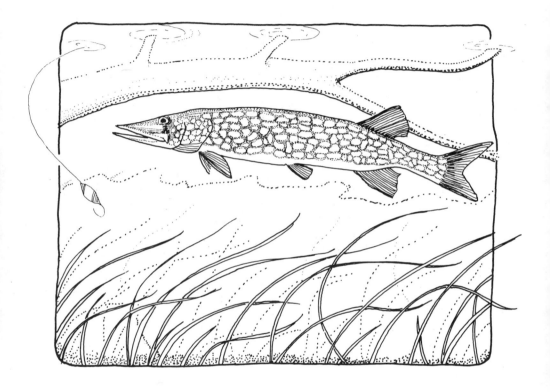

Ah! Those pickerel of Walden!...I am always surprised at their rare beauty, as if they were fabulous fishes, they are so foreign to the streets, even to the woods, foreign as Arabia to our Concord life. They possess a quite dazzling and transcendent beauty, which separates them from the cadaverous cod and haddock whose fame is trumpeted in our streets.

—Henry David Thoreau
Walden, 1854

Small members of the pike family, chain pickerel (*esox niger*) take their name from the intricately linked patterns that adorn their backs and sides. Though chain pickerel are very widely distributed throughout southern New England, one has to agree with Thoreau: their brilliant color, alligator's head, and torpedo body make them exotics.

The first one I saw was boldly positioned but so well camouflaged I had to look twice. Suspended in the Ipswich River, in a line of undulating eel grass, it ignored me and my canoe, but I remember being impressed by its stillness and composure, the way it lay waiting to launch itself like a green arrow.

As late as the mid-nineteenth century, the chain pickerel dominated the food chain in most of the region's warm lakes, ponds, and slow-moving backwaters. The only occasion when it got bumped from that position was when its own prized flesh appeared in turn upon local dinner tables. "The flesh is white and nutritious," wrote Dr. Jerome V. C. Smith in 1833, "and on the whole, it is one of the best table fishes in New-England, but only a comparatively small number find their way to the Boston market. In the western part of the state they occasionally attain the length of two feet and a half." Smith goes on to describe how, on hot summer days, basking pickerel were taken by slipping a noose around their necks with a long pole.

However, appreciation for the chain pickerel dwindled around the turn of our century. "In New England states," writes Dr. James Alexander Henshall, "it is regarded by many as not only a fine game-fish, but an excellent food fish as well. Others despise it on both counts, and there you are. To many a Yankee boy fishing for pickerel was the highest ideal of angling, but with the layer of experience of mature years his idol has been thrown from its pedestal."

Dr. Henshall, whose writings were popular in the 1890s, was one of the black bass's indefatigable boosters and certainly one of the forces behind its acceptance, prominence, and distribution nationwide. However, as the more fashionable largemouth and smallmouth bass were introduced into the pickerel's domain, the latter came to be regarded merely as a nuisance to bass fanatics. Just mastering his condescension, Dr. Henshall concludes that "while the pickerel is not a game fish of high degree, it is capable of furnishing a fair amount of sport with light black-bass tackle in waters not too weedy."

Today, in magazines and angling literature, the pickerel is given short shrift, if it is mentioned at all. In Walden Pond, of all places, Thoreau's admired pickerel seems to have been evicted by the arriviste bass and stocked trout. But even if you have been swept into the large-mouth bass's public relations campaign (which shows no sign of flagging), you might want to give the old favorite a chance.

Pickerel spawn early in spring, in the shallows, just after ice-out. An average female pickerel will distribute six thousand to eight thousand eggs in long strings over shoreline vegetation. Like the pike's reproductive pattern, this early hatching gives pickerel fry a jump on other species. Young pickerel start with insects but soon graduate to juvenile bait and panfish and will eventually consume adult fish, frogs, and even an occasional duckling. Pickerel are usually solitary, taking up a territory and defending it from their own kind. Thoreau called them "the swiftest, wariest, and most voracious of fishes," having seen one cannibalize "a brother pickerel half as large as itself."

Because young chain pickerel wear banded rather than chain markings, they are occasionally confused with redfin pickerel adults, *esox americanus americanus*. The redfin has a shorter snout, almost two dozen stripes, and distinctive orange fins. The redfin, also known as the banded pickerel, is a much smaller species that rarely reaches twelve inches in length and is not often sought.

Pickerel seldom live much longer than four years, but under ideal conditions they can grow to substantial size. While they average one to two feet and weigh just under a pound, the New Hampshire record fish weighed eight. Smaller pickerel prefer muddy shallows, hiding among the tangled vegetation that hugs the shore. (That tall lavender-flowered plant is called "pickerelweed" for a reason.)

Larger chain pickerel are found in deep water, under lily pads or among the dangling tendrils of aquatic weeds. Even the large pickerel can be taken on 6-pound-test line, but if you expect leviathans, you may wish to reinforce the end of your line with one foot or two feet of 25-pound-test line. Some anglers go so far as to add a half foot of steel leader, but it will usually prove unnecessary and will interfere with your lure's performance.

Very large pickerel, unlike large bass, seem arrogant rather than calculating, which may well be why one sees so few large specimens. (Either that or they are very wise and we never see them, but I fear the former is true.) It may take an effort to unhook and release one of these toothy, thrashing dragons, but the larger ones look a lot more impressive in the water than they do on a wall over the mantle.

One of the oldest and simplest methods of fishing was called "skittering." It required about eight feet of cane pole and an equal length of line tied to the end. This indelicate but practical instrument was used to drag a minnow, pork rind strip, or frog leg over lily pads and logs and would sooner or later precipitate a strike.

Today one has one's choice of spinning rod, baitcasting rod, or fly-rod. Baits, lures, and flies for chain pickerel are legion, and almost anything in the largemouth bass angler's arsenal will work: minnows, frogs, spoons, spinners, crankbaits, or plugs. If you are flyfishing, you will want a rig that can cast some of those wind-resistant bass bugs, frog and mouse imitations, and large streamer flies. Lures and flies that are shiny or red or both receive a lot of attention.

Come summer, chain pickerel become the pond's voluptuaries. When water temperatures climb past eighty and eighty-five degrees, and most other species retire to the cool depths, chain pickerel simmer happily. Feeding almost exclusively during daylight, pickerel rest in absolute stillness until a passing meal snaps them into action. Their giveaway, even if you can't see them, is a telltale **V**-shaped wake.

Because pickerel often suspend themselves perpendicular to the shoreline or cover, one of the best strategies is to make short casts parallel to their hiding places. Because you will probably be in weedy water cluttered with obstructions, lures with weedless single hooks will make fishing a lot less exasperating. A strip of pork rind can help conceal the hook, keep it from snagging, and soften a steel spoon's indigestible feel.

With both bait and lures, fast, erratic retrieval seems to precipitate the most strikes. More than once I've spotted an individual pickerel and dragged a lure within inches of its snout a half-dozen times without results. On the seventh pass I gave the line a quick pull, then a pause, and on the second pull instinct suddenly overruled the pickerel's indifference. Even then, however, they can change their minds in midswoop. Unlike many fish, pickerel may express interest in a lure after it has run by several times. They will hit a lure a second time if they miss, even if they have been hooked for a split second. If you see the fish follow a lure then change its mind, let it alone for a while and return.

Pickerel are bold and will occasionally glare at you as you approach the shore on foot or glide near them in a boat. They will follow a spinner to within a yard of you, then stop and fix you with what looks an awful lot like contempt before casually swimming away. The lesson here is not to let down your guard until your hook is out of the water.

While one often fishes the same waters, the same weed lines, for both largemouth and pickerel, there are a few critical differences that may determine which fish rises to the hook. Bass seem to ruminate over decisions longer, anxious not to make a mistake. The calculated cast that places a lure under a bass's nose, the patient count to ten, the tentative twitch and pull that will provoke a bass to indis-cretion, tend to elicit the pickerel equivalent of a yawn. Pickerel are far more impulsive: the shinier, faster, more recklessly driven vehicles are more apt to turn their heads. Though they will occasionally bite the tail off a passing rubber worm, and even get themselves hooked, fast-swimming lures and active bait are more likely to induce a strike.

Hooked pickerel explode with fury, leaping in the air in wiggling arcs, and quite frequently throw the hook. When you do get them up to the side of the boat, a landing net helps in welcoming the slippery fish aboard.

Like largemouth, bullheads, and other warm-water fishes that prefer weedy cover and muddy bottoms, pickerel flesh acquires the flavor of its environment by mid-July. Anglers are divided on the culinary vir-tues of pickerel, though pickerel taken through the ice are more uni-versally accepted on the table.

The chief complaint is the set of tiny Y-bones distributed along the pickerel's, pike's, and muskellunge's flanks. Don't despair: the bones can be removed in four cuts. First, place the gutted fish on its back and cut through the ribs on both sides of the backbone. Remove the backbone. Take half the fish, and keeping the fillet skin-side down, use your fingers to locate the Y-bones, which emerge from the flesh at an angle. Tracing this angle (about forty-five degrees), cut along both sides of the Y-bones. Remove and discard the freed bones and the flesh holding them together. Repeat on the other fillet. You end up with four pieces: a broad and a narrow strip from each fillet.

MAINE

—— Lakes and Ponds ——

Acton
  Great East Lake
Auburn
  Auburn Lake
Belgrade
  Messalonskee Lake
  Salmon Lake
Belgrade Lakes
  Long Pond
Bridgton
  Highland Lake
China
  China Lake
Cooper
  Cathance Lake
Crawford
  Crawford Lake
Damariscotta
  Biscay Pond
Danforth
  East Grand Lake
Dedham
  Hatcase Pond
  Phillips Lake
Denmark
  Hancock Pond
  Moose Pond
Dexter
  Wassookeag Lake
East Otisfield
  Thompson Lake
East Palermo
  Sheepscot Pond
Ellsworth
  Branch Lake
  Green Lake

Embden
  Embden Pond
Enfield
  Cold Stream Lake
Fayette
  Echo Lake
Fayette Township
  Parker Pond
Fryeburg
  Kezar Pond
  Lovewell Pond
Glenwood Plantation
  Wytopitlock Lake
Grand Lake Stream
  West Grand Lake
Greeley
  Sebec Lake
Hartland Township
  Moose Pond (Great Moose Lake)
Hermon
  Hermon Pond
Island Falls Township
  Pleasant Pond
Jacksonville
  Gardner Lake
Jefferson
  Damariscotta Lake
Lakeville
  Junior Lake
Liberty
  St. George Lake
Lincoln
  Mattanawcook Pond

Manchester
  Cobbosseecontee Lake
Meddybemps
  Meddybemps Lake
Millinocket
  Pemadumcook Chain of Lakes
Molunkus Township
  Molunkus Lake
Monmouth
  Cochnewagon Pond
New Vineyard
  Porter Lake
North Windham
  Little Sebago Lake
Orono
  Pushaw Lake
Orrington
  Brewer Pond
Otis
  Beech Hill Pond
Poland
  Range Ponds
Princeton
  Pocomoonshine Lake
Readfield
  Torsey Pond
Rome
  Great Pond
North Windham, Sebago Lake
  State Park
  Sebago Lake
Shapleigh
  Mousam Lake

Smithfield
  East Pond
  North Pond
South China
  Threemile Pond
Township 3, ND, Hancock
  County
  West Lake
Township 6, Range 1 NBPP,
  Penobscot County
  Scraggly Lake
Township 7, Range 9, Piscataquis
  County
  Millinocket Lake
Township 27, ED BPP
  Big Lake
Township 40, MD, Hancock
  County
  Nicatous Lake
Township 43, MD BPP,
  Washington County
  Third Machias Lake
Vassalboro
  Webber Pond
Waterboro
  Little Ossipee Lake
Wayne
  Androscoggin Lake
Winthrop
  Maranacook Lake
Woolwich
  Nequasset Pond

NEW HAMPSHIRE

Rivers and Streams

Connecticut River   *Merrimack River*
Exeter River

—— Lakes and Ponds——

Amherst
  Baboosic Lake

Barnstead
  Halfmoon Lake
  Lower Suncook Lake
  Upper Suncook Lake

Barrington
  Ayers Lake
  Swains Pond

Bradford
  Lake Massasecum

Canaan
  Canaan Street Lake
  Goose Pond

Chatham
  Kimball Pond

Chesterfield
  Spofford Lake

Conway
  Conway Lake

Deering
  Deering Reservoir

Derry
  Island Pond

Dublin
  Thorndike Pond

Enfield
  Crystal Lake
  Mascoma Lake

Errol
  Akers Pond
  Umbagog Lake

Franklin
  Webster Lake

Gilmanton
  Manning Lake
  Sunset Lake

Grafton
  Grafton Pond

Hebron
  Newfound Lake

Holderness
  Little Squam Lake
  Squam Lake
  White Oak Pond

Jaffrey
  Contoocook Lake

Kingston
  Country Pond
  Kingston Lake

Laconia
  Paugus Bay
  Winnisquam Lake

Madison
  Silver Lake

Manchester
  Massabesic Lake

Meredith
  Lake Waukewan
  Lake Winnipesaukee
  Pemigewasset Pond
  Wickwas Lake

Nelson
  Granite Lake
  Nubanusit Lake

New Durham
  Merrymeeting Lake

New London
  Little Sunapee Lake
  Pleasant Lake

Northwood
  Jenness Pond
  Northwood Lake

Nottingham, Pawtuckaway State
  Park
  Pawtuckaway Lake

Ossipee
    Dan Hole Ponds
    Ossipee Lake
Pittsburgh
    Lake Francis
Rindge
    Lake Monomonac
Rumney
    Stinson Lake
Salem
    Arlington Mills Reservoir
Stoddard
    Highland Lake
Strafford
    Bow Lake
Sunapee
    Sunapee Lake
Tamworth
    Chocorua Lake

Wakefield
    Balch Pond
    Great East Lake
    Pine River Pond
    Province Lake
Warren
    Lake Tarleton
Washington
    Ashuelot Pond
    Island Pond
Weare
    Horace Lake
Webster
    Lake Winnepocket
Windham
    Canobie Lake
Wolfeboro
    Lake Wentworth
    Rust Pond

VERMONT

—— Rivers and Streams ——

Barton River
Castleton River
Clyde River
Connecticut River
Lamoille River
Lewis Creek

Little Otter Creek
Missisquoi River
Otter Creek
Passumpsic River
Winooski River

—— Lakes and Ponds ——

Barnet
    Harveys Lake
Barton
    Crystal Lake
Brighton
    Island Pond
    McConnell Pond

Bristol
    Winona Lake
Brookfield
    Sunset Lake
Brunswick
    Dennis Pond
    Wheeler Pond

Burlington
  Lake Champlain
Cabot
  Molly's Falls Pond
  Mollys Pond
Castleton, Lake Bomoseen State Park
  Lake Bomoseen
Charleston
  Pensioner Pond
Concord
  Miles Pond
Craftsbury
  Great Hosmer Pond
  Little Hosmer Pond
Derby
  Brownington Pond
  Lake Salem
Derby Center
  Lake Derby
East Brighton
  Nulhegan Pond
Eden
  Long Pond
Eden Mills
  Lake Eden
Fairfield
  Fairfield Pond
Fairlee
  Lake Morey
Fletcher
  Metcalf Pond
Garfield, Morrisville Village Forest
  Green River Reservoir
Glover
  Daniels Pond

Greensboro
  Horse Pond
  Lake Eligo
  Long Pond
Groton
  Lake Groton
Groton, Groton State Park
  Ricker Pond
Hardwick
  Hardwick Lake
Hinesburg
  Lake Iroquois
Holland
  Holland Pond
Hortonville
  Lake Nineveh
Kents Corner
  Curtis Pond
Londonderry
  Lowell Lake
Ludlow
  Lake Rescue
Lunenburg
  Neal Pond
Morgan
  Seymour Lake
Marlboro
  Sunset Lake
Newbury
  Halls Lake
Newport
  Clyde Pond
  Lake Memphremagog
North Montpelier
  North Montpelier Pond
Peacham
  Fosters Pond

Plymouth
  Amherst Lake
  Woodward Reservoir
Pownal
  South Stream Pond
Readsboro, Howe Pond State
  Forest
  Howe Pond
Somerset
  Somerset Reservoir
South Ryegate
  Ticklenaked Pond
South Woodbury
  Sabin Pond
Stratton
  Grout Pond
Thetford
  Lake Fairlee
Tyson
  Echo Lake
Walden
  Coles Pond
  Lyford Pond

Wallace Pond
  Wallace Pond
Wallingford
  Wallingford Pond
West Danville
  Keiser Pond
West Glover
  Lake Parker
Wheelock
  Flagg Pond
Whitingham
  Sadawga Pond
Wilmington
  *Harriman Reservoir (Lake
    Whitingham)*
  Lake Raponda
Winhall
  Gale Meadows Pond
Woodbury
  Lake Greenwood
  Valley Lake
Worcester
  Worcester Pond

MASSACHUSETTS

—Lakes and Ponds —

Amesbury
  Lake Gardner
Andover
  Foster's Pond
Arlington
  Spy Pond
Ashburnham
  Lower Naukeag Pond
  Winnikeag Lake
Auburn
  Eddy Pond

Ayer
  Sandy Pond
Barnstable
  Chequaquet Lake
  Garretts Pond
  Mystic and Middle Pond
Becket
  Center Pond
  Yokum Pond
Belchertown
  Metacomet Lake

Bellingham
  Lake Hiawatha
Boston
  Jamaica Pond
Bourne
  Flax Pond
Boxford
  Baldpate Pond
Boylston
  Rocky Pond
Brewster
  Seymour Pond
  Upper Mill Pond
Bridgewater
  Lake Nippenicket
Brimfield
  Little Alum Pond
  Sherman Pond
Brookfield
  Quaboag Pond
Brookfield/Sturbridge
  Lake Quacumquasit
Brookline
  Brookline Reservoir
Carver
  Barrett Pond
  Sampson's Pond
Charlton
  Buffumville Reservoir
  Gore Pond
Chelmsford
  Hart Pond
Cheshire
  Cheshire Reservoir
Chicopee
  Chicopee Reservoir

Clinton
  Coachlace Pond
  Lancaster Mill Pond
  Mossy Pond
Douglas
  Wallis Reservoir
Dracut
  Long Pond
Dudley
  Hayden Pond
Dunstable
  Massapoag Pond
East Bridgewater
  Robbins Pond
East Brookfield
  Lake Lashaway
Easthampton
  Nashawannuck Pond
  Oxbow Pond
Erving State Forest
  Laurel Lake
Fall River
  Cooks Pond
Framingham
  Farm Pond
Gardner
  Dunn Pond
  Kendall Pond
Georgetown
  Pentucket Pond
  Rock Pond
Gloucester
  Cape Ann Club
Groton
  Baddacook Pond
  Duck Pond
  Knops Pond

Hadley
Lake Warner

Halifax
Monponsett Lakes

Hamilton
Beck Pond
Chebbaco Lake

Hanson
Indian Head Pond

Hardwick
Hardwick Pond

Harvard
Bare Hill Pond

Haverhill
Millvale Reservoir

Hinsdale
Ashmere Lake
Plunket Reservoir

Holden
Chaffin Pond

Holland
Hamilton Reservoir
Holland Pond

Hopedale
Hopedale Pond

Hopkinton
North Pond
Whitehall Reservoir

Hubbardston
Brigham Pond
Moosehorn Pond

Hudson
Boon Pond
Lake Boone

Huntington
Norwich Pond

Lakeville
Long Pond

Lancaster
Fort Pond

Lee
Goose Pond
Laurel Lake

Littleton
Long Lake

Ludlow
Chapin Pond

Lunenburg
Massapaug Pond
Shirley Reservoir

Lynn
Sluice Pond

Mashpee
Johns Pond
Mashpee-Wakeby Pond

Merrimac
Lake Attitash

Middleborough
Tispaquin Pond

Millbury
Singletary Lake

Monterey
Lake Buel
Lake Garfield

Natick
Morse Pond

Natick/Framingham
Lake Cochituate

New Salem
Quabbin Reservoir

North Reading
Martins Pond

Northborough
Bartlett Pond
Little Chauncy

Norton
Norton Reservoir
Winnecunnet Pond

Orange
Lake Mattawa

Orange/Athol
  Lake Rohunta
Orleans
  Pilgrim Lake
Otis
  Big Benton Pond
  Little Benton Pond
  Shaw Pond
Palmer
  Forest Lake
Pembroke
  Furnace Pond
  Oldham Pond
Petersham
  Connors Pond
Phillipston
  Bates Reservoir
  Queen Lake
Pittsfield
  Onota Lake
  Pontoosuc Lake
Plainfield
  Crooked Pond
  Plainfield Pond
Plainville
  Lake Mirimichi
Plymouth
  Billington Sea
  Bloody Pond
  Charge Pond
  Curlew Pond
  Ezekial Pond
  Fresh Pond
  Great Herring Pond
  Micajah Pond
  West Pond
Randolph
  Ponkapoag Pond
Richmond
  Richmond Pond

Rochester
  Marys Pond
  Snipatuit Pond
Royalston
  Tully Lake
Rutland
  Long Pond
Rutland State Park
  Whitehall Pond
Sandwich
  Lawrence Pond
Savoy
  South Pond
Sharon
  Lake Massapoag
Shutesbury
  Lake Wyola
Southwick
  Congamond Lakes
Spencer
  Howe Pond
Springfield
  Five Mile Pond
  Lake Lorraine
  Watershops Pond
Sterling
  East Waushaccum Pond
  *Quag and West Waushaccum
    Pond*
  Stuart Pond
Stockbridge
  Stockbridge Bowl
Stoughton
  Ames Long Pond
  Pinewood Pond
Sturbridge
  Big Alum Pond
  Cedar Pond
  East Brimfield Reservoir
  Leadmine Pond
  Walker Pond

Sutton
Manchaug Pond
Taunton
Lake Sabbatia
Prospect Hill Pond
Tolland State Forest
Otis Reservoir
Tyngsboro
Flint Pond
Mascopic Lake
Upton
Pratt Pond
Wildwood Lake
Wakefield
Lake Quannapowitt
Ware
Peppermill Pond
Warwick
Moore Lake
Webster
Webster Lake
Wellfleet
Long Pond
Wenham
Pleasant Pond
Westborough
Lake Chauncey
Suasco Site
West Boylston
Wachusett Reservoir
West Brookfield
Wickaboag Pond
Wickaboag Lake

Westfield
Buck Pond
Hampton Ponds
Pequot Pond
Westford
Forge Pond
Long Sought For Pond
Nabnasset Pond
Westminster
Wyman Pond Reservoir
Westport
Devol Pond
Sawdy Pond
South Watuppa Pond
Westwood
Buckmaster
Weymouth
Whitman Pond
Winchendon
Lake Dennison
Lake Monononac
Whitney Pond
Winchester
Wedge Pond
Windsor
Windsor Pond
Woburn
Horn Pond
Worcester
Coes Reservoir
Indian Lake
Lake Quinsigamond
Wrentham
Lake Pearl

CONNECTICUT

Lakes and Ponds

Bolton
Bolton Lakes

Bozrah
Fitchville Pond

Chester
Cedar Lake

Coventry
Eagleville Lake

Danbury
Candlewood Lake

Deep River
Messershmidts Pond

Eastford
Halls Pond

East Lyme
Pataganset Lake
Powers Lake

Ellington
Crystal Lake

Farmington
Batterson Park Pond

Glastonbury
Angus Park Pond
Smut Pond

Goshen
Dog Pond

Griswold
Pachaug Pond

Guilford
Quonnipaug Lake

Hampton
Hampton Reservoir
Pine Acres Lake

Kent
Hatch Pond
Leonard Pond
Waramaug Lake

Killingly
Alexander Lake
Killingly Pond
Ross Pond
Tetreault Pond
Wauregan Reservoir

Ledyard
Lantern Hill Pond
Long Pond

Lyme
Rogers Lake
Uncas Lake

Manchester
Salters Pond

Mansfield
Naubesatuck Lake

Meriden
Black Pond

Middlefield
Beseck Lake

North Stonington
Andersons Pond
Billings Lake
Lake of Isles
Wyassup Lake

Norwich
Bog Meadow Pond

Portland
Great Hill Pond

Preston
>   *Amos Lake*
>   *Avery Pond*

Salem
>   *Gardner Lake*
>   *Horse Pond*

Salisbury
>   *East Twin Lake*
>   *Wononscopomuc Lake*

Stonington
>   *Godfrey Pond*

Somers
>   *Somersville Mill Pond*

Stafford
>   *Whitney Flood Control Pond*

Suffield
>   *Congamond Lakes*

Thompson
>   *Keach Pond*
>   *Little Pond*
>   *Perry Pond*
>   *Quaddick Reservoir*

Union
>   *Breakneck Pond*
>   *Mashapaug Lake*
>   *Morey Pond*

Vernon
>   *Tankerhoosen Lakes*

Voluntown
>   *Beach Pond*
>   *Hazard Pond*
>   *Hodge Pond*

Wallingford
>   *North Farms Reservoir*

Winchester
>   *Winchester Lake*

Windsor
>   *Rainbow Reservoir*

Woodbury
>   *Quassapaug Lake*

Woodstock
>   *Black Pond*
>   *Muddy Pond*
>   *Roseland Lake*

RHODE ISLAND

Lakes and Ponds

Barrington
>   *Brickyard Pond*

Burrillville
>   *Herring Pond*
>   *Pascoag Reservoir*
>   *Peck Pond*
>   *Sucker Pond*
>   *Tarkiln Pond*
>   *Wakefield Pond*
>   *Wallum Lake*
>   *Wilbur Pond*
>   *Wilson Reservoir*

Charlestown
>   *Deep Pond*
>   *Pasquiset Pond*

>   *Schoolhouse Pond*
>   *Watchaug Pond*

Coventry
>   *Carbuncle Pond*
>   *Flat River Reservoir*
>   *Quidnick Reservoir*
>   *Tiogue Lake*

Cranston
>   *Blackamore Pond*
>   *Dyer Pond*
>   *Meshanticut Pond*
>   *Print Works Pond*
>   *Randall Pond*
>   *West Warwick Reservoir*

Cumberland
  Howard Pond
East Providence
  East Providence Reservoir
Exeter
  Beach Pond
  Boone Lake
  Breakheart Pond
  Browning Mill Pond
  Dawley Pond
Foster
  Shippee Saw Mill Pond
Glocester
  Bowdish Reservoir
  Mowry Meadow Pond
  Ponagansett Reservoir
  Smith & Sayles Reservoir
  Spring Grove Pond
  Waterman Reservoir
Hopkinton
  Alton Pond
  Asheville Pond
  Locustville Pond
  Long Pond
  Moscow Pond
  Wincheck Pond
  Yawgoog Pond
Johnston
  Lower Simmons Reservoir
  Oak Swamp Reservoir
  Upper Simmons Reservoir
Lincoln
  Butterfly Pond
  Olney Pond
New Shoreham
  Fresh Pond
North Kingstown
  Belleville Pond
  Pausacaco Pond
  Silver Spring Lake

North Smithfield
  Upper Slatersville Reservoir
Providence
  Upper Canada Pond
  Wanskuck Pond
  Wenscott Reservoir
Richmond
  Canob Pond
  Sandy Pond
Smithfield
  Georgiaville Pond
  Slack's Reservoir
  Woonasquatucket Reservoir
  Upper Sprague Reservoir
South Kingstown
  Barber Pond
  Glen Rock Reservoir
  Hundred Acre Pond
  Indian Lake
  Thirty Acre Pond
  Tucker Pond
  Worden Pond
  Yawgoo Pond
Tiverton
  Stafford Pond
Warwick
  Cranberry Bog
  Gorton Pond
  Warwick Pond
Westerly
  Chapman Pond
West Glocester
  Clarkville Pond
West Greenwich
  Mishnock Pond

11.
Northern Pike

The mighty Luce, or Pike, is taken to be the tyrant (as the salmon is the king) of the fresh waters...the pike is also observed to be a solitary, melancholy, and a bold fish: melancholy because he always swims or rests himself alone, and never swims in shoals or with company, as roach and dace and most other fish do: and bold, because he fears not a shadow, or to see or be seen of anybody, as the trout and chub and all other fish do.

—Izaak Walton
The Compleat Angler, 1676

The legendary northern pike, *esox lucius*, ranges all across the northern hemisphere in the vast collar of fresh waters below the Arctic Circle. In Europe it is the subject of superstitious practices and countless tall tales, several of which reached the willing ears of Izaak Walton. There are pike that live 200 years, pike that attack otters, mules, dogs, even attack women doing laundry. There are pike that fall victim to the wrath of frogs. But then Walton was wont to fall hook, line, and sinker for all sorts of stories and speculations. Among other things he endorses Swiss naturalist Gesner's theory that pike were bred "of a weed called pickerel weed."

But Gesner's most spectacular story is about the one that didn't get away, the nineteen-foot, 350-pound German monster taken in 1497, whose skeleton was preserved for some years in Mannheim Cathedral. It seems that on top of everything else, said pike was wearing a ring around its neck supposedly put in the pond 200 years earlier by Frederick II. This miraculous specimen continued to inspire anglers until some spoilsport counted the vertebrae and discovered that the pike was actually two pike, maybe even three.

The northern pike's fearlessness is an essential part of its mythology, though contemporary fisheries biologists are less easily impressed. Because a pike's brain tips the scales at less than a thousandth of its body weight, some skeptical members of the scientific community are inclined to attribute its boldness to simple stupidity. On the other hand, there is little in nature, excluding ourselves, that the pike need fear.

While the northern pike is considered a worthy quest in the United States and encouraged to flourish, in some parts of Canada it is seen as undesirable, as it depletes the trout population. Its native range in our region is confined to Lake Champlain and a few waters west of the Green Mountains. Many of those currently terrorizing southern New England were imported from the wilds of Michigan and Wisconsin and introduced into selective waters to control runaway populations of sunfish, perch, and suckers.

The pike is not only voracious but numbers among the fastest-growing freshwater fishes; in ideal conditions it can reach nearly a yard in length in three years. An average adult weighs between six and eight pounds, though hefty specimens have exceeded forty pounds.

The pike is olive with a pale belly and a host of light oval dashes distributed horizontally along its flanks. (These are disconnected, unlike the chain pickerel's linked pattern.) You can distinguish a pike from other members of its genus by the fact that the lower portion of its gill covers have no scales. Given its long body, prominent fins near the tail, and flat head, it is not difficult to understand how this formidable creature came to be named after a pointed weapon. In pursuit of a meal, a stationary pike can accelerate to speeds of up to ten miles an hour in a matter of seconds.

Nature equipped the pike with a mouthful of sharp teeth, and it isn't terribly particular about what it sinks them into. It is partial to fishes, including its own kind, but will also eat insects, leeches, frogs, salamanders, as well as ducklings and rodents. It has also been known to attack other hooked fishes on their way to the angler, fishes up to half its size. Along with sharks, pike have been described as "mere machines for the assimilation of other organisms" and have been found choked to death by their own gluttony.

Like pickerel and muskellunge, pike rely heavily on their eyes to find food and are almost exclusively daylight feeders. In general, they like the same water as largemouth bass and can be found among branches, in weeds, and under lily pads and logs. Like pickerel, the smaller ones can be found concentrated in coves along the shore while the heftier specimens haunt deeper water, ten or more feet beneath weed beds. Mornings are preferable fishing times, as they will not have fed since the previous evening. In summer, when they hold in deeper water, the same plastic worms used in bass fishing may offer good results in weedy water.

Bait fish should be relatively large, six or more inches, and hooked through the upper lip or hooked in tandem through the lip and the body. Perch and suckers are a good choice. Lures, of course, should imitate these fish, and whether plugs, spoons, spinners, or jigs, they should also be large. A strip of pork rind dangling from the hook is said by some anglers to make the lures even more attractive.

Pike will usually hit their prey from the side, swim off a short distance, then turn it around and swallow it headfirst. Hence, with bait one should wait a moment before striking; with lures, especially if they have a double or triple row of hooks, this hesitation isn't necessary. Once the fish has taken the bait or lure, the angler needs to hit hard for the hook to penetrate the pike's bony jaw. Keep in mind that if you are using treble hooks and you want to release your catch, you are going to be faced with an operation that resembles playing dentist to an ill-tempered shark. Use 10-pound-test line with six to ten inches of 20-pound-test-steal leader at the end.

After the initial fight, northern pike will occasionally play dead a moment until they are within sight of the boat or shore, then explode into one last furious run. The strategy often works—for them.

Pike spawn very early in the spring, when water temperatures reach forty degrees, spreading between seven thousand and five hundred thousand eggs over submerged grasses near shore. This reproductive head start gives them a competitve edge: their offspring reach sufficient size to overpower the emerging fry of other species. Adults, meanwhile, abstain from feeding during the spawn but begin feeding actively afterward. The best pike fishing is in the spring (May and June) and again later in the fall (October and November), when they are bat-tening for winter. They are most active in the shallows before the water temperature reaches sixty-five degrees.

In summer, especially in August, pike fishing slows down. This lull probably started the rumor that pike shed their teeth in August. The truth is they have plenty of bait to choose from and may not be that interested in what you've got in the pail. In addition, they abandon the suffocating shallows for the comfort of the depths where they are harder to find. Fishing picks up again as the water cools, and in winter they are frequently taken through the ice.

Pike are edible, but Native Americans held them in relatively low esteem as food. Like all members of the pike family, the northern has an extra row of Y-bones that run along its sides, which should be filleted out when cleaning the fish. Because their skin secretions are strong in flavor, the skin must also be completely removed or it will impart an unpleasant taste to the fish when it is cooked. Smoking the fish is popular with some anglers.

The pike has a relatively limited range in our region, but it has attracted a devoted following. Given their size, strength, teeth, and the need for steel leaders and large lures, both the pike and the muskellunge are the closest things to bluefish that an angler is likely to hook in New England's fresh waters. Unlike muskellunge, northern pike are persistent and not particularly selective about what they hit, and, in the presence of anglers, large specimens tend to disappear from a lake pretty quickly. But because they are more of a game fish than a table fish, anglers are encouraged to carefully return their catch.

VERMONT

—— Rivers and Streams ——

Connecticut River
Hubbardton River
Lemon Fair River
Lamoille River
Lewis Creek

Little Otter
Missisquoi River
Otter Creek
Winooski River

—— Lakes and Ponds ——

Addison
 Dead Creek
Bennington
 Lake Paran
Benson
 Sunrise Lake
 Sunset Lake
Bristol
 Winona Lake
Burlington
 Lake Champlain
Cabot
 Molly's Falls Pond
Castleton, Lake Bomoseen State Park
 Lake Bomoseen
Dorset
 Emerald Lake
 East Creek Site #1
Eden
 Long Pond
Elmore, Elmore State Park
 Lake Elmore
Fairfield
 Fairfield Pond
Fairlee
 Lake Morey

Franklin, Lake Carmi State Park
 Lake Carmi
Hubbardton
 Beebe Pond
Milton
 Arrowhead Mt. Lake
Monkton Ridge
 Cedar Lake
Norton
 Norton Pond
Readsboro
 Howe Pond
Salisbury, Salisbury Municipal Forest
 Lake Dunmore
Shelburne
 Shelburne Pond
Shoreham
 Richville Pond
Sudbury
 Burr Pond
 Lake Hortonia
Wells
 Little Pond

NEW HAMPSHIRE

—— Rivers and Streams ——

Connecticut River

—— Lakes and Ponds ——

Chesterfield
  Spofford Lake

MASSACHUSETTS

—— Lakes and Ponds ——

Amesbury
  Attitash Lake

Athol
  Rohunta Lake

Auburn
  Dark Brook Reservoir

Barnstable
  Wequaquet Lake

Becket
  Shaw Pond

Brimfield
  East Brimfield Reservoir

Brookfield
  Quaboag Pond

Charlton
  Buffumville Reservoir

Cheshire
  Cheshire Reservoir

Concord
  Concord River

East Brookfield
  Lashaway Lake
  Quaboag Pond

Framingham
  Cochituate Lake (North and Middle)

Granby
  Forge Pond

Holland
  Hamilton Reservoir

Hopkinton
  Whitehall Reservoir

Leverett
  Leverett Lake

Ludlow
  Red Bridge Pool

Lunenburg
  Massapoag Pond

Millbury
  Manchaug Pond

Monterey
  Buel Lake

Natick
  Charles River
  Cochituate Lake (North and Middle)

New Salem
  North Spectacle Lake
  Rohunta Lake

Norton
  Winnecunnet Pond

Orange
  Rohunta Lake

Oxford
     Buffumville Reservoir
Pittsfield
     Onota Lake
Rochester
     Snipatuit Pond
Sutton
     Manchaug Pond
Sturbridge
     East Brimfield Reservoir
Taunton
     Sabbatia Lake
Wayland
     *Cochituate Lake (North and
     Middle)*

Webster
     Webster Lake
Westborough
     A-1 Site
     Chauncey Pond
Wilbraham
     Red Bridge Pool
Wilmington
     Silver Lake
Worcester
     Indian Lake
     Quinsigamond Lake

CONNECTICUT

Rivers and Streams

Connecticut River

Lakes and Ponds

Brookfield
     Lake Lillinonah

Morris
     Bantam Lake

RHODE ISLAND

Rivers and Streams

Chipuxet River

Lakes and Ponds

Charlestown
     Pasquiset Pond
Coventry
     Flat River Reservoir
Glocester
     Waterman Reservoir

South Kingstown
     Hundred Acre Pond
     Thirty Acre Pond
     Worden Pond
Westerly
     Chapman Pond

12.
Muskellunge and Tiger Muskies

Whence and what are you, monster grim and great?
Sometimes we think you are a "Syndicate,"
For if our quaint cartoonists be but just
You have some features of the modern "Trust."
A wide, ferocious and rapacious jaw,
A vast, insatiate and expansive craw;
And like the "Trust," your chiefest aim and wish
Was to combine in one all the smaller fish,
And all the lesser fry succumbed to fate,
Whom you determined to consolidate.

—Wilcox, quoted in *American Food and Game Fishes*,
David S. Jordan and Barton W. Evermann, 1902

MUSKELLUNGE

If bigger is by some chance better, the muskellunge would undoubtedly be the best. The muskellunge, *esox masquinongy*, is the reigning member of the North American pike family and the largest freshwater game fish on the continent. In the nineteenth century, eight-foot, 100-pound specimens were reported, though today a large muskellunge would come in at about half that size and weight, which is still formidable. The staples in its diet are fish of all species with an occasional frog, duckling, squirrel, or muskrat thrown in for variety. The muskellunge's voracity, coupled with its tendency to stay near home, inevitably make it solitary. It will eat anything that strays into its territory (including its own kind), and one of the subtle signs of its presence is the eerie absence of other fish. Jordan and Evermann estimated that an 80-pound muskellunge represented "several tons of minnows, whitefish and the like."

The muskellunge's native range includes the Great Lakes region and Canada, where it prefers clear lakes and rivers, but it was recently introduced into a few Massachusetts lakes as a kind of living vacuum cleaner to control runaway panfish populations. Muskellunge can be relatively long-lived, the oldest on record having reached about thirty years of age, though the average is about eight and the majority don't make it past twelve years. They are also among the fastest-growing of the freshwater species. At five to seven years of age, a mature female may measure up to a yard long; males are smaller, maturing at four to five years of age, when they would measure about thirty inches long.

There are dozens of variations on the muskellunge's name and some controversy as to its origin. One school maintains the word is Ojibway, meaning "ugly fish." Physically, the muskellunge closely resembles the northern pike, though their coloration is different. The patterns on a muskie's flanks are dark on a light background; the pike's are light on dark. The pike's markings run horizontally and the muskie's vertically. The muskellunge's cheeks are only half covered with scales, while the pike's are entirely covered. Both, however, have the same massive mouths, lined with caninelike teeth on the mandible and short teeth on the upper jaw.

Though muskellunge spend most of their idle time in water deeper than thirty feet, when hungry they rise out of the depths to lurk in weed beds and at the edges of weed beds, especially near spots where shallow water drops off precipitously. They also haunt stumps, fallen trees, and overhanging branches, feeding early in the morning and late in the afteroon. Fishing improves on windy, overcast days. Many people troll to find them, though casting is no less reliable; if you bore easily, perhaps casting is more to your liking.

In any case, you'll need patience and faith bordering on devotion. Wisconsin's Bureau of Fisheries Management, an agency that sees an army of muskellunge fanatics annually, estimates that it takes about 100 hours on their waters before an angler meets up with a legal muskie. Finding a muskellunge, however, is only the beginning. The muskellunge, often described as the "fish of a thousand casts," has a reputation for sending anglers home with aching arms and empty creels quite a number of times before they are successful. Even if you find a fish, you may have to cast dozens of times, varying retrieves and lures, before you finally provoke the fish into a strike. In general, short casts and fast retrieves are considered most effective. The muskellunge hunts principally by sight but is far warier than other members of the pike family. It often studies its victim some time before coiling its long body like a snake and striking.

Muskellunge respond most often to noisy, flashy surface and subsurface lures, and there are a host of devices on the market equipped with propellers and spinners that wouldn't look out of place on a submarine. In the spring and the fall, large spinners dressed with bucktails are the preferred lure. Come summer, anglers switch to large plugs—eight-, ten-, and even twelve-inch plugs that would probably catch saltwater predators like bluefish or striped bass— though you need not go to that extreme. A five-inch-long lure should be more than adequate.

As for tackle, a spinning rod armed with 10- to 20-pound-test line should do if you reinforce the end of your line with steel leader. If you are casting large plugs you will probably prefer a fairly stiff rod that will give good contact with your lures. Many anglers, especially in other parts of the country, prefer bait-casting rigs, and flyfishing is also possible, though one would be using heavy saltwater tackle.

Muskellunge feel their appetite most keenly in waters of about sixty-eight degrees. September and October are very good months for muskellunge fishing, before temperatures drop substantially below that. Some anglers use live suckers or yellow perch the size of trout, especially late in the season. Very late in the year, when their metabolism has fallen significantly, muskellunge may seize the bait in the middle and hold it in their mouths until they are good and ready to eat. Under the cir-cumstances, one needs to wait for the fish to make the next move.

Like other members of the pike family, muskellunge will often follow a lure quite a ways and then abruptly change their minds. If the fish follows the lure up to the boat, one tactic that occasionally incites the fish into a strike is pushing the rod tip into the water and quickly tracing figure eights with the end so that the lure seems to have panicked. This is more awkward than it sounds, so you might want to rehearse a little.

When a fish picks up the lure or bait, if it doesn't hook itself immediately, let it move off a little before setting the hook. You should set the hook firmly several times to avoid losing the fish in the pyrotechnics that follow. Muskellunge have bony mouths, and when they fight they often leap out of the water and flip over. An alternative muskellunge ploy is to head for the bottom and do an imitation of a stump. Nevertheless, you will have to keep even pressure on the line, even when the fish charges the boat—a tactic muskellunge frequently use to throw a hook. If you have an outboard, be careful not to get your line wrapped around the prop. When the fish is finally played out, which can take up to an hour, you will probably want a large net to get it into the boat or, if you intend to keep it, a gaff.

Though muskellunge are in New England solely due to human intervention, you may want to release your catch and give it a chance to reach its full potential. If so, remember that using bait, or treble hooks, makes it harder to release fish unharmed. As a last resort, you can always cut through the hook with wire cutters, and it will disintegrate or fall out without harm to the fish. Many anglers consider muskellunge the best table fish in the pike family, and a few have gone so far as to compare it favorably with salmon.

TIGER MUSKIES

A fast-growing hybrid resulting from artificially crossing northern pike males and muskellunge females, the tiger muskie has also been introduced into Massachusetts to control runaway populations of smaller species. Unlike some earlier experiments in population management, the sterile tiger muskies are easily kept under control.

The tiger muskie's markings closely resemble its father's tiger stripes, but it inherits its slightly rounded fins from its mother. The same angling tactics and techniques that apply to muskellunge apply to tigers. The current Massachusetts record tiger muskie weighed nineteen pounds, four ounces.

MUSKELLUNGE

VERMONT

Rivers and Streams

Missisquoi River   Otter Creek

Lakes and Ponds

Burlington
  Lake Champlain

MASSACHUSETTS

Lakes and Ponds

Auburn
  Dark Brook Reservoir
Brimfield
  East Brimfield Reservoir
Brookfield
  Quaboag Pond
Charlton
  Buffumville Reservoir
East Brookfield
  Quaboag Pond
Framingham
  Cochituate Lake (Middle)
Hopkinton
  Whitehall Reservoir
Lunenburg
  Massapoag Pond
Ludlow
  Red Bridge Pool
Millbury
  Manchaug Pond

Natick
  Cochituate Lake (Middle)
Oxford
  Buffumville Reservoir
Sturbridge
  East Brimfield Reservoir
Sutton
  Manchaug Pond
Wayland
  Cochituate Lake (Middle)
Webster
  Webster Lake
Westborough
  A-1 Site
  Chauncey Pond
Wilbraham
  Red Bridge Pool
Worcester
  Indian Lake
  Quinsigamond Lake

TIGER MUSKIES

MASSACHUSETTS

Rivers and Streams

Ludlow
> *Chicopee River*

Lakes and Ponds

Arlington
> *Spy Pond*

Bridgewater
> *Nippenicket Pond*

Fall River
> *Cooks Pond*
> *South Watuppa*

Mashpee
> *Santuit Pond*

Natick
> *Lake Cochituate (Middle Pond)*

New Marlborough
> *Thousand Acre Swamp*

Northampton
> *Oxbow Pond*

Otis
> *Otis Reservoir*

Pittsfield
> *Pontoosuc Lake*

Plainfield
> *Plainfield Pond*

Plymouth
> *Bloody Pond*

Sandisfield
> *Upper Spectacle Pond*

Sharon
> *Massapoag Lake*

Tyngsboro
> *Flint Pond*

Wakefield
> *Quannapowitt Reservoir*

Wrentham
> *Pearl Lake*

13.
Walleye Pike

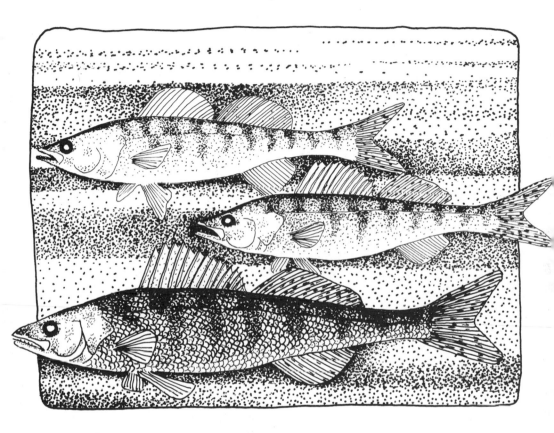

This important fish is a species of wide distribution. It is found from Lake Champlain westward throughout the Great Lakes region...Those who are acquainted with the wall-eyed pike as a food fish hold it in very high esteem. The flesh is firm, flaky, and white, and of delicious flavor.

—David S. Jordan and Barton W. Evermann
American Food and Game Fishes, 1902

Despite their name and elongated form, walleye pike, *stizostedian vitreum vitreum*, are not pike but the largest North American member of the perch family: in some parts of the United States they are known as "pike-perch." If one examines them only briefly, the shape of their heads and the tall crest of their dorsal fins give them away; if anything they look like a yellow perch that has been stretched out to twice its usual length. One of the taxonomic features that distinguishes them from their smaller cousins is the row of snaggly canine teeth that line their lower jaws—this may be their most pikelike feature. And, unlike the brightly colored yellow perch, they have dark olive backs, mottled with black, and pale pinkish bellies.

Regardless of how they got their surname, there's no question about how they got their given name. Their eyes, which have large, distinctively milky or white-marble pupils, gather so much light they glow in the dark and give them extraordinary night vision. One could think of walleyes as the submarine equivalent of owls, using their vision to advantage on the night-blind fish species that constitute the bulk of their diet.

Unfortunately, walleye pike have a narrow distribution in New England, and Vermont's Lake Champlain not only seems to be the most productive body of water in the region but marks the easternmost limit of their natural range. However, they have been introduced into the Connecticut, Merrimack, and Contoocook rivers and are flourishing there. Their prosperity in other fresh waters in New England varies from year to year and depends somewhat upon the overtaxed energies of the various state fisheries departments. In 1970, for example, a lone walleye was caught in New Hampshire's Spofford Lake; there could be more where that one came from, maybe not. It's worth contacting local state fisheries before committing time to scouring a lake for what may have gone the way of the mastodon.

Walleye favor clear water and hard bottoms and travel in schools whose members belong to the same generation. A popular fish in the Midwest, where they are more widely distributed, walleyes occasionally reach twelve pounds, though most weigh between one and four pounds. Mature females are larger than males and average fifteen inches in length, while males average about a foot. Since males reach sexual maturity at two or three years and females at four to five years, returning fish under fifteen inches will ensure that they have had the opportunity to breed before being caught.

Early in the spring, just after ice-out, male walleyes gather to spawn at the mouths of the rivers that feed Champlain. The females arrive a little later, each one scattering about fifty thousand eggs on the gravel in water usually no deeper than four feet. The eggs of one female are fertilized by several males (the males at these events outnumber females about seven to one). In the month following mating, the adults feed voraciously and most actively in water around sixty degrees.

Later in the year, in June and July, the walleyes leave the river mouths and distribute themselves along the lake's shore. Though nothing is as dauntingly featureless to the angler as a large body of fresh water, walleyes do favor certain places. Since they are not the sort of fish one can casually find from shore, a boat, and even a topographical map of the lake's or river's bottom, will be very useful in locating them. The first place to investigate is the water off a point of land. Sandbars, gravel bars, and shallow reefs are also gathering points where walleyes come together to prey on passing schools of bait fish. Their impatience to find food compounds the problem of locating them; unlike some species, they are not apt to hang around long waiting for dinner to arrive.

As a result, the wandering walleye has a well-earned reputation for being elusive and difficult to catch. In midsummer, when bait fish are plentiful, they are especially hard to find and to interest. The best fishing is in the spring and fall, and then in the evening, at night, or very early in the morning. While lanterns and lights attract some fish at night, they will repel mature walleyes. The devoted walleye angler is often a pale creature at home in the deep, clammy darkness.

During daylight hours, especially during warm, sunny weather, walleye retire to deep water. Weather plays an important part in their behavior: they tend to scatter during high-pressure periods, reassembling to feed heavily just before the arrival of a rainstorm. Also, wind of any duration concentrates bait fish on a lee shore, and that can certainly be of obvious advantage to the attentive angler.

Walleye feed principally on small yellow perch; in fact the two species feed on one another in a bizarre cyclical pattern—perch preying on walleye fry, walleye preying on adult perch. Walleye also eat baby shad, bullheads, and white suckers, among other species, so the preferred bait is live perch or minnows, either still-fished or trolled.

In shallow water, still-fish with a bobber and a number 4 or 6 hook, and give the fish enough slack to move off a ways before you set the hook. In very shallow water-diving plugs are also productive, and under those circumstances the flyfisher may be rewarded for trying a large streamer fly or one of those poppers designed for bass.

Though still-fishing is an unendurable waiting game to some anglers, roaring around the lake does little more than waste fuel if you're in a powerboat. Successful walleye anglers throttle down to slow speeds when trolling and trail live bait or lures. The simplest bait rig consists of little more than a hook, with or without a spinner, tied onto your line with a swivel and some sort of sinker above that to get the bait down. This can be as inelegant as a number 4 hook, worm, and split-shot or as involved as a minnow hooked onto a bass spinner or floating jig. Among lures, there is quite a bit of variety: six- to seven-inch swimming lures that imitate bait fish, red and white spoons, and spinners with pork rind all find partisans. If you are using swimming lures you will need a sinker attached about a yard above to get the lure down. A three-way swivel is the best way to keep things from getting tangled. Despite the walleye's teeth, no special leader is required at the end of your line.

Walleye congregate within two feet of the bottom. Giving your line an occasional tug will make your lure dart around and appear more like a feeding bait fish and will often provoke a strike. Because walleye tend to be a bit demure at mealtime, it takes concentration and some experience to detect a hit. Once they take the hook, they are strong rather than flashy fighters, pulling stubbornly for the bottom.

Once a school is located, anglers change tactics. The boat is stopped, an anchor dropped, and everyone switches to casting, lures or bait, or still-fishing with bait fish, worms, crayfish, or leeches. Baiting with fish seems to work better in spring and fall, the other baits being reserved for summer.

Fishing with light-colored jigs dressed with maribou feathers is also popular: they are easily cast, can be made more attractive with the addition of bait, and require no sinker. A quarter-ounce jig on 6-pound-test line is ideal.

Though not particularly attractive creatures, walleye are wonderful table fish, firm of flesh and free of bones. They are very lean and, as a result, freeze well.

NEW HAMPSHIRE

Rivers and Streams

Connecticut River
Contoocook River

Merrimack River (below Hooksett)

Lakes and Ponds

Chester
  Spofford Lake

VERMONT

Rivers and Streams

Connecticut River
Lamoille River
Lewis Creek
Missiquoi River
Otter and Little Otter Creek

Wells River
West River
White River
Winooski River

Lakes and Ponds

Brighton
  Island Pond

Burlington
  Lake Champlain

Castleton, Lake Bomoseen State
  Park
  Lake Bomoseen

Derby
  Lake Salem

Milton
  Arrowhead Mountain Lake

Newport
  Clyde Pond
  Lake Memphremagog

Shelburne
  Shelburne Pond

Waterbury, Mt. Mansfield State
  Forest
  Waterbury Reservoir

MASSACHUSETTS

Rivers and Streams

Connecticut River (above Turners Falls)

CONNECTICUT

Lakes and Ponds

Brookfield
  Lake Lillinonah

Monroe
  Lake Zoar

14.
Yellow Perch

The Common Perch, *Perca flavescens*, which name describes well the gleaming, golden reflections of its scales as it is drawn out of the water, its red gills standing out in vain in the thin element, is one of the handsomest and most regularly formed of our fishes...It is a tough and heedless fish, biting from impulse, without nibbling, and from impulse refraining to bite, and sculling indifferently past.

—Henry David Thoreau
A Week on the Concord and Merrimack Rivers, 1849

Though New England's yellow perch possesses a subtle beauty all its own, I suspect that we tend to take it for granted. Perhaps this is because the European perch, more than double ours in size and weight, is so similar that the invaders from across the sea would have immediately recognized it and possibly dismissed it as a dwarf variation on an Old World prototype.

The dark olive on the backs of both runs down yellow sides in vertical bands (six to eight bands in the New World, five to six in the Old), ending on the verge of a pale belly. Izaak Walton's description of his perch deftly sketches our own. "The Perch is a very good and a very bold-biting fish," he wrote, "he has a hooked or hog back, which is armed with sharp and stiff bristles, and all his skin armed or covered over with thick dry hard scales, and hath (which few other fish have) two fins on his back." By extending these dorsal fins with your fingers, you can appreciate the perch's appearance underwater where it bristles like a Mohawk warrior. This show of finery is completed with red orange pectoral and anal fins, these colors becoming pronounced in the male during mating season.

The healthiest New England specimens inhabit cold-water lakes and ponds and slow-moving rivers; when they are found in warmer, weedier water, perch are sometimes infested with parasitic worms. They are a slow-growing fish and will only reach a pound after about a decade, which is old for a perch. The New Hampshire record perch weighed two pounds, six ounces. Yellow perch average between six and ten inches, occasionally up to twelve or fourteen inches. Though not great fighters, their firm flesh and excellent taste make them popular. Only 1 percent of their body weight is fat, so they tend to store fewer pollutants than larger predatory species. If you are looking to put fish on the table, the yellow perch is an excellent candidate: obliging, tasty, and widely distributed throughout the region. Like other panfish, however, when they overpopulate a body of water, their growth is stunted and they become, from the angler's perspective, small, bait-stealing pests.

Feeding exclusively during daylight hours, most active early in the morning, around noon, and before sunset, adult perch eat minnows, crustaceans, leeches, and subsurface insects. If fishing with live bait, worms or one- to two-inch minnows work well; grasshoppers or crickets also make good bait in late summer and autumn.

Because yellow perch travel in large spindle-shaped schools of 50 to 200 or more fish, catching them is usually an all or nothing proposition. Fishing from shore or from a dock or pier greatly limits your chances: you really need a canoe or small boat. Even then, you have to locate them by trial and error, both vertically and horizontally. Many anglers begin by trolling or drift-fishing the deepest part of the lake.

Once a school is found, you can catch them almost as fast as you can bait your line, and the more they feed, even with members disappearing from their midst, the more excited they seem to become. Some anglers believe that leaving a struggling fish in the midst of its fellows a moment or two before reeling it in whets the entire school's appetite. Walton would seem to confirm this. Ever on the lookout for an opportunity to moralize, he fancied yellow perch as marching together in troops, doomed by their greed to collective perdition. "If there be twenty or forty in a hole, they may be at one standing all catched one after another, they being...like the wicked of the world, not afraid, though their fellows and companions perish in their sight." If fishing in the evening, however, be prepared for the school to disperse almost the instant the light fails; once they lose sight of one another they settle to the bottom for the night.

Because of the perch's staggering reproductive powers, one can leave one's luck, conscience, or appetite to govern the size of the catch. Perch are prolific, and in ideal circumstances they are an important bait fish, feeding the larger predatory species as well as the angler. You may have noticed that many swimming lures manufactured for taking bass are baby perch imitations. Trout are the unfortunate exception to the rule: left in a natural state, perch will quickly remove trout fry, and hence trout, from an ecosystem.

On the average, perch live to about seven years of age and reach sexual maturity in their second or third year. In April or May, perch gather at points where feeder streams empty into a lake or pond; in the absence of such they will seek a shallow cove in which to mate. The female distributes her eggs in long, transparent, ropelike strands. These may reach several feet in length and contain up to two hundred thousand eggs, though the average is closer to twenty-eight thousand. About twenty males will fertilize one of these strands, which afterward tangle in vegetation near shore and hatch a little over a week later.

Spring is one of the few times one is apt to find yellow perch of any size in water under ten feet. For the rest of the year, they cruise near the bottom, sometimes as deep as forty-five feet. In summer, when they frequent sandy bottoms at depths between twenty and thirty feet, the most effective approach is a rig with one or two hooks (number 4 or 6) spaced a foot or a foot and a half apart, tied above a small bell sinker. Three-way swivels help keep the hooks separated from the line. Keeping the line taut, this assembly will cover a couple feet above the bottom while preventing the hooks from snagging on vegetation or submerged branches. If you don't catch anything after a few minutes, try reeling in a couple feet at a time, as the schools (especially in summer) may be suspended several feet over the bottom. Perch also respond to spinners, brightly colored jigs (such as shad darts), streamer flies, bucktails, and small nymph imitations. All of these need to be fished slowly and deliberately. You can combine small pieces of worm with any of the above hardware. Since perch congregate in schools of the same generation, if you catch one that is too small you should move off as the remainder won't vary much in size. In general, the smaller fish tend to school in shallower water.

Perhaps out of curiosity, or possibly from their schooling instincts, perch are attracted by bright colors and reflected light. Some anglers festoon their anchor lines with bright strips of cloth or plastic to attract a school. In the same vein, adding red or yellow beads or thread to your line near the hook, or bits of aluminum foil or any shiny material above the hook, may catch a marauding school's attention.

Fishing close to the surface is occasionally productive in the spring and fall or on summer evenings before sunset. If they are feeding near the surface, perch betray their presence by rippling the water as they chase bait fish. On these occasions, all one needs is a bobber with a piece of split-shot fastened a foot above the hook or a floating flyline and a streamer fly.

Whether the fish are near the surface or the bottom, you will quickly discover the perch's deftness in cleaning worms off a hook without paying the consequences. They may be willing but they're not gullible. If you wait to feel the second or third nibble, you will find your hook stripped clean. If you strike too soon you will pull the bait from their mouths. As soon as you feel a nibble, pull the rod back firmly and evenly, and they will usually hook themselves. Slow jigging can also encourage incautious strikes. When handling your catch be careful of the spines on the perch's dorsal fins: I discovered by experience that they are sharp enough to puncture the less-expensive inflatable boats.

Fishing with minnows as bait requires a different strategy: a brief delay before setting the hook. Like pickerel and pike, perch will strike a minnow from the side, move off with it, then swallow it head first. Because small fishes make up more and more of the perch's diet as it matures, minnows will be of greater interest to large perch.

When the summer fades, you might think of yellow perch as autumn's last resort. When you cannot get yourself to surrender to winter, when everything else in the lake is immobilized by cold, when the shore dons a thin collar of ice, it is often possible to find just one last school of perch before the pond closes over. Even after that, in the dead of winter, they are probably the most sought-after species fished for through the ice.

MAINE

——Lakes and Ponds——

Acton
    Great East Lake
Allens Mills
    Clearwater Pond
Attean
    Wood Pond
Attean Township
    Attean Pond
Auburn
    Auburn Lake
Belgrade
    Messalonskee Lake
    Salmon Lake
Belgrade Lakes
    Long Pond
Bridgton
    Highland Lake
Chain of Ponds Township,
    Franklin County
    Chain of Ponds
China
    China Lake
    Threemile Pond
Cooper
    Cathance Lake
Crawford
    Crawford Lake
Damariscotta
    Biscay Pond
Danforth
    East Grand Lake
Denmark
    Hancock Pond
    Moose Pond
Dexter
    Wassookeag Lake

East Otisfield
    Thompson Lake
East Palermo
    Sheepscot Pond
Ellsworth
    Branch Lake
    Green Lake
Embden
    Embden Pond
Enfield
    Cold Stream Lake
Fayette
    Echo Lake
Fayette Township
    Parker Pond
Fryeburg
    Kezar Pond
    Lovewell Pond
Glenwood Plantation
    Wytopitlock Lake
Grand Lake Stream
    West Grand Lake
Greeley
    Sebec Lake
Greenville
    Moosehead Lake
Hermon
    Hermon Pond
Hobbstown Township
    Spencer Lake
Island Falls Township
    Pleasant Pond
Jacksonville
    Gardner Lake
Jefferson
    Damariscotta Lake

Lakeville
   Junior Lake
Liberty
   St. George Lake
Lincoln
   Mattanawcook Pond
Linneus
   *Drews Lake (Meduxnekeag
      Lake)*
Manchester
   Cobbosseecontee Lake
Meddybemps
   Meddybemps Lake
Millinocket
   Pemadumcook Chain of Lakes
Molunkus Township
   Molunkus Lake
Monmouth
   Cochnewagon Pond
New Vineyard
   Porter Lake
North Windham
   Little Sebago Lake
North Windham, Sebago Lake
   State Park
   Sebago Lake
Orono
   Pushaw Lake
Orrington
   Brewer Pond
Poland
   Range Ponds
Princeton
   Pocomoonshine Lake
Rangeley
   Dodge Pond
Rangeley, Rangely Lake State
   Park
   Rangeley Lake

Readfield
   Torsey Pond
Rome
   Great Pond
Shapleigh
   Mousam Lake
Smithfield
   East Pond
   North Pond
Township 1, Range 11, Piscat-
   aquis County
   Nahmakanta Lake
Township 3 ND, Hancock
   County
   West Lake
Township 3, Range 12, WELS,
   Piscataquis County
   Chesuncook Lake
Township 3, Range 14, WELS,
   Piscataquis County
   Lobster Lake
Township 6, Range 8, WELS,
   Piscataquis County
   Matagamon Lake
Township 7, Range 9, Piscataquis
   County
   Millinocket Lake
Township 7, Range 14,
   Piscataquis County
   Caucomgomoc Lake
Township 16, Range 5, WELS,
   Aroostook County
   Square Lake
Township 17, Range 5, Aroostook
   County
   Cross Lake
Township 27, ED BPP
   Big Lake

Township 43, MD BPP,
  Washington County
    Third Machias Lake
Vassalboro
    Webber Pond
Waterboro
    Little Ossipee Lake
Wayne
    Androscoggin Lake

Wilton
    Wilson Pond
Winthrop
    Maranacook Lake
Woolwich
    Nequasset Pond

NEW HAMPSHIRE

Rivers and Streams

Connecticut River
Exeter River

Lamprey River
Merrimack River

Lakes and Ponds

Amherst
    Baboosic Lake
Barnstead
    Halfmoon Lake
    Lower Suncook Lake
    Upper Suncook Lake
Barrington
    Ayers Lake
    Swains Pond
Bradford
    Lake Massasecum
Canaan
    Canaan Street Lake
    Goose Pond
Chatham
    Kimball Pond
Chesterfield
    Spofford Lake
Conway
    Conway Lake
Deering
    Deering Reservoir
Derry
    Island Pond

Dublin
    Dublin Pond
    Thorndike Pond
Enfield
    Mascoma Lake
Errol
    Akers Pond
    Umbagog Lake
Franklin
    Webster Lake
Gilmanton
    Crystal Lake
    Manning Lake
    Sunset Lake
Grafton
    Grafton Pond
Hebron
    Newfound Lake
Holderness
    Little Squam Lake
    Squam Lake
    White Oak Pond
Jaffrey
    Contoocook Lake

Kingston
  Country Pond
  Kingston Lake
Laconia
  Winnisquam Lake
  Paugus Bay
Madison
  Silver Lake
Manchester
  Massabesic Lake
Meredith
  Lake Waukewan
  Lake Winnipesaukee
  Pemigewasset Pond
  Wickwas Lake
Nelson
  Granite Lake
  Nubanusit Lake
New Durham
  Merrymeeting Lake
New London
  Little Sunapee Lake
  Pleasant Lake
Northwood
  Northwood Lake
Nottingham, Pawtuckaway State
  Park
  Pawtuckaway Lake
Ossipee
  Dan Hole Ponds
  Ossipee Lake
Rindge
  Lake Monomonac

Rumney
  Stinson Lake
Salem
  Arlington Mills Reservoir
Stoddard
  Highland Lake
Strafford
  Bow Lake
Sunapee
  Sunapee Lake
Wakefield
  Balch Pond
  Great East Lake
  Lovell Lake
  Pine River Pond
  Province Lake
Warren
  Lake Tarleton
Washington
  Ashuelot Pond
  Island Pond
Weare
  Horace Lake
Webster
  Lake Winnepocket
Windham
  Canobie Lake
Wolfeboro
  Mirror Lake
  Rust Pond

VERMONT

Rivers and Streams

Barton River
Black River
Clyde River

Connecticut River
Hubbardton River
Lamoille River

Lemon Fair River
Lewis Creek
Little Otter Creek
Missisquoi River
Otter Creek

Passumpsic River
Rock River
Williams River
Winooski River

——Lakes and Ponds ——

Addison
   Dead Creek
Barnard
   Silver Lake
Benson
   Sunrise Lake
   Sunset Lake
Brighton
   Island Pond
   McConnell Pond
Bristol
   Winona Lake
Brunswick
   Dennis Pond
   Paul Stream Pond
   Wheeler Pond
Burlington
   Lake Champlain
Cabot
   Molly's Falls Pond
   Mollys Pond
Chittenden
   Chittenden Reservoir
Concord
   Miles Pond
Craftsbury
   Great Hosmer Pond
   Little Hosmer Pond
Danby
   Danby Pond
Danville
   Joes Pond

Derby
   Brownington Pond
   Lake Salem
Derby Center
   Lake Derby
Dorset, Emerald Lake State Park
   Emerald Lake
Eden
   Long Pond
Eden Mills
   Lake Eden
Elmore, Elmore State Park
   Lake Elmore
Essex
   Indian Brook Reservoir
Fairfield
   Fairfield Pond
Fairlee
   Lake Morey
Fernville
   Fern Lake
Fletcher
   Metcalf Pond
Glover
   Daniels Pond
   Shadow Lake
Greensboro
   Caspian Lake
   Horse Pond
   Long Pond
Groton
   Lake Groton

Groton, Groton State Park
Ricker Pond
Guilford
Weatherhead Hollow Pond
Hinesburg
Lake Iroquois
Hubbardton
Beebe Pond
Halfmoon Pond
Kents Corner
Curtis Pond
Londonderry
Lowell Lake
Ludlow
Lake Rescue
Lunenburg
Neal Pond
Marlboro
Sunset Lake
Marshfield
Marshfield Pond
Marshfield, Groton State Park
Kettle Pond
Milton
Arrowhead Mountain Lake
Monkton Ridge
Cedar Lake
Montpelier, Writsville State Park
Wrightsville Reservoir
Morgan
Seymour Lake
Newbury
Halls Lake
Newport
Clyde Pond
North Bennington
Lake Paran

North Montpelier
North Montpelier Pond
Peacham
Fosters Pond
Peacham Pond
Perkinsville
Stoughton Pond
Plymouth
Amherst Lake
Woodward Reservoir
Readsboro, Howe Pond State Forest
Howe Pond
Shelburne
Shelburne Pond
Shoreham
Richville Pond
Somerset
Somerset Reservoir
South Ryegate
Ticklenaked Pond
South Woodbury
Sabin Pond
Stamford
Lake Hancock
Stratton
Grout Pond
Sudbury
Burr Pond
Lake Hortonia
Thetford
Lake Fairlee
Tinmouth
Chipman Lake
Tyson
Echo Lake

Walden
  Coles Pond
  Lyford Pond
Wallingford
  Wallingford Pond
Wells
  Little Pond
West Castleton
  Glen Lake
West Charleston
  Charleston Pond (Lubber Lake)
West Danville
  Keiser Pond
West Glover
  Lake Parker
Westmore
  Lake Willoughby

Whitingham
  Sadawga Pond
  Sherman Reservoir
Wilmington
  Harriman Reservoir (Lake Whitingham)
  Lake Raponda
Winhall
  Gale Meadows Pond
Woodbury
  Buck Lake
  Lake Greenwood
  Nichols Pond
  Valley Lake
Worcester
  Worcester Pond

MASSACHUSETTS

Rivers and Streams

Amherst
  Fort River
  Mill River
Ashland
  Sudbury River
Charlemont
  Maxwell Brook
Heath
  Mill Brook
Holden
  Trout Brook
Holyoke
  Broad Brook
Pepperell
  Nissitissit River

Princeton
  East Wachusett Brook
Rehoboth
  Palmer
South Hadley
  Bachelor Brook
Southwick
  Munn Brook
Spencer
  Cranberry River
Tyringham
  Hop Brook
Williamsburg
  Mill River, West Branch

——Lakes and Ponds——

Amherst
Factory Hollow Pond

Arlington
Spy Pond

Ashburnham
Lower Naukeag Pond

Ashland State Park
Ashland Reservoir

Barnstable
Hathaway Pond
Mystic and Middle Pond

Becket
Greenwater Pond
Yokum Pond

Belchertown
Metacomet Lake

Bellingham
Lake Hiawatha

Boston
Jamaica Pond

Boxford
Baldpate Pond

Brewster
Long Pond
Seymour Pond
Upper Mill Pond

Bridgewater
Lake Nippenicket

Brimfield
Little Alum Pond

Brimfield State Forest
Dearth Hill Pond

Brookfield
Quaboag Pond

Brookline
Brookline Reservoir

Carver
Barrett Pond
Johns Pond
Sampson's Pond

Charlton
Buffumville Reservoir
Glenecho Lake
Gore Pond

Chicopee
Chicopee Reservoir

Clinton
Coachlace Pond
Lancaster Mill Pond
Mossy Pond

Concord
Walden Pond

Douglas
Wallis Reservoir

Douglas State Forest
Wallum Pond

Dudley
Hayden Pond

Dunstable
Massapoag Pond

East Bridgewater
Robbins Pond

East Brookfield
Lake Lashaway

Easthampton
Oxbow Pond

Fall River
Cooks Pond

Gardner
Kendall Pond

Groton
Baddacook Pond

Hadley
  Lake Warner
Halifax
  Monponsett Lakes
Hamilton
  Chebbaco Lake
Hamilton-Wenham
  Beck Pond
Hanson
  Indian Head Pond
Hardwick
  Hardwick Pond
Harvard
  Bare Hill Pond
Hinsdale
  Ashmere Lake
  Plunket Reservoir
Holland
  Hamilton Reservoir
Hopedale
  Hopedale Pond
Hopkinton
  North Pond
  Whitehall Reservoir
Hubbardston
  Asnacomet Pond
  Brigham Pond
  Moosehorn Pond
Hudson
  Boon Pond
  Lake Boone
Lakeville
  Long Pond
Lancaster
  Fort Pond
Lee
  Goose Pond
  Laurel Lake

Ludlow
  Chapin Pond
Lunenburg
  Massapaug Pond
  Shirley Reservoir
  Whalom Pond
Mashpee
  Mashpee-Wakeby Pond
Middleborough
  Tispaquin Pond
Mendon
  Nipmuc Pond
Montague
  West Pond
Monterey
  Lake Buel
  Lake Garfield
Natick
  Morse Pond
Northborough
  Bartlett Pond
  Little Chauncy
Norton
  Norton Reservoir
Orange
  Lake Mattawa
Orleans
  Pilgrim Lake
Palmer
  Forest Lake
Petersham
  Connors Pond
Pittsfield
  Onota Lake
Pittsfield State Forest
  Berry Pond
Plainfield
  Crooked Pond

Plymouth
  Little Pond
  Long Pond
Randolph
  Ponkapoag Pond
Richmond
  Richmond Pond
Rochester
  Marys Pond
  Snipatuit Pond
Rutland
  Demond Pond
  Long Pond
Rutland State Park
  Whitehall Pond
Sandwich
  Lawrence Pond
Sharon
  Lake Massapoag
Spencer
  Howe Pond
Springfield
  Five Mile Pond
  Lake Lorraine
  Loon Pond
Sterling
  Stuart Pond
Stockbridge
  Stockbridge Bowl
Stoughton
  Ames Long Pond
Sturbridge
  Cedar Pond
  East Brimfield Reservoir
Sutton
  Manchaug Pond
  Ramshorn Pond
Taunton
  Lake Sabbatia
  Prospect Hill Pond

Tolland State Forest
  Otis Reservoir
Tyngsboro
  Flint Pond
Upton
  Pratt Pond
  Wildwood Lake
Wakefield
  Lake Quannapowitt
Warwick
  Moore Lake
Warwick State Forest
  Sheomet Pond
Webster
  Webster Lake
Wellfleet
  Long Pond
Westborough
  Lake Chauncey
  Suasco Site
West Brookfield
  Wickaboag Pond
Westfield
  Buck Pond
  Hampton Ponds
  Pequot Pond
Westford
  Forge Pond
  Nabnasset Pond
Westminster
  Wyman Pond Reservoir
Westport
  Devol Pond
  Sawdy Pond
Weymouth
  Whitman Pond
Winchendon
  Lake Dennison
  Lake Monononac

Windsor
  Windsor Pond

Worcester
  Carbuncle Pond
  Lake Quinsigamond

CONNECTICUT

Lakes and Ponds

Andover
  Bishop Swamp

Bolton
  Bolton Lakes
  Bolton Notch Pond

Branford
  Lake Saltonstall

Chester
  Cedar Lake

Coventry
  Eagleville Lake
  Waumgumbaug Lake

Danbury
  Candlewood Lake
  Lake Kenosia

Deep River
  Messershmidts Pond

Eastford
  Halls Pond

East Haddam
  Moodus Reservoir
  Shaw Lake

East Lyme
  Dodge Pond
  Gorton Pond
  Pataganset Lake
  Powers Lake

East Windsor
  Broad Brook Mill Pond

Ellington
  Crystal Lake

Farmington
  Batterson Park Pond

Glastonbury
  Angus Park Pond
  Salmon Brook Pond
  Smut Pond

Goshen
  Tyler Pond
  West Side Pond

Griswold
  Glasgo Pond
  Hopeville Pond
  Pachaug Pond

Guilford
  Quonnipaug Lake

Hamden
  Lake Wintergreen

Hampton
  Hampton Reservoir

Hebron
  Gay City Park Pond
  Holbrook Pond

Kent
  Hatch Pond
  Leonard Pond
  Waramaug Lake

Killingly
  Alexander Lake
  Killingly Pond
  Tetreault Pond
  Wauregan Reservoir

Ledyard
   Lantern Hill Pond
   Long Pond
Lyme
   Norwich Pond
   Rogers Lake
   Uncas Lake
Middlefield
   Beseck Lake
   Pistol Shop Pond
Middletown
   Crystal Lake
   Dooley Pond
Monroe
   Lake Zoar
North Stonington
   Andersons Pond
   Billings Lake
   Hewitt Flyfishing Pond
   Lake of Isles
   Wyassup Lake
Norwich
   Bog Meadow Pond
Plainfield
   Moosup Pond
Portland
   Great Hill Pond
Preston
   Amos Lake
Ridgefield
   Mamanasco Lake
Salem
   Gardner Lake
Salisbury
   East Twin Lake
   Wononscopomuc Lake

Sharon
   Indian Pond
   Mudge Pond
Somers
   Somersville Mill Pond
Stonington
   Godfrey Pond
Suffield
   Congamond Lakes
Thompson
   Keach Pond
   Little Pond
   Perry Pond
   Quaddick Reservoir
Union
   Breakneck Pond
   Hamilton Reservoir
   Mashapaug Lake
   Morey Pond
Vernon
   Tankerhoosen Lakes
   Walkers Reservoir
Voluntown
   Beachdale Pond
   Beach Pond
   Hazard Pond
   Hodge Pond
Winchester
   Highland Lake
   Winchester Lake
Woodbury
   Quassapaug Lake
Woodstock
   Black Pond
   Muddy Pond
   Roseland Lake

RHODE ISLAND

—— Lakes and Ponds ——

Barrington
  Brickyard Pond
Burrillville
  Herring Pond
  Pascoag Reservoir
  Peck Pond
  Sucker Pond
  Tarkiln Pond
  Wakefield Pond
  Wallum Lake
  Wilbur Pond
  Wilson Reservoir
Charlestown
  Deep Pond
  Pasquiset Pond
  Schoolhouse Pond
  Watchaug Pond
Coventry
  Carbuncle Pond
  Flat River Reservoir
  Quidnick Reservoir
  Tiogue Lake
Cranston
  Blackamore Pond
  Meshanticut Pond
  Print Works Pond
  Randall Pond
  West Warwick Reservoir
East Providence
  East Providence Reservoir
Exeter
  Beach Pond
  Boone Lake
  Breakheart Pond
  Browning Mill Pond

Glocester
  Bowdish Reservoir
  Keech Pond
  Mowry Meadow Pond
  Ponagansett Reservoir
  Smith & Sayles Reservoir
  Spring Grove Pond
  Waterman Reservoir
Hopkinton
  Alton Pond
  Asheville Pond
  Locustville Pond
  Long Pond
  Moscow Pond
  Wincheck Pond
  Yawgoog Pond
Johnston
  Lower Simmons Reservoir
  Oak Swamp Reservoir
  Upper Simmons Reservoir
Lincoln
  Olney Pond
New Shoreham
  Fresh Pond
  Middle Pond
  Sands Pond
North Kingstown
  Belleville Pond
  Pausacaco Pond
  Silver Spring Lake
North Smithfield
  Upper Slatersville Reservoir
Providence
  Wenscott Reservoir

Richmond
    Canob Pond
    Sandy Pond
Smithfield
    Georgiaville Pond
    Slack's Reservoir
    Upper Sprague Reservoir
    Woonasquatucket Reservoir
South Kingstown
    Barber Pond
    Glen Rock Reservoir
    Hundred Acre Pond
    Indian Lake
    Thirty Acre Pond
    Tucker Pond
    Worden Pond
    Yawgoo Pond

Tiverton
    Stafford Pond
Warwick
    Gorton Pond
    Warwick Pond
Westerly
    Chapman Pond
West Glocester
    Clarkville Pond
West Greenwich
    Carr Pond
    Loutitt Pond
    Mishnock Pond

15.
Sunfish:
Bluegills, Pumpkinseeds, and Redbreasted Sunfish

Slowly upward, wavering gleaming,
Rose the Ugudwash, the sun-fish,
Seized the line of Hiawatha,
Swung with all his weight upon it,
Made a whirlpool in the water,
     * * *
But when Hiawatha saw him
Slowly rising through the water,
Lifting up his disc refulgent,
Loud he sounded in derision
"Esa! Esa! Shame upon you,
You are Ugudwash, the Sunfish;
You are not the fish I wanted.
You are not the King of Fishes."

—Henry Wadsworth Longfellow
The Song of Hiawatha, 1855

135

Ugudwash the Ubiquitous. When you are bass fishing, he nips the tail of your plastic worm or manages to hook himself on a balsa minnow he couldn't possibly swallow. If you are still-fishing for pout, pickerel, or perch, he repeatedly assaults your bait until it's in shreds. When you lay a Hendrickson or Cahill under a branch with a cast you will never repeat, a cast no trout could resist, up pops Ugudwash.

Anglers in their prime, especially in company, regard sunfish with condescension, even disgust. Boys and girls are ever in a hurry to count "kibbies" or "sunnies" among the things they have outgrown. On the other hand, anglers in their autumn years wax shamelessly sentimental over the little buggers.

"The pumpkinseed or 'sunny' of fragrant memory," rhapsodizes Dr. James Henshall. "It is enshrined in the heart of many an American angler as his first love, when with pin hook, thread line, and willow wand he essayed its capture in the nearest brook or millpond...Looking backward over an angling career of half a century, the gamesome 'sunny' with its coat of many colors shines out as a bright particular star among those of greater magnitude."

I remember an elderly woman gently casting her hook and bobber, instructing two rapt grandchildren in the gentle art of sunfishing, and I wondered if perhaps the sunfish wasn't the alpha and omega of the angler's life.

What we commonly refer to as sunfish are actually five or more distinct species. In New England we would be talking about pumpkinseeds, bluegills, redbreasted sunfish, green sunfish, and banded sunfish. All these species are flat and oval-shaped, and because they resembled the European bream, early colonists and even some people today refer to them by that name. Pumpkinseeds, bluegills, and redbreasted sunfish are the most widely distributed and pursued. The green and the banded are generally too small or rare to be given serious consideration.

The sunfish's diet consists primarily of insects, but the sunfish will also consume crustaceans, fish eggs, very small fish, and even algae. They have small mouths, but they keep them very busy. From dawn until dusk, you will hear them making a kissing sound as they snap insects off the surface of a pond or splashing as they leap to pluck an insect on the wing. Feeding will even continue after dark if there's a clear sky and a full moon.

The bluegill, pumpkinseed, and the redbreasted sunfish are all polygamous and have very similar breeding behavior. Spawning begins when water temperatures rise over sixty-five degrees. The nests are constructed by the males, who then round up one or more females and drive them into this corral to lay eggs. After the male fertilizes the eggs, he drives the female off and she in turn goes to deposit more eggs in some other Romeo's bower. The male remains, fanning the eggs with his tail until they hatch, defending the young until they can care for themselves.

Thoreau closely observed the sunfish nesting in the shallows, hovering over its crater "hollowed in the sand, over which it is steadily poised through the summer hours on waving fin. Sometimes there are twenty or thirty nests in the space of a few rods, two feet wide by half a foot in depth, and made with no little labor, the weeds being removed, and the sand shoved up on the sides, like a bowl."

Though sunfish, particularly bluegills, are notorious predators of eggs, they don't care to have other fish return the favor. They have been reported chasing largemouth bass and even muskellunge from the waters around their nests.

"The breams are so careful of their charge," writes Thoreau, "that you may stand close by in the water and examine them at your leisure. I have thus stood over them half an hour at a time, and stroked them familiarly without frightening them, suffering them to nibble my fingers harmlessly, and seen them erect their dorsal fins in anger when my hand approached their ova."

If you are fishing during the breeding season, which is not unethical with the prolific, competitive bluegill, they will often strike short of your lures, especially larger lures. Though they will accidentally hook themselves while chasing intruders from their nests, smaller lures are more likely to be interpreted as food.

Because there has been some crossbreeding in many lakes and ponds, separating the species from the hybrids can be challenging even to biologists, but one or two distinctive characteristics will usually allow you to hazard a guess.

Our most widespread native sunfish is the pumpkinseed, *lepomis gibbosus*, most easily identified by the scarlet trim on the back of the dark blue opercula, a flap that is present on all three species. (This characteristic flap is located about where you would expect to find an ear if a fish had one.)

All Solomon's glory would look like the most conservative gray pinstripe next to the raiment of an average pumpkinseed. Bright as a parrot or a toucan, an outright tropical dandy compared with drab neighbors like the bass and the horned pout, the pumpkinseed has an olive dorsal area, an orange breast, electric blue lines radiating from its mouth to its gills, and flanks flecked with rust and silver.

Though they are widespread in New England, pumpkinseeds lay fewer than three thousand eggs a season. They are often found in lakes with other species of sunfish like the bluegill, but they generally favor slightly cooler and shallower water and sometimes live in slow-moving rivers. Although they have smaller mouths than the other sunfish species, fish are part of their diet, and the larger individuals can be coaxed into hitting small bait fish or inch-long streamers.

Although the pumpkinseed's body is flat and it seldom weighs more than a half pound, its length (five to seven inches, occasionally reaching eight or nine) makes it only a little smaller than most of the supposedly much nobler wild or stocked brook trout caught in New England. If the water is cool enough, they may indeed share the same river.

The redbreast, *lepomis auritus*, another native sunfish, resembles a pumpkinseed: it has the same orange belly, though the orange portion is usually larger and brighter and extends to the fins. The wavy blue lines around the mouth do not extend much behind the eye. It grows slightly larger than the pumpkinseed, reaching eight to ten inches and just under a pound. A long black "ear" flap and rounded rather than pointed pectoral fins distinguish it from its cousins.

Redbreasts prefer clear, slowly flowing water and will even live in brackish streams. In general, they feed near the bottom, but when they rise after insects along a shady overhang, like the pumpkinseeds, they can fool trout anglers and significantly raise heartbeats. I would venture that redbreasts, especially the larger individuals, are cagier than the other species and need to be approached more warily and presented to with a bit more grace.

The bluegill, *lepomis macrochirus*, potentially the largest and certainly the most prolific of our sunfishes, was introduced to New England from outside the region. Except for Lake Champlain, where they were native, the bluegill's original range began in western New York and extended southward to Florida and westward to the Rockies, but stocking has spread it all over the nation. It is probably the most conservatively dressed of the sunfish, being mostly dark blue or violet, with silver or paler blue showing through. A half-dozen vertical bars mark its flanks, and a pale blue arc follows the edge of its gills. It is most easily distinguished by the blue patch located near the end of the dorsal fin.

Bluegills thrive in still rather than moving water and feed most actively when water temperatures reach eighty-one small insects. Southern bluegill can grow to more than four pounds, but they don't come close to that in New England. In our waters, in a richly vegetated environment with an active number of predators to keep its population down, the bluegill can grow to about fourteen inches long and about a pound in weight.

Unfortunately, these conditions are unusual; typically, the bluegill just takes over and the whole pond becomes an overcrowded colony of midgets. Bluegill were introduced in Rhode Island in 1914, for example, and since then have all but eliminated the pumpkinseeds sharing their waters and greatly curbed the growth of other species as well.

Breeding begins late in the spring and doesn't stop until fall, by which time a bluegill may have raised two or three broods. The female can produce between twelve thousand and twenty-seven thousand eggs per spawn. Compounding the problem is its affection for the eggs of other fish, including those of the largemouth bass. With a digestive rate twice that of pickerel, the bluegill has an insatiable appetite. Few predators can get their jaws around the flat, spiky bodies of any of the sunfish, especially the adults. As a result, fisheries and wildlife departments in several states encourage anglers to cart them home, if not for food then for fertilizer. Whatever you do, don't introduce bluegill into waters foreign to them.

If you have never fished, or you are not ashamed of enjoying the smaller things in life, the guileless sunfishes will almost always oblige, except perhaps in early spring. While many other species are ravenous in this season, the sunfish is fairly torpid until May or June. Come the hot days of summer, however, they are irrepressible. Though they take refuge in shade or in cooler water when they can find it, they are seldom found deeper than fifteen to twenty feet during the middle of the day. In the mornings and evenings they come inshore in force. They can also be caught through the ice in winter.

As a consequence of being easily caught, they are a good fish to start children on, though very small children may require help removing them from the hook because of the fish's spiny dorsal fins. A small hook (number 8 to 12) baited with a portion of worm or grub or a whole insect, suspended from a small bobber, will bring a strike even if the angler is plainly visible, attired in bright red, and blowing a trumpet between casts. When using bait, long-shanked hooks will be easier to disgorge from those tiny mouths. Don't use split-shot or in any way inhibit the free movement of your bait. Small jigs are also effective, as are small spinners (though less so).

If you are learning to flyfish, sunfish are particularly vulnerable to wet flies in the spring and dry flies in the summer. Wet flies can be tied in tandem or even suspended beneath a bobber. Dry flies work particularly well if you give them a slight twitch after they have settled a moment. Those small spidery lures designed for bass are also very effective if you trim off some of the extra hair and cork. The fish will either hit the flies immediately or study them for just a second beforehand.

While sunfish will forgive some very clumsy presentations, they fight nearly as tenaciously as brook trout. By turning their flat sides to the line's pressure, they create a lot of resistance for their size. They generally head for the bottom, but once in a while they indulge a modest jump before being brought to bay.

Though they feed close to shore and are easily caught, it takes a dozen plump sunfish of any variety to make a meal. On the other hand, if you are flyfishing and don't have to rebait a hook between casts, you can, without exaggeration, harvest hundreds in a single day. Bring along a bucket, keep it filled with water, and sort out the big ones later.

Euell Gibbons includes the sunfish in his inventory of easily available edibles, and it is, despite its size, a truly tasty morsel. In a poorer country, or perhaps in one less addicted to beef, sunfish would undoubtedly be a staple. At one time it was quite popular. "As a food-fish the bluegill is of much importance," wrote Jordan and Evermann in 1902, "and of all the species it is the one most often sent to market, where it always brings a good price. As a pan-fish it is excelled, among fresh-water fishes, only by the yellow perch."

Because of its diminutive size, filleting is a project. Many anglers prepare their catch by simply removing the head and fins, gutting and scaling them, then frying what remains.

Sunfish of one species or another populate nearly every body of fresh warm water in the region, and one could go so far as to say that everyone in New England, even city dwellers, are within a hike, or even a short walk, of sunfishes. I will not list all the waters where they are found because it would take less space to note where they are not found.

Pumpkinseeds and redbreasted sunfish are widespread over all six states. Redbreasted sunfish are particularly well represented in the

Merrimack and Connecticut river watersheds. Bluegills are rare in Maine and New Hampshire but widespread in Massachusetts. In New Hampshire they are limited to the Merrimack River below Nashua and to four other bodies of water: Baboosic Lake in Amherst; Deer Meadow Pond, Chichester; Horseshoe Pond, Merrimack; and Sip Pond, Fitzwilliam. Rhode Island has representatives of all three species, but bluegills have overrun most of the waters where they were introduced.

16.
Black Crappie
(and White Crappie)

Probably no other fish has gathered a greater variety of colloquial names than the crappie. In New England they are most commonly known as calico bass...my theory is that fishermen, unable to stomach such a delicious and popular fish being refered to as *crappy*, simply came up with their own more colorful (and certainly more appetizing) titles.

—Peter G. Mirick
"The 'Sunny' Always Shines," *Massachusetts Wildlife*,
summer 1986

The black crappie, *pomoxis nigromaculatus*, has collected over two dozen nicknames. A partial inventory includes croppie, calico or speckled bass, speckled or bachelor perch, papermouth, tinmouth, and lamplighter. Taken together, a sampling of these names begins to build a composite description: crappie are speckled members of the sunfish family (as are largemouth bass), they school somewhat like perch, they have delicate mouths, and they often appear near the surface at dusk. The bachelor nickname may refer to the way the male alone guards the eggs, fanning them with his tail and protecting the fry after they've hatched.

Regardless of what you call it, the black crappie is a creature of subtle beauty. Its dark, olivaceous back seems to dissolve into random speckles over its pale gold flanks and fins, giving the creature the handsome look of hammered antique metal. Most black crappies grow to about a foot in length. Though they seldom weigh a pound, an occasional large specimen may grow to two pounds; in waters south of the Mason-Dixon line, where the growing season is longer, the black crappie can double the weight of its northern counterparts.

Originally native to the Great Lakes and Mississippi Valley, it seems to have been introduced here without fanfare and has become a permanent and self-sustaining part of our ecological scheme. Though a popular object of anglers in other parts of the United States, one seldom meets anyone in New England who sets out fervently in pursuit of it. In our region, the black crappie is probably most often landed accidentally by anglers fishing for largemouth bass with minnows. In the New England angler's assessment, black crappie seem to occupy some dubious middle ground among the sunfishes: a consolation prize greater than a pumpkinseed yet lesser than the dreadnaught largemouth bass. When hooked, it fights vigorously for but a few seconds, then surrenders.

The black crappie thrives in clear ponds, reservoirs, lakes, and slow-moving rivers and is broadly distributed over the northern United States. It gathers in loose schools around the branches of sunken trees, clusters of reed, or among submerged structures. It also frequents the edges of drop-offs, so a contour map of the water you are fishing may prove useful. As with perch and bluegill, overpopulation in a particular body of water leads to schools of stunted individuals. The black crappie's diet consists principally of small fish and larval insects.

The black crappie would be highly esteemed on any angler's plate; its flesh is sweet and firm and, unlike its more coveted neighbor the largemouth bass, it seldom acquires that characteristically weedy taste. The reason for this, however, is probably that, unlike the largemouth, it is difficult to find and catch in midsummer. The best fishing is in the spring—April, May, and June—and later again in the fall. On a spring evening or very early in the morning, black crappie will school in water as shallow as one to three feet. Occasionally, they crappies can be seen working together to flush schools of minnows to the surface. When they gather to spawn, try fishing the mouths of any tributary streams that may feed into the main body of water or in the coves. At this time of year it is relatively easy to catch them, and they make a good quarry for beginning anglers, whether children or adults.

The most difficult black crappie fishing is probably in daylight hours, in the heat of summer, when the schools retire to deeper, cooler water that holds more oxygen. They will still often return to the shallows in the evening. Though they tolerate temperatures from sixty to seventy-five degrees, they definitely prefer the cooler end of that range. In deeper water, as in shallow water, they are attracted by structure, gathering around rocks, submerged logs, and branches. Occasionally, they may also be found suspended in water without any physical features, so if you are desperate, try deep areas at random.

In deeper water, crappie jigs (metal-headed lures with plastic bodies and tails dressed with hair or feathers) are particularly successful. To the human eye, most of these jigs look less like minnows than some species of garish synthetic grub, but the fish are apparently less concerned than the angler with aesthetics. In general, the lighter the jig, the better. The weights run from a very light 1/64 ounce all the way up to a 1/4 ounce for use in deep water. At the light extreme your line weight won't exceed a pound or two, but then ultralight tackle is probably the best match of fish and equipment. Popular jig colors run toward the red, orange, and yellow end of the spectrum, though white is also productive. While small spinners and spoons fished near the bottom are also successful under these conditions, the jigs, because the hook point rides upside-down, are least likely to hang up on submerged branches.

Fishing among branches, carefully poking your rod into a pond-side thicket, and plunking the bait or lure into the water may not allow you the "ennobling" gesture of a cast well made, but it will get fish. For the record, this is probably the most ancient method of taking fish with rod and line. It was originally practiced by gradually moving the pole's end over the fish, then untwining hook and line by slowly rotating the pole. I mention it in this context because in some other parts of the country, one finds bamboo "crappie poles"; instead of storing line on a reel, the angler wraps it around the butt end of the pole.

Black crappie have mouths hinged to extend around their prey in an accordion arrangement. The tissue here is paper thin, and too much pressure or speed setting the hook may tear it loose. This accordion motion takes a little longer than the motion used by bass or panfish, and consequently, if you slow down you will have greater success. Instead of striking when you feel a tap, slowly lift your rod tip and you will usually hook the fish.

Minnows are the ideal live bait, secured above the spine or through the lips on a number 2 or number 4 hook and suspended from a small bobber. When purchasing bait, ask for minnows on the small side: two inches and under. On summer evenings, crappies will hit other live bait, like floating grasshoppers or crickets or worms fished near the surface, but you will often find yourself with a lot of smaller sunfish on your line.

If you prefer not to use live minnows as bait, carved balsa imitations, two inches and slightly under, are very effective. Cast near a brush pile, allow the ripples to subside, then twitch the lure and allow it to settle again, retrieving it a few inches at a time all the way home. The fish may follow the lure to within a few feet of the shore or boat before striking.

Flyfishing for crappies requires none of the elaborate caution or strategy needed for bass or trout, and again, patterns that resemble minnows are most effective: muddler minnows and streamer flies like the Mickey Finn or the Grey Ghost. Allow the fly to sink a foot or so below the surface, then retrieve it slowly. The fish will often follow for a few yards and then strike when the fly approaches the surface. If you are fishing in the evenings, you will probably find that you need to fish slower still as the light fails.

A third strategy combines elements of both fly- and spin fishing. You can suspend a streamer fly, wet fly, or nymph a foot or so below a small bobber; the bobber gives the fly sufficient weight to be cast, but you get the very seductive, minnowlike movement or the erratic movement of an insect nymph from the nearly weightless fly.

Though "calico bass" may be one of the black crappie's most attractive and familiar names in our region, it technically refers to their nearest relative, the white crappie, *pomoxis annularis*. If the black crappie's range in New England is relatively limited, the white crappie's is extremely so. Common in the southern United States, the white crappie grows larger than its black relative, reaching a maximum weight of four pounds. The white differs physically in that its dorsal fins have only six spines as opposed to seven or eight on the black, and the speckles on the white are arranged in vertical bars instead of being scattered. Otherwise, their behavior is very similar and the means of angling for them identical.

BLACK CRAPPIE WATERS
MAINE
Lakes and Ponds

Acton
: *Mousam Lake*

Newport
: *Sebasticook Lakes*

Sebago
: *Sebago Lake*

NEW HAMPSHIRE

Lakes and Ponds

Hollis
: *Pennichuck Reservoir*

Hopkinton
: *Clements Pond*

Londonderry
: *Scobie Pond*

Merrimack
: *Horseshoe Pond*

Nashua (below Nashua)
: *Merrimack River*

Wakefield
: *Balch Pond*

VERMONT

Lakes and Ponds

Burlington
: *Lake Champlain*

Castleton
: *Lake Bomoseen*

MASSACHUSETTS

Rivers and Streams

Waltham
: *Moody Pool (Charles River)*

Lakes and Ponds

Braintree
: *Old Quincy Reservoir*

Bridgewater
: *Nippenicket Lake*

Boxford
: *Baldpate Pond*

Carver
: *Federal Pond*
: *Vaughn Pond*

Cheshire
: *Cheshire Reservoir*

Duxbury
  Island Creek Pond
Hinsdale
  Ashmere Lake
Holland
  Holland Pond
Lanesborough
  Pontoosuc Lake
Monterey
  Buel Lake
New Bedford
  Turner Pond
New Salem
  Quabbin Reservoir
Northborough
  Bartlett Pond
  Little Chauncy Pond
Shrewsbury
  Mill Pond

Springfield
  Watershops Pond
Taunton
  Sabbatia Lake
Westborough
  Assabet River Reservoir (A-1)
West Newbury
  Artichoke Reservoir
Winchendon
  Dennison Lake
  Monomonac Lake
  Whitney Pond
Woburn
  Horn Pond
Worcester
  Indian Lake
  Lake Quinsigamond

CONNECTICUT

Rivers and Streams

Connecticut River

Lakes and Ponds

Berlin
  Silver Lake
Branford
  Lake Saltonstall
Brookfield
  Lake Lillinonah
Danbury
  Candlewood Lake
Deep River
  Messershmidts Pond
Eastford
  Halls Pond
East Haddam
  Bashan Lake

East Lyme
  Dodge Pond
  Gorton Pond
  Pataganset Lake
Easton
  Saugatuck Reservoir
Farmington
  Batterson Park Pond
Glastonbury
  Smut Pond
Hebron
  Holbrook Pond
Kent
  Hatch Pond

Killingly
Wauregan Reservoir

Ledyard
Lantern Hill Pond
Long Pond

Monroe
Lake Zoar

Morris
Bantam Lake
Mount Tom Pond

North Stonington
Andersons Pond
Lake of Isles

Norwich
Bog Meadow Pond

Portland
Great Hill Pond

Salem
Gardner Lake

Salisbury
East Twin Lake

Somers
Somersville Mill Pond

Stonington
Godfrey Pond

Thompson
Keach Pond
Quaddick Reservoir

Union
Breakneck Pond
Hamilton Reservoir

Woodstock
Roseland Lake

RHODE ISLAND

Lakes and Ponds

Cranston
West Warwick Reservoir

Exeter
Beach Pond
Browning Mill Pond

Hopkinton
Locustville Pond
Wincheck Pond
Yawgoog Pond

Lincoln
Olney Pond

New Shoreham
Sachem Pond

North Smithfield
Upper Slatersville Reservoir

Westerly
Chapman Pond

WHITE CRAPPIE

MASSACHUSETTS

Lakes and Ponds

Hopkinton
North Pond
Whitehall Reservoir

Waltham
Moody Pool (Charles River)

Westborough
Assabet River Reservoir (A-1)

17.
Largemouth Bass

"Kiss my bass."

—A bumper sticker headed north on Interstate 95

Let me assure the trout anglers and the otherwise faint of heart that you can pursue the largemouth black bass, *micropterus salmoides*, without first scheduling a lobotomy. You need not take up witless T-shirts, hats that advertise motor oil, chewing tobacco, nor that awful beer that comes in red-and-white cans. You need not subscribe to periodicals with names like *Bait & Bucket* nor enter a bass tournament. Nor do you have to refer to said innocent fish as Ol' Mr. Bass, Bucketmouth, or a Hawg. You can spare your prep school diction such truncated expressions as bassin', trollin', or flippin'.

There are only two difficult things about the largemouth bass: the vulgarity of the tackle industry that claims it for a mascot and the weeds. The first you can try to ignore: stay off the mailing lists if you can; the weeds you can come to terms with.

So what is all the fuss about? Well, the largemouth is large, puts up a good fight for its size, and is nowhere near as spooky as a trout. You don't have to drive to Aroostook County to find one. It's easier to clean than pickerel, and when other large fish are hiding in the thermocline—which coincides with many summer vacations—the bass is still available. It will be found thriving in water that verges on primordial swill. It also tolerates powerboats and water skiers. It appears on television. And, it's large...well, sometimes it's large.

The truth is, the largemouth is a worthy fish, but before considering its merits, perhaps a little gratuitous deflation is in order just to bring this beady-eyed and ugly phenomenon into perspective. First of all, this mighty creature isn't technically a bass: it's a large member of the sunfish family. Second, there's nothing especially virile about it: it has no teeth to speak of, and the humble bluegill will reproduce circles around it, compete with it for food, prey on its eggs, and even drive it from preferred nesting sites. Third, it tastes relatively uninteresting and sometimes downright swampy. Fourth, compared with the smallmouth it acts like an old linebacker too long on steroids.

As a historical footnote, its introduction to New England brought about a precipitous decline in the size and number of native chain pickerel. This resulted in an explosion in the panfish population, which in turn stunted the bass in many confined waters.

The largemouth's original range ran from Ontario, through the Great Lakes, and down the Mississippi to Florida. Most American anglers associate it with the Deep South, where anglers with names like Bubba wrench twenty-pound, yard-long specimens from the simmering bayous. New England's lakes and ponds boast no such leviathans. Though they may live a decade or more, bass in our region grow slowly. After three years, a healthy fish may just be passing the one-foot mark. On the average they will weigh two or three pounds and occasionally get up to five, even eight or ten. The farther north, the smaller. In Connecticut, large fish weigh ten pounds; in Vermont more like six.

Regardless of heft, whether Alabama swamp fighter or Pawtuckaway Lake lunker, the largemouth is given to the same sullen patience and unpredictable appetite. It feeds principally by ambush—it doesn't hunt so much as lurk. Since the advent of its cult, bait and sporting goods stores stock a staggering inventory of lures: chuggers, poppers, sputter and jitter bugs, spooks, creepers, crawlers, bombers, and torpedos. A few magazine photographers make a living shooting telephoto views down the yawning maw of bass impaled on balsa wood minnows, metalflake plastic worms, red metal spoons, and lures that seem to resemble nothing so much as extraterrestrial spiders crossbred with safety pins.

All this leads you to suspect the awful truth: this fish will eat anything that moves. Small bass will strike at medium-size insect imitations, but larger fish will opt for substance: small fish, large insects (they will leap out of the water after dragonflies), field mice, frogs, tadpoles, and salamanders. Someone once swore to me that his brother had a friend who lived across the street from a guy who saw one gobble up a careless chickadee perched on a low branch over the water.

The unpredictable nature of bass make them interesting. Some days they are spooky, darting from view into the shadow of a weed bed; other days they may see you, watch you tie a lure with trembling fingers, and watch with a remarkably human imitation of contempt while you lead the lure right past their noses. On other days they may strike at that same lure regardless of your obvious presence.

Bass are at their best in muddy, weedy, shallow, warm, still waters. In the spring they remain torpid until water temperatures reach fifty-five to sixty degrees. When it warms to the low to midsixtiess, they start thinking about spawning. Like the smaller sunfishes, the male builds a nest near shore, though these bowers are often in slightly deeper water and are sloppy affairs compared with the pumpkinseed's work. When the water reaches sixty-four degrees, the female deposits two thousand to seven thousand eggs per pound of body weight, and the male guards them. Largemouth bass mature at two to three years of age; the females grow faster and live longer than males.

Bass are particularly vulnerable to angling in spring. They feed heavily before spawning, then cease. When the males are on their nests, they can be easily hooked because they will maul anything that approaches the eggs. Bass taken from their nests should be returned immediately. The best way to release a bass is to hold it firmly between thumb and forefinger by the lower jaw, leaving the body in the water. The fish acts paralyzed, and the hook can be easily extracted. At least consider forgoing treble hooks, which are difficult to extract.

Early in the season, bass will be in relatively open water because there's no vegetation to hide in. When surface water is cold, bass prefer deeper, warmer water. Their ideal temperature range is between sixty-eight and seventy-two degrees, but early in the season they will still be sluggish. Deep fishing with safety-pin spinnerbaits and regular spinners is the best strategy, but they need to be fished slowly, alternately pumping them up and allowing them to sink.

Once the water warms and the weeds come in, you can switch to surface fishing. In general, bass are stay-at-homes, remaining all their lives within a few hundred feet of where they were born. They have no affection for open water or direct sunlight. Middle-aged bass occasionally form loose groups that work together to encircle schools of bait fish, but for the most part they are solitary fish with an individual territory. Because of this, in small ponds, large bass will quickly disappear from the most accessible spots. If you are fishing a pond that forbids motorboats, rowing or paddling those few extra yards can make a difference. If on foot, the same strategy applies. Waders and belly boats may win you catcalls from the bass-boat fraternity, but they allow considerable stealth and give you unparalleled contact with the environment. There's nothing like getting right into that soup with them. For the most part you will be casting toward shore, retrieving toward shore, or retrieving through weed beds.

Too many anglers are in the habit of pulling up with a boat, carpet-bombing a cove with rods rigged three different ways, concluding there are no fish, then tearing off to the next spot. While boat engines do not tend to spook bass for long, if you approach quietly and observe for a moment, you can sometimes see the fish make a move before you cast, and you can take down the bass's exact address.

If you can't see evidence of fish, they are usually at the intersection of shade, protection, and a weedless corridor that will admit food or a makeshift diving board like a branch or lily pad where dinner will oblige by walking the plank. Even if the cove is bereft of bass, it's a rare day when you won't catch a pickerel or see a turtle, frog, water lily, mouse, muskrat, bat, hawk, diving beetle, freshwater jelly fish, red-winged blackbird, or something that will make you glad you kept your peace and took your time.

In the daytime bass prefer a canopy overhead, whether it's weed, water lily, or overhanging branches. In the largemouth real estate market it's structure, structure, structure. They will hold near sunken logs and stumps, brush-tangled islands, or up against shady banks of pickerel weed or purple loosestrife. They can be incredibly close to shore if there's water deep enough to hold them. Before the surface water gets too warm is a great time for flyfishing hair bugs and poppers. Though this will be possible summer evenings, in late spring the weeds are not yet all the way to the surface, and the fish are not hiding on the bottom. A System 8 flyrod is ideal but 7 and 6 will also work well, though they can make throwing bulky flies a labor. You don't need leader anywhere near the length you would use for trout: six feet of leader that will test to ten or twelve pounds should do fine.

Structure, the novice also soon learns, is anything that will snag a lure or tangle a line. If you like bass fishing, don't fall in love with your lures. This is not the time to become possessive of that three-dollar spinner or you may go home in tears. One of the most difficult things is the fact that at least some of the time, when you think you are hung up on a branch, a bass has delayed your lure a moment and then spat it out. If you suspect this, inevitably you will overstrike the next time the lure pauses and get hung up on a submerged log with the displacement of the Titanic. The heroic solution is terrific casting that puts your lure or fly precisely in the space between three lily pads, or one inch from the edge of a tree trunk. But because hooks plus weeds equal snags, many anglers use "weedless" lures and line up to 10-pound-test. Even some of the hair bugs used by flyfishers have their hooks shielded by monofilament hook guards.

In really hot weather, especially during daylight hours, you have to penetrate the clutter on the surface and get down five to fifteen feet. You have only a few alternatives: bait, weedless spoons, or rubber worms. Minnows need to be weighted to get them under the lily pads. Weedless spoons are equipped with a pair of flexible wire skids that allow them to be dragged over lily pads and stumps without snagging, then plopped into the open mouth of your quarry. Old-timers often dress these with pork tails so they taste a little less like toy car fenders. There are also weedless rubber lures that resemble frogs or are designed as jig-headed fish.

Plastic worms made their debut in the 1950s and were so successful that at least one state considered outlawing them. At first people were mystified; the devices resembled nothing in the bass's diet, yet bass struck at them time and again. I suspect the worms may have some living precedent in salamanders and eels, but who knows? Black, blue, purple, and a color often described as "motor oil" are popular. If the fish takes the worm near the top, it tends to be a violent strike. Once the worm is on the bottom, fish it very slowly. The bass may examine it for some time, tap at it a few times, even pick it up and swim with it. In my experience, if the fish is swimming away from you, or across your path, you can usually set the hook immediately. If the fish is swimming even slightly toward you, give it a moment to swallow the worm, then hit.

The advent of a late afternoon storm will occasionally precipitate a feeding frenzy. This is a productive time to fish, provided you leave before the lightning begins to strike. If you are foolhardy enough to linger, you will find that the fish themselves stop striking when the thunder gets close. Don't wait for "one last cast."

Midsummer, when daylight temperatures peak, bass will feed near the surface only in the early morning, evening, or after dark. As with most other fish, one of the most exciting times to pursue bass is at dusk when clouds of mosquitoes are rising and the silvery surface of the water is broken by the furtive wake of a field mouse or the boisterous crashing of muskrats. On a hot, humid evening, as the light wanes, you can hear bass exploding to the surface after moths, small muskrats, or frogs. Witnessing a baby field mouse disappear in an explosion of bass appetite will forever wean the observer from any greeting-card sentiments he or she may have entertained about Nature's peaceable kingdom. Spinners worked across the surface like a mouse pumping for dear life across an open stretch of water will often provoke a spectacular attack.

Complete darkness is also an exciting medium to fish in, but it's not as easy as it sounds. In general, you are better off fishing spots you know well, looking them over carefully during the day, memorizing the positions of stumps, logs, and low branches. There is nothing more frustrating than hearing a feeding bass a few yards away when your lure is snagged six feet above the water on a branch you forgot about. Flyfishing is even more complicated in the dark, so keep it as simple as possible.

Vibrating lures and even crankbaits loaded with a rattling BB are most useful at night or in murky water where the bass relies on sound and movement rather than on sight to find its prey. Floating plastic and balsa lures, or dark fly patterns that imitate wounded minnows, all work well. Fish them slowly, twitching them, letting them sit, moving them again, allowing the bass to zero in.

In September and October, two lovely and underfished months in New England, bass return to shallower water to beef up for winter. Be there.

MAINE

Lakes and Ponds

Belgrade
  Messalonskee Lake
  Salmon Lake

Belgrade Lakes
  Long Pond

Bridgton
  Highland Lake

China
  China Lake

Denmark
  Hancock Pond

East Otisfield
  Thompson Lake

Fayette
  Echo Lake

Fayette Township
  Parker Pond

Fryeburg
  Kezar Pond

Hermon
  Hermon Pond

Manchester
  Cobbosseecontee Lake

Monmouth
  Cochnewagon Pond

North Windham
  Little Sebago Lake

North Windham, Sebago Lake
State Park
  Sebago Lake

Rome
  Great Pond

Smithfield
  East Pond
  North Pond

South China
  Threemile Pond

Vassalboro
  Webber Pond

Wayne
  Androscoggin Lake

Winthrop
  Maranacook Lake

Woolwich
  Nequasset Pond

NEW HAMPSHIRE

Rivers and Streams

Connecticut River
Exeter River
Lamprey River

Merrimack River
Saco River

——Lakes and Ponds——

Amherst
: *Baboosic Lake*

Barnstead
: *Halfmoon Lake*

Barrington
: *Ayers Lake*
: *Swains Pond*

Canaan
: *Canaan Street Lake*
: *Goose Pond*

Chesterfield
: *Spofford Lake*

Derry
: *Island Pond*

Enfield
: *Mascoma Lake*

Gilmanton
: *Manning Lake*

Jaffrey
: *Contoocook Lake*

Kingston
: *Country Pond*
: *Kingston Lake*

Laconia
: *Paugus Bay*

Meredith
: *Lake Winnipesaukee*
: *Wickwas Lake*

Northwood
: *Northwood Lake*

Nottingham, Pawtuckaway State Park
: *Pawtuckaway Lake*

Salem
: *Arlington Mills Reservior*

Stoddard
: *Highland Lake*

Wakefield
: *Balch Pond*
: *Province Lake*

Washington
: *Ashuelot Pond*
: *Island Pond*

Weare
: *Horace Lake*

Windham
: *Canobie Lake*

Wolfeboro
: *Mirror Lake*

——VERMONT——

——Rivers and Streams——

Connecticut River
Lamoille River
Lemon Fair River
Lewis Creek
Little Otter Creek

Missisquoi River
Otter Creek
Rock River
Winooski River

——Lakes and Ponds——

Addison
  Dead Creek

Belmont
  Star Lake

Benson
  Sunrise Lake

Bristol
  Winona Lake

Burlington
  Lake Champlain

Castleton, Lake Bomoseen State Park
  Lake Bomoseen

Chittenden
  Chittenden Reservoir

Danby
  Danby Pond

Derby
  Lake Salem

Derby Center
  Lake Derby

Dorset, Emerald Lake State Park
  Emerald Lake

Fairlee
  Lake Morey

Fernville
  Fern Lake

Glover
  Daniels Pond

Guilford
  Weatherhead Hollow Pond

Hinesburg
  Lake Iroquois

Hortonville
  Lake Nineveh

Hubbardton
  Halfmoon Pond

Kents Corner
  Curtis Pond

Londonderry
  Lowell Lake

Ludlow
  Lake Rescue

Monkton Ridge
  Cedar Lake

Newbury
  Halls Lake

Newport
  Clyde Pond
  Lake Memphremagog

North Bennington
  Lake Paran

North Hartland, North Hartland State Park
  North Hartland Reservoir

North Montpelier
  North Montpelier Pond

North Springfield, North Springfield State Park
  North Springfield Reservoir

Plymouth
  Amherst Lake
  Woodward Reservoir

Salisbury, Salisbury Municipal Forest
  Lake Dunmore

Sherburne
  Kent Pond

Shoreham
  Richville Pond

South Poultney
  Lake St. Catherine
Sudbury
  Burr Pond
  Lake Hortonia
Thetford
  Lake Fairlee
Tinmouth
  Chipman Lake
Walden
  Lyford Pond

Wells
  Little Pond
West Castleton
  Glen Lake
West Glover
  Lake Parker
Wheelock
  Flagg Pond
Whitingham
  Sadawga Pond
Winhall
  Gale Meadows Pond

MASSACHUSETTS

Rivers and Streams

Assabet River
Charles River
Chicopee River
Concord River
Connecticut River

Ipswich River
Nashua River
Parker River
Quinebaug River

Lakes and Ponds

Ashland State Park
  Ashland Reservoir
Beartown State Forest
  Benedict Pond
Belchertown
  Metacomet Pond
Billerica
  Nuttings Pond
Boston
  Jamaica Pond
Bridgewater
  Nippenicket Pond
Carver
  Sampsons Pond

Charlton
  Buffumville Reservoir
  Gore Pond
Chelmsford
  Crystal Lake
Cheshire
  Cheshire Reservoir
Douglas
  Wallis Reservoir
Dunstable
  Massapoag Pond
Fall River
  Cooks Pond
  South Watuppa

Framingham
   Cochituate Lakes
   Farm Pond
Groton
   Baddacook Pond
   Knops Pond
Hadley
   Warner Lake
Hamilton
   Chebbaco Lake
Hanson
   Monponsett Lakes
Harvard
   Bare Hill Pond
Haverhill
   Saltonstall Lake
Holland
   Hamilton Reservoir
Hopkinton
   North Pond
   Whitehall Lake
Hubbardston
   Comet Pond
Hudson
   Fort Meadow Pond
Lakeville
   Long Pond
Lancaster
   Fort Pond
Lee
   Goose Pond
   Laurel Lake
Littleton
   Spectacle Pond
Methuen
   Forest Lake
Millbury
   Dorothy Pond
   Singletary Lake

Natick
   Cochituate Lakes
   Dug Pond
Needham
   Cutler Pond
New Salem
   Quabbin Reservoir
Norton
   Norton Reservoir
Palmer
   Forest Lake
Pittsfield
   Onota Lake
Randolph
   Ponkapoag Pond
Rochester
   Snipatuit Pond
Rutland
   Demond Pond
Sandwich
   Lawrence Pond
Southwick
   Congamond Lakes
Sterling
   East Waushacum Pond
Sturbridge
   Big Alum Pond
   Cedar Pond
   East Brimfield Reservoir
Sunderland
   Cranberry Lake
Taunton
   Sabbatia Lake
Tyngsboro
   Althea Lake
   Flint Pond
Wakefield
   Quannapowitt Lake

Wareham
    Mill Pond

Webster
    Webster Lake

Westborough
    A-1 Site

West Boxford
    Stiles Pond

West Boylston
    Wachusett Reservoir

West Brookfield
    Wickaboag Pond

Westfield
    Hampton Pond

Westford
    Forge Pond

Winchendon
    Whalom Pond
    Whitney Pond

Wrentham
    Pearl Lake

CONNECTICUT

Lakes and Ponds

Andover
    Bishop Swamp

Berlin
    Silver Lake

Bolton
    Bolton Lakes
    Bolton Notch Pond

Bozrah
    Fitchville Pond

Branford
    Lake Saltonstall

Brookfield
    Lake Lillinonah

Brooklyn
    Lawton Pond

Chester
    Cedar Lake
    Pataconk Lake

Colchester
    Pickerel Lake

Coventry
    Eagleville Lake

Danbury
    Candlewood Lake
    Lake Kenosia

Deep River
    Messershmidts Pond

Eastford
    Halls Pond

East Haddam
    Bashan Lake
    Moodus Reservoir
    Shaw Lake

East Lyme
    Dodge Pond
    Gorton Pond
    Pataganset Lake

Easton
    Saugatuck Reservoir

East Windsor
    Broad Brook Mill Pond

Ellington
    Crystal Lake

Farmington
    Batterson Park Pond

Glastonbury
  Angus Park Pond
  Smut Pond
Goshen
  Dog Pond
  Tyler Pond
  West Side Pond
Granby
  Manitook Lake
Griswold
  Glasgo Pond
  Hopeville Pond
  Pachaug Pond
Guilford
  Quonnipaug Lake
Hamden
  Lake Wintergreen
Hampton
  Hampton Reservoir
  Pine Acres Lake
Hebron
  Holbrook Pond
Kent
  Hatch Pond
  Leonard Pond
  Waramaug Lake
Killingly
  Alexander Lake
  Killingly Pond
  Ross Pond
  Wauregan Reservoir
Ledyard
  Lantern Hill Pond
  Long Pond
Lyme
  Rogers Lake
  Uncas Lake

Manchester
  Salters Pond
Mansfield
  Bicentennial Pond
  *Mansfield Training School
    Ponds*
  Naubesatuck Lake
Meriden
  Black Pond
Middlefield
  Beseck Lake
  Pistol Shop Pond
Middletown
  Crystal Lake
  Dooley Pond
Monroe
  Lake Zoar
Morris
  Bantam Lake
New Fairfield
  Ball Pond
New Hartford
  West Hill Pond
North Stonington
  Andersons Pond
  Billings Lake
  Hewitt Flyfishing Pond
  Lake of Isles
  Wyassup Lake
Norwich
  Bog Meadow Pond
Portland
  Great Hill Pond
Preston
  Amos Lake
  Avery Pond
Redding
  Starret Pond

Ridgefield
    Mamanasco Lake
Salem
    Gardner Lake
Salisbury
    East Twin Lake
    Wononscopomuc Lake
Sharon
    Indian Pond
    Mudge Pond
Shelton
    Housastonic Lake
Somers
    Somersville Mill Pond
Stonington
    Godfrey Pond
Suffield
    Congamond Lakes
Thompson
    Keach Pond
    Little Pond
    Perry Pond
    Quaddick Reservoir
    West Thompson Lake
Torrington
    Burr Pond
Trumbull
    Twin Brooks Park Pond

Union
    Bigelow Pond
    Breakneck Pond
    Hamilton Reservoir
    Mashapaug Lake
    Morey Pond
Vernon
    Tankerhoosen Lakes
Voluntown
    Beachdale Pond
    Beach Pond
    Hazard Pond
    Hodge Pond
Wallingford
    North Farms Reservoir
Watertown
    Black Rock Pond
Winchester
    Highland Lake
    Park Pond
    Winchester Lake
Windsor
    Rainbow Reservoir
Woodbury
    Quassapaug Lake
Woodstock
    Black Pond
    Muddy Pond
    Roseland Lake

RHODE ISLAND

Lakes and Ponds

Barrington
    Brickyard Pond
Burrillville
    Herring Pond
    Pascoag Reservoir

Sucker Pond
Tarkiln Pond
Wakefield Pond
Wallum Lake
Wilbur Pond
Wilson Reservoir

Charlestown
  Deep Pond
  Pasquiset Pond
  Schoolhouse Pond
  Watchaug Pond
Coventry
  Carbuncle Pond
  Flat River Reservoir
  Quidnick Reservoir
  Tiogue Lake
Cranston
  Blackamore Pond
  Dyer Pond
  Mashpaug Pond
  Meshanticut Pond
  Print Works Pond
  Ralph Pond
  Randall Pond
  West Warwick Reservoir
Cumberland
  Howard Pond
East Providence
  East Providence Reservoir
Exeter
  Beach Pond
  Boone Lake
  Breakheart Pond
  Browning Mill Pond
Foster
  Shippee Saw Mill Pond
Glocester
  Bowdish Reservoir
  Keech Pond
  Ponagansett Reservoir
  Smith & Sayles Reservoir
  Spring Grove Pond
  Waterman Reservoir
Hopkinton
  Alton Pond
  Locustville Pond

Long Pond
  Moscow Pond
  Wincheck Pond
  Yawgoog Pond
Johnston
  Oak Swamp Reservoir
Lincoln
  Butterfly Pond
  Olney Pond
Newport
  Lily Pond
New Shoreham
  Fresh Pond
  Middle Pond
North Kingstown
  Belleville Pond
  Pausacaco Pond
  Silver Spring Lake
North Smithfield
  Upper Slatersville Reservoir
Providence
  Wanskuck Pond
  Wenscott Reservoir
Richmond
  Canob Pond
  Sandy Pond
Smithfield
  Georgiaville Pond
  Slack's Reservoir
  Upper Sprague Reservoir
  Woonasquatucket Reservoir
South Kingstown
  Barber Pond
  Glen Rock Reservoir
  Hundred Acre Pond
  Indian Lake
  Thirty Acre Pond
  Tucker Pond
  Worden Pond
  Yawgoo Pond

Warwick
　Gorton Pond
　Warwick Pond
Westerly
　Chapman Pond
West Glocester
　Clarkville Pond

West Greenwich
　Carr Pond
　Loutitt Pond
　Mishnock Pond

Part III

Cold-Water Species

18.
Smallmouth Black Bass

The black bass is eminently an American fish. He has the faculty of asserting himself and making himself completely at home wherever placed. He is plucky, game, brave, and unyielding to the last when hooked. He has the arrowy rush of the trout, the untiring strength and bold leap of the salmon...I consider him, inch for inch and pound for pound, the gamest fish that swims.

—Dr. James A. Henshall
The Book of the Black Bass, 1881

In any red-blooded, patriotic discussion of the smallmouth, which was once popularly known as the black bass, one is obligated to trot out Dr. James A. Henshall's Final Word on the subject. My apologies to those who have been down that paragraph before, but it does bear rereading. One might be tempted to say that a less-prejudiced opinion might extend that praise, perhaps ounce for ounce, to the smaller sunfishes, but we will not quibble with a Kentucky gentleman.

Perhaps it was the American predilection for things large that relegated the smallmouth black bass, *micropterus dolomieui*, to second-class status after its better-known cousin, the largemouth bass. The smallmouth is lighter in weight, usually in the one- to three-pound range, but can grow to five or six pounds. Both fish occasionally occupy the same waters, particularly in large deep lakes, and though their physical differences seem inconsequential at first glance, several distinctions are in order.

When its mouth is closed, the largemouth's jaw usually extends back beyond the middle of its eye; the smallmouth's does not. The large-mouth's dorsal fin is divided, nearly notched, into a front and back; the smallmouth's is continuous. Finally, the largemouth often has a dark band that runs from front to back.

The smallmouth prefers cooler, clearer lakes, deeper than twenty-five feet, and can also be found in streams. It likes rocky or gravel bottoms and enjoys sunlight more than its sullen cousin. There is often a color difference, the largemouth tending to a greenish hue and the smallmouth more to bronze, hence its nickname, "bronzeback."

The original range of the smallmouth bass included the St. Lawrence watershed, the Great Lakes, and the upper Mississippi, but in the years following the Civil War, it rode like a hobo over the American landscape, a guest of the railroad companies. The fish was stocked in many places to encourage weekend outings and, in some cases, proved to be yet another insult to trout populations already struggling with environmental change. In addition to the railroad's free passes, many anglers who learned of the smallmouth's reputation took it upon themselves to pay the fish's way to their neighborhoods.

One such self-appointed fisheries manager was Mr. Samuel Tisdale, who, in 1856, apparently impatient with the rails, imported the first twenty-seven specimens to Massachusetts. They arrived from Saratoga, New York, and were deposited in Flax Pond, Wareham. By the follow-ing decade the species was being seeded into New Hampshire and probably around that time into Maine as well.

A solid fishery was quickly established and lasted until the large-mouth made its debut in a second invasion about forty years later. Although both species occasionally still inhabit the same lakes, largemouths and bluegills will tend to drive out smallmouths pretty quickly. Rhode Island authorities, for example, considered favoring the smallmouth in a few ponds but admitted that they could not keep anglers from planting largemouths in smallmouth waters. (A recent examination of the state's lakes and ponds indicated that through illegal stocking, 68 of the 101 waters surveyed contained large-mouth.)

The smallmouth has other strikes against it: it maturesslowly, taking up to three years, and grows slowly as well. Four or five years may pass before a smallmouth attains a foot in length. In addition, a parasitic worm, *proteocephalus ambloplites*, though not fatal, restricts the success-ful reproductive rate of the smallmouth. The parasite often moves from lake to lake when the largemouth is casually stocked.

This prejudice for the largemouth is a pity on two counts: despite the superficial resemblance of the two fish, the smallmouth has an entirely different personality and, some will argue, more merit than its larger relative. Perhaps the most apt analogy would be to compare the larger fish to a heavyweight and the smaller to a bantamweight. The smallmouth is more cautious, better eating, and, forgive my bias, somehow just a cleaner, brasher fish. What they may lack in quantity they more than compensate for in quality. They are agile, athletic, and noted for spectacular leaps and runs.

Nevertheless, in New England today the smallmouth is a prize less often sought or found than it once was, and it tends to prosper in northern rather than southern New England waters. The smallmouth is most successful in waters whose temperatures do not rise above eighty degrees or drop below sixty degrees in the summer; its ideal is in the lower seventies. Southeastern Maine, for example, is considered one of the best smallmouth regions in the country.

In lakes and ponds, smallmouth will not begin to feed until the water temperature rises to about fifty degrees. At that time they can be taken by flyfishing several streamer and bucktail patterns including the Black Nose Dace, Muddler Minnow, Mickey Finn, Grey Ghost, and various maribou streamers. They will also take many dry flies off the surface. Trolling with streamers is a popular way to find them, and anglers using spinning tackle should try small spinners, spoons, and crankbaits.

The black bass is hungry but wary in the springtime. The fish are intimidated by loud noises, so you may be better off with an electric motor, or with no motor—paddle, row, or sail. In any case, use fairly long lines so the boat is removed from the scene before the fish sees the lure. It likes to loiter about sunken reefs in water ten feet or less, often as shallow as two to three feet. However, it's important to remember that this doesn't always mean along the shore: productive reefs can be anywhere in a lake.

Feeding is interrupted as water temperatures reach the low to mid-sixties, and smallmouth males begin building nests. In southern New England this usually means late April or May; in the north, it can be as late as June. The male builds a nest in water relatively deep for a sunfish, from a foot or two all the way down to twenty feet, but afterward he abides by the mores of the other members of the sunfish family, driving up to three females into it and fertilizing their eggs. Females lay between two thousand and ten thousand eggs and then retire to the bottom to recover for a few days. The fry turn black after about a week, and the male remains to protect them until they reach about an inch long and are ready to disperse.

There is some controversy as to whether fishing should be allowed during spawning season, because the males will attack anything that strays within a few feet of their nests. Some biologists feel that the fish is too vulnerable during this season; others believe that in smaller, overpopulated lakes, culling a number of smallmouths will benefit the community.

Once the adults disperse after spawning, two distinct forms of behavior emerge. Some black bass strike out as individuals, staking out a territory—as would a largemouth; others begin schooling—more like bluegill. In summer, smallmouths become harder to take using artifical tackle, except early in the morning or on evenings when they feed in the shallows. In the shallows they may take the same sort of hair bugs and poppers that work on the largemouth, but these flies must be presented quietly and worked with a lot less flair. Large terrestrial patterns like hoppers and crickets will attract attention, and if you are spinning, try quietly fishing small crankbaits and balsa minnows.

During hot summer days, smallmouths still exhibit a preference for rocky shoals and bars, but these browsing grounds now tend to be deeper, in the twenty- to thirty-foot range. Most lures lose their attraction, or are difficult to get down that far, so many anglers switch to live bait. Though smallmouths will feed on small frogs, hellgrammites, and minnows, their craving for crayfish is legendary. The smallmouth's fervor for freshwater crustaceans could be compared to that of a vacationing tourist's craving for Maine lobster. Your best bet is to hook a crayfish through the tail with a number 4 or number 6 hook. Keep it on the bottom with a small piece of split-shot. Some tackle companies make a small rubber imitation of crayfish, which can be slowly jigged through the rocks. Other lead-headed jigs like plastic grub patterns in weights from 1/8 to 1/4 ounce are good as well.

In September and October, lake and pond smallmouth often gather in schools to chase bait fish in waters as shallow as one to three feet. Small crankbaits that can dive to the bottom, rise, and dive again will frequently turn their heads. By November the bass are again in deep water, and jigging with plastic grubs and small spoons may get you a few more before the season is over.

In the summer, just when catching smallmouths in still water is starting to get taxing and trout are starting to look for cold water, smallmouth fishing is at its peak in streams. River and stream fishing for smallmouth closely resembles trout fishing. The fish are solitary and territorial. Early in the season they may occupy the same water as brook trout, though, being more tolerant of warm temperatures, smallmouth will remain in it longer.

The Connecticut River and the rivers that empty into it from Vermont, New Hampshire, Massachusetts, and Connecticut (roughly above Hartford) all contain considerable smallmouth populations. Even the perennially polluted Millers River in Massachusetts has some wonderful bass. One June afternoon, just after midday, I took over a dozen in a hundred yards of water. None was edible because of the PCBs in the water, but the fish at least appeared healthy.

Like trout, smallmouths hover where they can wait for food to drift by: behind boulders and islands, in the calm water at the edges of current, in pools below riffles, or in the eddies behind sunken logs. Just as with trout, precision casting counts. In streams, along with the bucktails and streamers already mentioned, try a few large nymphs. Again, bait would include hellgrammites and crayfish with just enough split-shot to get them down. Small spinners and spoons also work; crankbaits and poppers need to be fished conservatively. Imitating wounded or panic-stricken bait fish with a lure will tend to spook a smallmouth rather than instigate them to strike.

MAINE

Lakes and Ponds

Acton
   Great East Lake
Allens Mills
   Clearwater Pond
Auburn
   Auburn Lake
Belgrade
   Messalonskee Lake
   Salmon Lake
Belgrade Lakes
   Long Pond
Bridgton
   Highland Lake
China
   China Lake
Cooper
   Cathance Lake
Crawford
   Crawford Lake
Damariscotta
   Biscay Pond
Danforth
   East Grand Lake
Dedham
   Hatcase Pond
   Phillips Lake
Denmark
   Moose Pond
Dexter
   Wassookeag Lake
East Orland
   Toddy Pond
East Otisfield
   Thompson Lake

East Palermo
   Sheepscot Pond
Ellsworth
   Branch Lake
   Green Lake
Embden
   Embden Pond
Fayette
   Echo Lake
Fayette Township
   Parker Pond
Fryeburg
   Lovewell Pond
Grand Lake Stream
   West Grand Lake
Greeley
   Sebec Lake
Greenville
   Wilson Ponds
Hermon
   Hermon Pond
Island Falls Township
   Pleasant Pond
Jefferson
   Damariscotta Lake
Lakeville
   Junior Lake
Liberty
   St. George Lake
Lincoln
   Mattanawcook Pond
Manchester
   Cobbosseecontee Lake

Meddybemps
: *Meddybemps Lake*

Molunkus Township
: *Molunkus Lake*

Monmouth
: *Cochnewagon Pond*

Newport
: *Sebasticook Lake*

North Windham
: *Little Sebago Lake*

North Windham, Sebago Lake State Park
: *Sebago Lake*

Orland
: *Alamoosook Lake*

Orono
: *Pushaw Lake*

Poland
: *Range Ponds*

Princeton
: *Pocomoonshine Lake*

Readfield
: *Torsey Pond*

Rome
: *Great Pond*

Shapleigh
: *Mousam Lake*

Smithfield
: *East Pond*
: *North Pond*

South China
: *Threemile Pond*

Sullivan
: *Flanders Pond*

Township 3, Range 12, WELS, Piscataquis County
: *Chesuncook Lake*

Township 6, Range 1, NBPP, Penobscot County
: *Scraggly Lake*

Township 7, Range 2, NBPP, Washington County
: *Pleasant Lake*

Township 27, ED BPP
: *Big Lake*

Township 40 MD, Hancock County
: *Nicatous Lake*

Township 43, MD BPP, Washington County
: *Third Machias Lake*

Vassalboro
: *Webber Pond*

Waterboro
: *Little Ossipee Lake*

Wayne
: *Androscoggin Lake*

Winthrop
: *Maranacook Lake*

NEW HAMPSHIRE

Rivers and Streams

Connecticut River
Exeter River

Merrimack River

——Lakes and Ponds——

Andover
   Highland Lake
Barnstead
   Halfmoon Lake
   Lower Suncook Lake
   Upper Suncook Lake
Barrington
   Ayers Lake
   Swains Pond
Bradford
   Lake Massasecum
Canaan
   Canaan Street Lake
   Goose Pond
Chatham
   Kimball Pond
Chesterfield
   Spofford Lake
Conway
   Conway Lake
Deering
   Deering Reservoir
Derry
   Island Pond
Dublin
   Thorndike Pond
Enfield
   Crystal Lake
   Mascoma Lake
Franklin
   Webster Lake
Gilmanton
   Crystal Lake
   Manning Lake
   Sunset Lake
Grafton
   Grafton Pond

Harrisville
   Silver Lake
Hebron
   Newfound Lake
Holderness
   Squam Lake
   Little Squam Lake
Kingston
   Country Pond
Laconia
   Paugus Bay
   Winnisquam Lake
Madison
   Silver Lake
Manchester
   Massabesic Lake
Meredith
   Lake Waukewan
   Lake Winnipesaukee
   Pemigewasset Pond
   Wickwas Lake
Nelson
   Granite Lake
New Durham
   Merrymeeting Lake
New London
   Little Sunapee Lake
   Pleasant Lake
Northwood
   Jenness Pond
Nottingham, Pawtuckaway State Park
   Pawtuckaway Lake
Ossipee
   Dan Hole Ponds
   Ossipee Lake
Rumney
   Stinson Lake

Salem
    Arlington Mills Reservoir
Stoddard
    Highland Lake
Strafford
    Bow Lake
Sunapee
    Sunapee Lake
Tamworth
    Chocorua Lake
Wakefield
    Balch Pond
    Great East Lake
    Lovell Lake
    Province Lake

Warren
    Lake Tarleton
Washington
    Ashuelot Pond
Weare
    Horace Lake
Webster
    Lake Winnepocket
Windham
    Canobie Lake
Wolfeboro
    Lake Wentworth
    Rust Pond

VERMONT

Rivers and Streams

Barton River
Black River
Clyde River
Connecticut River
Huntington River
Lamoille River
Lemon Fair River
Lewis Creek
Little Otter Creek
Mad River

Middlebury River
Missisquoi River
Otter Creek
Passumpsic River
Stevens River
Wells River
White River
Williams River
Winooski River

Lakes and Ponds

Addison
    Dead Creek
Barton
    Crystal Lake
Brighton
    Island Pond
    Spectacle Pond

Burlington
    Lake Champlain
Cabot
    Molly's Falls Pond
Castleton, Lake Bomoseen State
Park
    Lake Bomoseen

Charleston
  Echo Lake
Concord
  Miles Pond
Craftsbury
  Great Hosmer Pond
  Little Hosmer Pond
Danville
  Joes Pond
Derby
  Brownington Pond
  Lake Salem
Dorset, Emerald Lake State Park
  Burr Pond
Eden Mills
  Lake Eden
Elmore, Elmore State Park
  Lake Elmore
Fairfield
  Fairfield Pond
Fairlee
  Lake Morey
Fletcher
  Metcalf Pond
Franklin, Lake Carmi State Park
  Lake Carmi
Greensboro
  Lake Eligo
Groton
  Lake Groton
Groton, Groton State Park
  Ricker Pond
Hinesburg
  Lake Iroquois
Hortonville
  Lake Nineveh
Hubbardton
  Beebe Pond

Kents Corner
  Curtis Pond
Londonderry
  Lowell Lake
Ludlow
  Lake Rescue
Lunenburg
  Neal Pond
Marshfield
  Marshfield Pond
Milton
  Arrowhead Mountain Lake
Morgan
  Seymour Lake
Newport
  Clyde Pond
  Lake Memphremagog
North Calais
  Lake Mirror
North Hartland, North Hartland
  State Park
  North Hartland Reservoir
North Springfield, North
  Springfield State Park
  North Springfield Reservoir
Plymouth
  Amherst Lake
  Woodward Reservoir
Pownal
  South Stream Pond
Salisbury, Salisbury Municipal
  Forest
  Lake Dunmore
Shelburne
  Shelburne Pond
Somerset
  Somerset Reservoir
South Poultney
  Lake St. Catherine

South Ryegate
  Ticklenaked Pond
South Woodbury
  Forest Lake (Nelson Pond)
  Sabin Pond
Stamford
  Lake Hancock
Stratton
  Grout Pond
Sudbury
  Burr Pond
  Lake Hortonia
Thetford
  Lake Fairlee
Tyson
  Echo Lake
Walcott
  Walcott Pond
Walden
  Lyford Pond

Wallingford
  Wallingford Pond
Waterbury, Mount Mansfield
  State Forest
  Waterbury Reservoir
West Castleton
  Glen Lake
Whitingham
  Sherman Reservoir
Willington
  Lake Raponda
Wilmington
  Harriman Reservoir (Lake Whitingham)
Windsor
  Lake Runnemede
Woodbury
  Buck Lake
  Lake Greenwood
  Valley Lake

MASSACHUSETTS

Rivers and Streams

Assabet River
Concord River
Deerfield River
Millers River

Quaboag River
Quinebaug River
Swift River
Westfield River

Lakes and Ponds

Amesbury
  Lake Gardner
Barnstable
  Chequaquet Lake
  Garretts Pond
  Lovells Pond
  Mystic and Middle Ponds

Becket
  Center Pond
  Greenwater Pond
  Shaw Pond
Brewster
  Seymour Pond
Concord
  Walden Pond

Eastham
  Herring Pond
Harwich
  Long Pond
Hubbardston
  Comet Pond
Huntington
  Norwich Lake
Lakeville
  Long Pond
Lee
  Goose Pond
Mashpee
  John's Pond
  Mashpee Pond
Monterey
  Garfield Lake
  Lake Buel
New Salem
  Quabbin Reservoir

Otis
  Benton Pond
  East Otis Reservoir
  Pig Pond
Plainfield
  Plainfield Pond
Randolph
  Ponkapoag Pond
Sandisfield
  Lower Spectacle Pond
Sandwich
  Snake Pond
  Triangle Pond
Sturbridge
  Big Alum Pond
Sutton
  Manchaug Pond
Tolland
  Noyes Pond
West Boylston
  Wachusett Reservoir

CONNECTICUT

Lakes and Ponds

Bolton
  Bolton Lakes
Brookfield
  Lake Lillinonah
Chester
  Cedar Lake
Colebrook
  Colebrook Flood Control
    Impoundment
Coventry
  Eagleville Lake
  Waumgumbaug Lake

Eastford
  Halls Pond
East Haddam
  Bashan Lake
Easton
  Saugatuck Reservoir
Ellington
  Crystal Lake
Guilford
  Quonnipaug Lake
Hartland
  West Branch Reservoir

Kent
   Waramaug Lake
Killingly
   Alexander Lake
   Killingly Pond
   Wauregan Reservoir
Monroe
   Lake Zoar
Morris
   Bantam Lake
New Hartford
   Lake McDonough
   West Hill Pond
North Stonington
   Wyassup Lake
Norwich
   Bog Meadow Pond

Salem
   Gardner Lake
Shelton
   Housatonic Lake
Thompson
   Keach Pond
   West Thompson Lake
Union
   Hamilton Reservoir
   Mashapaug Lake
Voluntown
   Beach Pond
   Hazard Pond
Woodstock
   Black Pond

RHODE ISLAND

Lakes and Ponds

Black Hut Management Area
   Spring Lake
Burrillville
   Wallum Lake
Charlestown
   Watchaug Pond
Coventry
   Quidnick Reservoir
   Tiogue Lake
Exeter
   Beach Pond
Hopkinton
   Asheville Pond
Lincoln
   Olney Pond

Richmond
   Sandy Pond
South Kingstown
   Barber Pond
   Indian Lake
   Worden Pond
   Yawgoo Pond
Tiverton
   Stafford Pond
Warwick
   Gorton Pond
   Warwick Pond
West Greenwich
   Carr Pond
   Mishnock Pond

19.
Brown Trout

It is a bad day; the sun is up; the trout are not feeding. We fail again and again. But fishing teaches a stern morality; inculcates a remorseless honesty. The fault may be with ourselves.

—Virginia Woolf
"Fishing," 1947

The brown trout, *salmo trutta*, is the hallowed European fish of Dame Juliana Berners, of Izaak Walton and Charles Cotton, and, after it arrived in the United States, of the studious and reclusive master fly designer, Theodore Gordon. Some will tell you that this is the "true" trout—that the brookie is merely a char, that stocked rainbows are for anglers more impressed by full stringers than real fishing. Others will tell you that the brown is a fussy foreigner brought in to cater to the tastes of those persnickety Anglophiles and that it has contributed to the decline of the native trout.

When farming and timbering deforested vast tracts of New England in the eighteenth and nineteenth centuries, waters without a canopy of foliage warmed, and the brook trout's domain shrank. Because the brown tolerated water temperatures five degrees higher than its American cousins, portions of many rivers seemed ideal for the new fish. It needed less oxygen than the natives, would tolerate more pollution, and consequently could thrive in slower-moving waters, either farther downstream or in lakes.

For those anglers devoted to it, the brown trout is more than a fish, it's an institution. Nearly synonymous with flyfishing, no other fish swims in the shadow of such a huge and sometimes pedantic corpus of literature, no other has museums devoted to enshrining the paraphernalia and memorabilia of those who fish for it. Not even the bass angler can marshal such a daunting arsenal of precisely crafted equipment. The brown's cult can transform ordinary mortals into Type-A anglers, into amateur entomologists muttering Latin like archbishops, into journeymen engineers discussing the relative tensile strength of 1X tippets. Neophyte anglers often feel compelled to enroll in flyfishing courses even before daring to wet their feet—or rather their three-hundred-dollar waders.

But, back for the moment to the fish. The first brown trout eggs to reach these shores were imported from England by one W. L. Gilbert of Plymouth, Massachusetts, in 1882. Those few that hatched were joined in the next decade by other imports. The principal strains were German Von Behr browns and Scottish Loch Leven browns, but after a while, in the spirit of the new continent, they intermingled into a sort of American mutt. By 1885 they had reached Maine and New Hampshire, by 1892 Vermont, and they have been with us ever since.

Dark brown on its back and golden along its flanks, the brown has coarser scales than either the rainbow or the brook trout. Its flanks are stippled with faintly haloed black or brown spots with a few red or orange ones thrown in by Nature just to make it look like a better tweed. The spots fade or disappear along the tail. It can be physically distinguished from the others by the teeth that line the roof of its mouth. On an average it grows to between six and fifteen inches and has a heavier-set build than the sleek brookie or rainbow. In New England, it generally runs from one or two on up to eight pounds; in the Old World, Scotland's thirty-nine-and-a-hal-pound record still stands, and we haven't yet reached half that.

The new fish did not exactly rush to impale itself on the hooks of anglers accustomed to the careless ways of the brook trout. Time and again, when fisheries personnel surveyed streams that anglers considered bereft of fish, they discovered that indeed there were few brook trout, but dozens of browns were hiding in the nooks. By one estimate, in Maine, anglers catch five brookies for every brown. In addition, the brown has longevity on its side; at three years of age, when most brook trout are getting ready to pass on to that big stream up yonder, browns are just reaching maturity and have two to five years to go. There even have been a few isolated ten-year-olds. The new fish not only competes with the brook trout, it eats it. For this reason, because brook trout are defenseless against them, today browns are only stocked in water that is no longer suitable for self-sustaining brook trout populations.

Quite simply, the brown is a sly and cautious creature, the wiliest, not only of the trouts but possibly of all New England fish, period. One stumble on the bottom, one clumsy cast, and it's gone. Sometimes, for no explicable reason, it seems to be fasting. For some anglers, like Theodore Gordon and his disciples, this elusiveness only incited greater perseverance. "Should it be an off day, when the fish are glued to the bottom of the stream, how hard we work to tempt them! We feel a certain animosity against the trout. 'Confound them! They must rise at something'...If it was always easy to take trout, surely we would not be so fond of fly-fishing."

In April, when it quickens from the torpor of winter, the brown trout will be more likely to feed from midmorning to midafternoon. Though some purists choose to go after it with nymphs, it is particularly difficult to tempt a brown on any kind of a fly this time of year. In the roiling early spring streams, browns are more easily taken on worms, minnows, or, dare I say it—marshmallows—drifted near the bottom. Number 6 and number 8 hooks are good for bait fishing. This is tricky fishing until one gains a good feel for the bottom—too high and the trout ignore the bait, too low and you hang up on rocks and branches. In lakes, trolling flashy spinners and spoons, even plugs, will often provoke a fish.

Though they can live in fast water, most brown trout will settle into relatively slow pools downstream from the other two trout species. They are attracted to interesting addresses—sunken logs, undercut banks, branches that arch low over the water, even old tires. Fishing for a trout firmly ensconced in its jumble of rocks or tangled overhang or twisted tree trunk can turn into a campaign. Bait has to appear as if it had casually floated downstream, yet arrive right on the fish's doorstep.

Later in the spring, brown trout feed mostly in twilight and into the night. The younger browns will eat crayfish and hellgrammites when available, but as the weather warms, three families of insects and their larvae—the mayfly, caddis fly, and stonefly—dominate their diet. This enthusiastic appetite for *ephemeroptera*, *trichoptera*, and *plecoptera*, as the families are known to taxonomy, has led their pursuers to design hundreds of patterns to imitate all stages of these insects' life cycles. There are flies that represent the immature nymph, the emerging dun, the mating spinner, even flies to represent the fallen, spent Icarus as he is swept away by the stream.

Because hundreds of books have been written on the subject—some of them virtual manifestos—we will oversimplify the subject here. In a nutshell, the angler first tries to locate the fish by its rises. Slowly rising fish will usually consider taking whatever comes along. Quick rises indicate major insect hatches, and the trout become fixated in their insistence upon the creature of the moment. Although many anglers in Britain cast only to rises, in America if there are no rises in evidence, we rudely attempt to provoke them by casting to what appear to be likely spots.

To achieve the desired effect, you have to approach unsuspected and present the fly perfectly; if the fish doesn't like the way it looks on the plate, you seldom get a second shot at it that evening. Because you are casting partly upstream, be sure that when the fly floats above the fish, it isn't dragging in the current. In the beginning, it's disappointing. Don't despair. I would rather not count the times I have spotted a rise, wriggled into my waders, crept like an assassin into the stream, and blew it all with one overexcited cast that landed more like a stone than a stonefly. The earliest successes I had with trout were accompanied by an obliging breeze that ruffled the surface sufficiently to disguise a less than respectable showing. Unfortunately, these breezes are about as far apart in the evening as taxis in a downpour.

Prominent dry flies include Adamses, Hendricksons, Cahills, and the Quill Gordon. If there is a shop that sells flies near the stream, it's their business to know what insects are rising and even their aproximate sizes. Equivalent dry flies usually run from number 12 to 18; if you cast to a fish and it does not take your fly but continues to rise, try a smaller version of the same fly. Use as fine and as long a leader as you can manage well. The tippet should test about one and a half pounds. You will need longer leader, up to twelve feet, on lakes.

Even perfect presentation of the right flies will be far more apt to attract smaller rather than larger fish. Maturing brown trout turn increasingly to a diet of fish, and even masters of the dry fly will often turn to bucktails and streamers when pursuing a big one.

In later years, past the age of breeding, these large and solitary fish can grow into ancient dictators, tyrannizing their neighborhoods, gorging on bait fish and other small trout including their own kind, and dying of old age before they can be caught. Late at night, especially in hot months like July and August, these large fish will emerge from their lairs and actively patrol pools for bait fish. Such solitary browns are located more by ear than by eye. Drifting live grasshoppers on the surface, using a bobber, or casting large flies and even bass bugs may receive a warm reception. (Be sure to check individual state regulations on fishing for trout at night—New Hampshire, for example, forbids fishing from two hours after sundown to one hour before sunrise.)

Should the trout accept your offering under any of these circumstances, it may resist capture by tangling or snapping your line on a branch or even getting purchase on whatever it can grab with its mouth.

The brown trout spawns in the fall, anytime from October to December. As the fish begin moving upstream, usually in September, they feed heavily and may fall to large streamers or spinners. By the middle of October, when they begin to arrive at their river's headwaters, feeding ceases. The female, like the salmon, digs a nest in the gravel. She deposits between 200 and 6,000 eggs, which winter over and hatch in spring. The young mature in two to three years and repeat the cycle. Lake-bound communities spawn in gravel near shore. Though many waters are supplemented with hatchery fish, the brown can, unlike the rainbow, establish a self-sustaining population. In the years to come, if the region's trout waters continue to deteriorate, the brown trout's star will probably rise even further, despite or perhaps because of its admirable tendency to remain elusive.

You can spend a lifetime studying the brown trout—its habits, its food, its seasons—and the culture anglers have built around it. You can immerse yourself in the evolutions of its flies and the biographies of the men and the women who created them. You can transform a visit to Vermont's Batten Kill River into a pilgrimage. Yet regardless of the physical, social, literary, and historical baggage you drag down to the stream, in the end it's you and the fish. Practice your casting. Go gently. Stay low. But remember: it's a fish, and a fish doesn't know a twelve-hundred-dollar Tonkin cane rod from a plumber's helper.

(See also "Sea Run Trout," chapter 5.)

MAINE

Rivers and Streams

Abagadasset River
Cathance River
Eastern River
Great Works River
Kennebunk River
Little River
Magalloway River
Merriland River

Piscataqua River
Saco River
St. George River
Sebasticook River
Sheepscot River
South River
Webb River
Wilson Stream

Lakes and Ponds

Acton
    Great East Lake
    Mousam Lake
Auburn
    Auburn Lake
Bridgton
    Highland Lake
China
    China Lake
Damariscotta
    Biscay Pond
Davis Township
    Kennebago Lake
Dedham
    Phillips Lake
Denmark
    Hancock Pond
Ellsworth
    Branch Lake
Fryeburg
    Kezar Pond
    Lovewell Pond
Grand Lake Stream
    West Grand Lake
Gray
    Little Sebago Lake

Hancock County
    Nicatous Lake
Hartland
    Moose Pond (Great Moose
    Lake)
Island Falls Township
    Pleasant Pond
Liberty
    St. George Lake
Magalloway Township
    Richardson Lakes
Molunkus Township
    Molunkus Lake
Monmouth
    Cochnewagon Pond
Oakland
    Salmon and McGrath Lakes
North Windham
    Sebago Lake
Palermo
    Sheepscot Pond
Rangeley
    Rangeley Lake
Rome
    Great Pond

South Vassalboro
    Threemile Pond

Sullivan
    Flanders Pond

Sullivan Township
    Tunk Lake

Vassalboro
    Webber Pond

Waterboro
    Little Ossipee Lake

Winthrop
    Maranacook Lake

NEW HAMPSHIRE

Rivers and Streams

Androscoggin River
Ashuelot River
Connecticut River
Exeter River
Gale River
Lamprey River

Mascoma River
Saco River
Soughegan River
Sugar River
Swift River

Lakes and Ponds

Conway
    Conway Lake

Derry
    Island Pond

Errol
    Akers Pond
    Umbagog Lake

Manchester
    Lake Massabesic

Pittsburgh
    Back Lake
    Lake Francis

Wakefield
    Great East Lake

VERMONT

Rivers and Streams

Barton River
Batten Kill (and West Branch)
Black River
Browns River
Castleton River
Clarendon River
Clyde River
Cold River

Connecticut River
Deerfield River
Dog River
Green River
Hoosic River
Huntington River
Lamoille River (and North Branch)
Lewis Creek

Mad River
Middlebury River
Mill River
Missisquoi River
Moose River
New Haven River
Nulhegan River Otter Creek
Ompompanoosuc River
Ottauquechee River
Passumpsic River
Poultney River
Saxtons River
Trout River

Tyler Brook
Waits River
Walloomsic River
Waterbury river
Wells River
West River
White River (and First Branch,
    Second Branch, Third Branch)
Williams River
Willoughby River
Winhall River
Winooski River (and North Branch,
    Kingsbury Branch)

——Lakes and Ponds——

Averill
    Forest Lake
Brighton
    Island Pond
    Spectacle Pond
Burlington
    Lake Champlain
Cabot
    Molly's Falls Pond
Castleton, Lake Bomoseen State
    Park
    Lake Bomoseen
Charleston
    Echo Lake
Chittenden
    Chittenden Reservoir
Danville
    Joes Pond
Groton
    Lake Groton
Jamaica
    Ball Mountain Reservoir

Marlboro
    South Pond
Marshfield
    Marshfield Pond
Morgan
    Seymour Lake
Newport
    Lake Memphremagog
Peacham
    Peacham Pond
Perkinsville
    Stoughton Pond
Plymouth
    Woodward Reservoir
Pownal
    South Stream Pond
Somerset
    Somerset Reservoir
Townshend
    Townshend Reservoir
Wallace Pond
    Wallace Pond

Whitingham
  Sherman Reservoir
Wilmington
  *Harriman Reservoir (Lake
    Whitingham)*

Winhall
  Gale Meadows Pond
Windsor
  Mill Pond
Woodbury
  Lake Greenwood

MASSACHUSETTS

Rivers and Streams

Millers River

Lakes and Ponds

Barnstable
  Hathaway Pond
Brewster
  Cliff Pond
  Flax Pond
Concord
  Walden Pond
East Brookfield
  South Pond
Florida
  North Pond
Hubbardston
  Asnacomet Pond

Lee
  Goose Pond
Plymouth
  Big Sandy Pond
  Long Pond
Springfield
  Lake Lorraine
Warwick
  Shemet Pond
West Boylston
  Wachusett Reservoir

CONNECTICUT

Rivers and Streams

Farmington River

Salmon River

Lakes and Ponds

Danbury
  Candlewood Lake
Ellington
  Crystal Lake

New Hartford
  West Hill Pond
Union
  Mashapaug Lake

RHODE ISLAND

Lakes and Ponds

Burrillville
  Tarkiln Pond
  Wallum Lake
Charlestown
  Watchaug Pond
Exeter
  Beach Pond
  Dawley Pond
Glocester
  Bowdish Reservoir
  Mowry Meadow Pond
  Spring Grove Pond

Johnston
  Oak Swamp Reservoir
North Kingstown
  Silver Spring Lake
Portsmouth
  Melville Pond
South Kingstown
  Tucker Pond

20.
Rainbow Trout

...he had a way of describing trout as if they were a precious and intelligent metal.

Silver is not a good adjective to describe what I felt when he told me about trout fishing.

I'd like to try to get it right.

Maybe trout steel. Steel made from trout. The clear snow-filled river acting as foundry and heat.

—Richard Brautigan
Trout Fishing in America. 1967

The first time I remember well. It was May in Massachusetts, and a heady dose of Hemingway sent me and my yard-sale flyrod in pursuit of the noble rainbow trout. Aglow with that naive devotion that shields the rank beginner from reality's sharp edges, and armed with an impressive array of Royal Coachmen, Blue Duns, and Quill Gordons, I arrived at a slow, murky stream whose identity I would blush to disclose. After a day of casting to what I thought were rises, I accidentally connected with a single specimen of the creature I had come to meet.

The trout jumped and danced across the water but was no match for the angler. "Fish," I said under my breath, "you fought well, fish," and I fervently put him on a stringer. Slipping the stringer over one side of the boat, I pulled up the bottle of Chablis cooling on the other. Sometime while I was rowing wearily back, I felt a sharp tug on the stringer. Hand over hand I retrieved what was left of my hard-earned fish, just glimpsing the hind legs of a massive snapping turtle disappearing in the tea-colored water.

I beached my boat near a bridge where a man and his son showed me a dozen trout in a Styrofoam cooler. They had been murdering them, they told me, and I was about to ask what flies they were using when I saw the bag of fluorescent marshmallows. It was then, Pilar, that I learned disillusionment.

The rainbow trout, *salmo gairdneri,* a fish fair as its name, is native to the Pacific watersheds west of the Rocky Mountains. It thrives in those waters, living up to ten years and occasionally reaching remarkable dimensions—the record is an Idaho specimen that came to the net at thirty-seven pounds.

Rainbows have conspicuous scales peppered with black spots that radiate along their tails. While they are dark when viewed from above, with backs ranging from blue to green to brown, their handsome flanks have a silvery sheen tinged with washes of yellow, green, gray, and pink. On the average they are larger than brook trout, growing to between eight and fifteen inches, and even larger when settled into lakes and streams with good forage. The region's record, fourteen pounds, was caught in the Connecticut River. Nevertheless, how large they are in New England usually depends on how large they were when released from the hatchery. Few survive more than a season.

In 1878 New Hampshire imported its first rainbow eggs from California's McCloud River. Maine followed suit in 1880, bringing in fifty thousand fingerlings. The truth is, the rainbow was introduced into eastern waters to fill a conspicuous hole. "It is believed," wrote Jordan and Evermann in 1902, "that this species will serve for stocking streams formerly inhabited by the eastern brook trout in which the latter no longer thrives owing to the clearing of the lands about the sources of the streams."

Even then there was ambivalence. Jordan and Evermann go on to praise the rainbow as "a fish whose gameness will satisfy the most exacting of expert anglers and whose readiness to take any proper lure will please the most impatient of inexperienced amateurs." But, they confessed that there is "no comparison between the rainbow in its California mountain streams and those introduced into eastern waters, where the warmer water temperature has enervated them, and where they have grown large and fat and sluggish."

Though rainbow trout prosper in temperatures just below sixty-eight degrees, if there is sufficient oxygen in the water, they can weather temperatures over eighty degrees for brief periods. Because they can be bred and grown so quickly in captivity, they have become the darlings of fisheries and wildlife operations nationwide, not to mention the farms in Idaho and Utah that ship them to your local supermarket. In some circles they are known as hatchery Herefords or government-issue trout, and in truth, fishing for them in ponds and sluggish streams resembles hunting Thanksgiving dinner on a turkey farm.

Every spring, and sometimes a second time in the fall, over much of the United States, various fisheries and wildlife departments back the trout truck up to local ponds, and anglers line the banks, some with flyrods, more often with sacks of fluorescent marshmallows, and everyone fishes for a few weeks until either every last trout is taken or is suffocated by the warming water. A percentage of these are hatchery brook trout, but the majority are rainbows.

Participating in this now perennial rite of spring requires little more than a spinning rod and some split-shot fixed a foot to a foot and a half from the end of your line to carry a number 6 hook to the bottom. Hatchery fish tend to hang together to some degree and browse the bottom five to ten feet down. You can also fish with a bobber, your hook suspended a yard or so below it. The rainbows that swim in a local pond are not much more difficult to catch than sunfish. Accustomed to seeing their feeders, they are nowhere near as timorous as wild fish and will take worms, salmon eggs, cheese, or corn kernels.

For those who prefer more active methods, flyfishing streamers or dry flies or spin-casting small spinners and spoons is also effective. In general, stocking rainbows plays to the worst part of an angler's human nature, elevating catching a famous fish far above the art of fishing itself.

In clean lakes and cold-water ponds fed by cool springs, the rainbow may survive several seasons, and the longer it lasts in a "wild" state, eating insects, the more challenging it becomes and the more its flavor improves. The rainbow will remain near the surface until water temperatures exceed seventy degrees. As waters warm, it will appear near the surface in the evenings, feed there through the night, and descend again in the morning. Those that make it through the spring live deep in the pond in the warm months. At these times, and as the rainbow gets older, it will begin supplementing its diet with small fishes.

In the cold, fast-moving waters of Vermont and New Hampshire, the rainbow is far more challenging and more apt to live up to its reputation. Especially when they rise to the top after insect hatches, rainbows become ideal quarry for flyfishers with dry flies and long leaders. Casting flies to a fish that rises to meet the invitation on the very verge that separates us is undeniably appealing. That it is more apt than a brown trout to feed off the surface has no doubt added to its popularity.

Though still not exactly wily, in tumbling water a rainbow is far less of a sitting duck. In streams, rainbows are partial to faster water more than either brook trout or brown trout, preferring riffles or areas right below waterfalls. Considering a river as a whole, rainbow trout tend to occupy water downstream from the brook trout and upstream from browns. From an angler's perspective, they also fall in the middle: harder to catch than brookies and easier to catch than browns.

Early spring stream fishing tends to be problematical, especially for flyfishers. In states with an "opening day," a few committed anglers will try bumping weighted nymph patterns or streamers near the bottom, but most anglers turn to worms or whatever live nymphs they can find under rocks, on a line loaded with enough split-shot to take it deep. These they cast slightly upstream and allow to bounce down with the water. When trout take bait or a lure in this kind of water, the angler tends to feel only a tap and needs to set the hook immediately.

Between April and the end of June, rainbows live almost entirely on insects: either on the larvae in the water or those flying above. Rainbows will leap out of the water after hovering mayflies and, on rarer, heart-stopping occasions, will jump after a slowly presented angler's fly, even before it has settled. This is the classic flyfishing season, and anglers attempt to grab and examine the insects rising off the water.

In the fall, when insect hatches diminish, flyfishers turn to wet flies, streamers, and bucktails. They cast upstream and allow the fly to float down, then hang a moment in the current. The fish will often follow it downstream and then hit. If it doesn't, retrieve the fly slowly, vary the retrieve with a few sharp pulls, and repeat.

In spring, unlike other fall-spawning trout, the rainbow reproduces in the gravelly riffles of its stream—or it tries to. Unfortunately, New England's waters are naturally too acidic for it to succeed. Consequently, the few self-sustaining populations are concentrated in the region's handful of alkaline streams.

Another thing that keeps the rainbow from successfully settling in New England is its propensity for migration. The McCloud River rainbow descends to the sea after about three years and returns as the steelhead, essentially a sea-run rainbow. At one time a strain of rainbow known as *salmo shasta*, a sort of landlocked rainbow, would have been the ideal progenitor of a self-sustaining population. Somehow these two strains, with human help, accidentally crossbred, and the "landlocked" tendency of the shasta disappeared. Today, stocked fish are hybrids of the two and sooner or later begin slipping downstream looking for the ocean.

While the genuine steelhead is still unknown in New England, the rainbows that venture into Lake Champlain and feed on its provender return to their native streams (the Willoughby River, for example) with far greater weight than their stream and small-pond cousins. However, some recent catches of large rainbows in the St. Lawrence River are leading biologists to speculate that rainbow refugees from Champlain are trying to find salt water even farther afield.

As much as one would like rainbows to settle in New England, after a century of stocking, it doesn't look like they really belong here. It takes little imagination to see that the rainbow is the victim of a vast put-and-take operation. In some situations, rainbows are useful in that they lure anglers away from brook trout or relieve fishing pressure on young browns. One cannot help but wonder how much things might have improved if the money that went into stocking had been spent on restoring some of the region's brook trout waters rather than creating the transparent illusion of a healthy trout fishery. Stocking can hardly be said to teach anglers restraint or anything else about the environment. If anything, it extends disposable consumption to angling. In Yosemite, the week after trout are stocked, rangers begin finding them in trash barrels.

Now that the region's anglers are turning increasingly to bass and landlocked salmon fishing, the rainbow's days may be numbered here. At this writing, Maine has already abandoned raising and stocking them. Their only success was on the Kennebec River.

On the bright side, stocking rainbow trout in urban ponds gives inner-city children an opportunity they might not otherwise enjoy and gives amateurs a chance to practice and dream of Montana and the Madison River.

MAINE

Rivers and Streams

Kennebec River

NEW HAMPSHIRE

Rivers and Streams

Ammonoosuc River
Androscoggin River
Ashuelot River
Connecticut River
Exeter River
Isinglass River
Lamprey River

Mad River
Mascoma River
Pemigewasset River
Saco River
Soughegan River
Sugar River
Swift River

Lakes and Ponds

Andover
    Highland Lake
Chesterfield
    Spofford Lake
Derry
    Island Pond
Enfield
    Crystal Lake
Harrisville
    Silver Lake
Manchester
    Massabesic Lake

Nelson
    Granite Lake
    Nubanusit Lake
Pittsburgh
    Back Lake
    Lake Francis
    Third Connecticut Lake
Rumney
    Stinson Lake
Stewartstown, Coleman State Park
    Diamond Ponds
Windham
    Canobie Lake

VERMONT

Rivers and Streams

Barton River
Black River
Browns River
Castleton River

Clarendon River
Clyde River
Cold River
Connecticut River

Dog River
Huntington River
Lamoille River, North Branch
Lamoille River
Lewis Creek
Mad River
Middlebury River
Mill River
Missisquoi River
Moose River
New Haven River
Nulhegan River
Ompompanoosuc River

Ottauquechee River
Otter Creek
Passumpsic River
Stevens River
Trout River
Waits River
Walloomsic River
Waterbury River
Wells River
White River, First Branch, Third Branch
Willoughby River
Winooski River

——Lakes and Ponds——

Averill
  Little Averill Pond
Barnet
  Harveys Lake
Barton
  Crystal Lake
Belmont
  Star Lake
Benson
  Sunset Lake
Brighton
  Island Pond
Brookfield
  Sunset Lake
  Baker Pond
Burlington
  Lake Champlain
Cabot
  Molly's Falls Pond
Charleston
  Echo Lake
Chittenden
  Chittenden Reservoir
Concord
  Shadow Lake

Danville
  Joes Pond
Derby
  Brownington Pond
Eden Mills
  Lake Eden
Glover
  Shadow Lake
Goshen
  Sugar Hill Reservoir
Greensboro
  Caspian Lake
  Lake Eligo
Holland
  Holland Pond
Hortonville
  Lake Nineveh
Hubbardton
  Halfmoon Pond
Leicester
  Silver Lake
Maidstone, Maidstone Lake State Park
  Maidstone Lake

Marlboro
South Pond
Marshfield, Groton State Park
Kettle Pond
Newark
Center Pond
Newport
Lake Memphremagog
North Bennington
Lake Paran
North Calais
Lake Mirror
Norton
Norton Pond
Peacham
Ewell Pond
Perkinsville
Stoughton Pond
Plymouth
Amherst Lake
Woodward Reservoir
Pownal
South Stream Pond
Reading, Reading Town Forest
Knapp Brook Ponds
Salisbury, Salisbury Municipal
Forest
Lake Dunmore
South Poultney
Lake St. Catherine

South Woodbury
Forest Lake (Nelson Pond)
Sabin Pond
Strafford
Miller Pond
Thetford
Lake Fairlee
Townshend
Townshend Reservoir
Tyson
Echo Lake
Wallace Pond
Wallace Pond
West Castleton
Glen Lake
Westmore
Bald Hill Pond
Lake Willoughby
Whitingham
Sherman Reservoir
Wilmington
Harriman Reservoir (Lake
Whitingham)
Lake Raponda
Windsor
Mill Pond
Woodbury
East Long Pond
Lake Greenwood
Nichols Pond

MASSACHUSETTS

Rivers and Streams

Acushnet River
Agawam River
Asabet Brook
Cold River
Coonamesset River

Deerfield River
Farmington River
Hoosic River
Indian Head River
Ipswich River

Mattapoisett River
Millers River
Nissitissit
North River
Parker River
Plymouth River

Quaboag River
Sudbury River
Swift River
Westfield River
Williams River

——Lakes and Ponds——

Ashland
 Ashland Reservoir

Barnstable
 Hamblin Pond

Becket
 Greenwater Pond

Boston
 Jamaica Pond

Boxford
 Stiles Pond

Concord
 Walden Pond

Easthampton
 Nashawannuck Pond

Erving
 Laurel Lake

Falmouth
 Ashumet Pond

Groton
 Baddacook Pond

Lancaster
 Fort Pond

Lunenburg
 Whalom Lake

Mashpee
 Mashpee-Wakeby Pond

Milton
 Houghtons Pond

Monterey
 Lake Buel

Orange
 Lake Mattawa

Plymouth
 Long Pond

Rochester
 Mary's Pond

Sandwich
 Spectacle Pond

Springfield
 Watershops Pond

Stockbridge
 Stockbridge Bowl

Ware
 Peppermill Pond

Wenham
 Pleasant Pond

Woburn
 Horn Pond

Worcester
 Lake Quinsigamond

Wrentham
 Lake Pearl

CONNECTICUT

Rivers and Streams

Farmington River

Salmon River

Lakes and Ponds

Danbury
Candlewood Lake

New Hartford
West Hill Pond

Union
Mashapaug Lake

RHODE ISLAND

Lakes and Ponds

Burrillville
Peck Pond
Tarkiln Pond

Charlestown
Watchaug Pond

Coventry
Carbuncle Pond

Exeter
Beach Pond
Breakheart Pond

Glocester
Mowry Meadow Pond
Spring Grove Pond

Lincoln
Olney Pond

North Kingstown
Silver Spring Lake

Portsmouth
Melville Pond

Richmond
Sandy Pond

South Kingstown
Tucker Pond

Tiverton
Stafford Pond

21.
Brook Trout

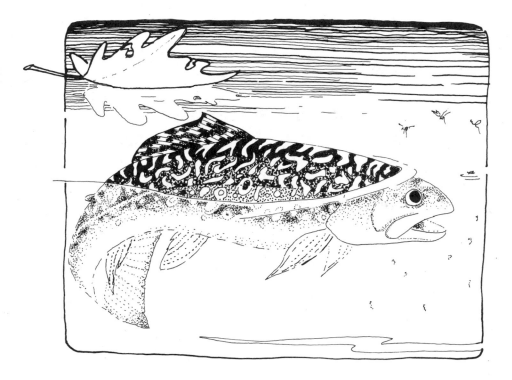

I dreamed of trout fishing; and, when at length I awoke, it seemed a fable that this painted fish swam there so near my couch...So I arose before dawn to test its truth, while my companions were still sleeping. There stood Ktaadn with distinct and cloudless outline in the moonlight; and the rippling of the rapids was the only sound to break the stillness. Standing on the shore, I once more cast my line into the stream, and found the dream to be real and the fable true.

—Henry David Thoreau
The Maine Woods, 1864

The eastern brook trout, *salvelinus fontinalis*, perhaps New England's loveliest native fish, is actually a member of the char rather than the trout family. Its smoothly scaled skin points to a kinship with the Arctic chars, as well as the sunapee, blueback, and lake trouts.

Thoreau describes brook trout as "bright fluviatile flowers," and they are undeniably creatures of rare and subtle beauty. Their dorsal color varies from green to gray to black, mottled to camouflage them in the lambency in which they live. Their neutral-toned flanks are stippled with red and blue spots, the leading edges of their ventral fins are streaked with white, and they have the closest thing to a square tail of any of the trouts.

Because brook trout are living testaments to a stream's purity, it will come as no surprise that most of them today have to be stocked for the season. For brook trout to thrive, water must be clean, cold, and oxygen-rich. Their preferred temperature range lies between the high fifties and about sixty-eight degrees; temperatures in the high 70s are fatal. In a few streams, where the water remains cold enough, you can fish for brook trout all summer, but usually the season is short. After spring the fish retire to deeper water, where they are more difficult to reach.

The brookie's native range in eastern North America once ran from Hudson Bay to Georgia. In colonial America it was our most common cold-water fish, living in streams, ponds, and lakes. Its early range is almost inconceivable today: no one needed to travel to the north country to find a brook trout, and its nearly ubiquitous presence was not lost on the colonies' early anglers. John Rowe, a member of the Massachusetts House of Representatives, imported a fishing rod from England to pursue local trout and perch. Ladies and gentlemen of the Boston gentry accompanied Rowe on piscatorial outings that culminated in picnics under the shade trees. In Rowe's diary, dated June 1766, we find that the fishing in "a trout brook which empties into the Charles River about a mile and a half beyond the Dedham Causeway" (Saw Mill Brook in Dover) was "middling." Would that a few brooks within 100 miles of Boston could make that boast today.

Perhaps more than any other factors, lumbering and clearing land for farming destroyed vast sections of the brook trout's habitat. What we think of as forest today is at best second-growth timber, and by one estimate nearly four-fifths of New England was cleared for farming in the nineteenth century. Even before heavy chemical and wastewater pollution, waters bereft of an arboreal canopy warmed, waters adjacent to plowed fields and timbering operations silted, nutrients disappeared, and the trout went with them.

In addition, the brook trout was so easily caught that its enthusiasm for wet flies soon became legendary. Visiting Europeans, accustomed to the caution of their brown trout, expressed contempt for the brook trout and went so far as to reject it as a serious sporting fish. For their part, contemporary Americans referred to trout fishing as "killing trout," and kill they did. Anglers pursued the brookie with the unbridled greed of children after candy. Using worms or scraps of pork for bait, anglers took fish by the hundreds: pools were fished out in an hour, whole brooks in a matter of days. Even Thoreau writes of an expedition to Maine where the "speckled trout," as it was known in those days, "swallowed the bait as fast as we could throw [it] in." As the fish were landed on a boat a little way out, the company tossed them ashore, and "one who had lost his hook, stood on shore to catch them as they fell in a perfect shower around him." Frying great messes of trout for breakfast quickly became an inseparable part of the wilderness experience.

Five- and six-pound brook trout are a staple of nineteenth-century angling literature. These giants lived in Rangeley and Moosehead lakes and disappeared at the turn of the century, soon after the state decided the landlocked salmon should make its debut in those waters. Though brookies in lakes are generally a little larger than those in streams, anglers who feel a need to take large brook trout today fly into the Canadian wilderness to find them. The record is a Canadian fish caught in 1916 and weighing fourteen and a half pounds.

For a brook trout to grow that large, conditions need to be near perfect for close to a decade, but because few brookies now live more than three years, they seldom reach a fraction of that size. Today an average fish is five to eight inches, especially in small streams, though it may occasionally reach three pounds if left undisturbed. Because natural reproduction is too slow to meet the American angler's "needs," massive management programs stock domestic brook trout, along with rainbows, all over the region.

"Not that trout will cease to be," wrote the Reverend Myron W. Reed, almost a century ago. "They will be hatched by machinery and raised in ponds, and fattened on chopped liver, and grow flabby and lose their spots...gross feeding and easy pond-life will enervate and deprave him. The trout that the children will know only by legend is the gold-sprinkled living arrow of the white water; able to zig-zag up the cataract; able to loiter in the rapids; whose dainty meat is the glancing butterfly."

Indeed, hatchery fish are not as timid as their wild kin and are often caught quickly or make fast food for herons. Unfortunately, though they will seldom survive, when mixed with wild fish the domestic strains compete with and stress the natives. In the skillet, the wild brook trout's flesh is sweet and tends to be pink; that of the hatchery fish paler and poorer in flavor.

The brook trout, mostly a daytime feeder, subsists almost entirely on larval and adult insects and tiny crustaceans, supplemented on occasion by small fishes, making it an ideal candidate for the flyfisher. Brook trout will also take worms and, for some reason, perhaps mistaking them for tiny fish, will strike at small spinners.

Early in the season the brookie is easier to catch on worms bounced along the bottom, but as the water warms it will turn to mayflies, caddis flies, and stoneflies, insects whose life cycles are inextricably bound to the stream. As summer progresses and the hatches of these insects diminish, the fish will substitute terrestrial insects (those that fall into the water accidentally) such as ants, moths, grasshoppers, and crickets.

In lakes and ponds fishing is pretty straightforward. You can fish with light tackle down to 1-pound-test, either bottom-fishing or floating bait under a bobber. For flyfishing, System 5 flyline is more than adequate unless there is a lot of wind. After the water begins to warm, fishing is most productive mornings and evenings.

While fishing in ponds and lakes may bring larger fish, there is nothing like an up-country gravel stream to erase civilization's discontents. A mixture of light and shade, deep and shallow, swift and seemingly still, brook trout streams shoulder their way between loaves of stone, rush over smaller rocks, and rest in pools. Splashed on your cheeks, the water refreshes, and its constant, plangent chorus is sublimely narcotic. An hour turns into three, then four. Shadows lengthen, and the sound of the stream enters your blood.

Small streams can be particularly challenging for anglers accustomed to still water or even larger rivers. Again, unless you anticipate wind, very light tackle has the advantage. The problem is finding the fish. Even viewed through polarized sunglasses, the bottom is a jumble of pink, olive, and slate pebbles. Against this background, fish dissolve into invisibility. It takes something akin to an act of faith to accept that innumerable fish can secret themselves in this relatively shallow and transparent water. Though the trout lose themselves, you are quite obvious. Every time you stumble or wave your hands to balance yourself or kick a stone, trout scatter, whether you can see them or not. After scaring them in your excitement, you eventually settle down, and it's then that a brookie may strike what you present and drag your line across the stream or dive to the bottom of a pool.

In textbook stream fishing, the fish face upstream when at rest, holding behind or in front of rocks, at the edges of the current, or in pools waiting for the water to bring their food. Gently bouncing a worm downstream on a small hook will probably take fish easier than any other method. Unlike rainbow trout, which are partial to the faster motion of riffles and channels, brook trout prefer pools, but both spend their lives absorbed almost entirely in motion, either their own or the medium around them.

If you are dry flyfishing, you are working upstream. Because of its modest scale and volume, a novice flyfisher, possibly flush with success on slower-moving water, may initially feel the river will be no match for his or her wiles. Nothing could be further from the truth. After a few casts you realize that even where it is only a few feet wide, the river is a laboratory of variables. The wind can change direction, the trouts' dietary preferences alter by the hour, and the current, conspiring with the stones and logs and branches, alternately tangles, slackens, drags, and obstructs your line. Wet flyfishing, downstream, offers an easier alternative, and some of the traditional patterns include the celebrated Parmachene Belle and the Royal Coachman. Streamers and bucktails like the Black Nosed Dace, Mickey Finn, and Muddler Minnow are also effective. Allow the current to carry your fly to a pocket in front of or behind a boulder and retrieve line slowly in short six-inch pulls.

Where the stream follows a road, anglers will concentrate wherever they can leave their cars, and two or three anglers can quickly make a crowd. Because of easy access, these areas are also more likely to be stocked with relatively tame fish. A pleasant alternative is surveying such streams from the seat of a bicycle. Four-piece flyrods and telescoping spinning rods make it possible to tote your gear on two wheels instead of four, and you can pull over wherever you like.

The majority of anglers, like the majority of "campers," will seldom stray far from a parking area, so any legwork invested on your part will usually guarantee solitude and often calmer fish as well. Water depth varies from between a few inches to waist-deep favoring the use of hip or chest waders or, for the exceptionally warm-blooded, a combination of shorts and sneakers.

If you are looking for the less-frequented areas, study a map and try a river's small feeder streams. Narrow streams that have trees on the south side usually remain cooler through the year than exposed waters, as do those that flow on a north–south axis and only get sun midday. Packing in with a pair of waders and a few select pieces of tackle will often allow you to probe places no one has tried for years.

Both the upper sections of the main river and these smaller streams offer challenging flyfishing, but if you are a beginner, or frustrate easily, the lower parts may be more suitable. But if at the end of a long day you can sit amid the butterflies and wild strawberries listening to the lowing of dairy cattle, satisfied with one or two fish, or an empty creel, you will have found more peace in a day than some people find in a lifetime.

Even in southern New England, unadvertised tangles of bush and bramble obscure the domain of a persevering few fish. It will take time, exploration, and hard work before they yield their small but significant rewards. "Wild trout live in a fairy land," writes Ted Williams,

> where any fairy would be driven mad by the black flies and brambles. The best pools are ringed with muck moats that suck at your boots and bubble with foul vapors as you slog through. There will be...slimy rocks that send you sprawling; and alder fingers that reach out to make cat's cradles with your line. You will sweat, swear, and scratch. You will be anything but relaxed; (whoever prescribed fishing as a nerve tonic never hunted wild trout in Massachusetts). You will stagger bleary-eyed and bloody from the woods at dusk with a handful of trout in your jacket pocket (the crusty one the cat likes to chew), and you will be supremely satisfied.

In these sorts of waters the fish are difficult to locate and even harder to catch because of the thickets that hide not only the fish but often the brook itself. One means of taking these is to float worms, grasshoppers, or crickets downstream with an open bailer. A short flyrod (under eight feet, maybe under seven) is to your advantage, otherwise you can't even hope for a roll cast. One ancient but successful method is dapping, the tactic of poking a rod through the brush and allowing a wet or dry fly, or a live insect, to be carried a short distance downstream or downwind to the trout.

Brook trout spawn from September to November in New England. Like the maple leaves above its streams, the male brook trout's breast flushes a lovely orange to scarlet in autumn. He grows a kype to do battle with other males, and the stream-bound species migrates far upstream into shallow gravel to spawn. Egg production depends upon the size and age of the fish: a yearling female may only deposit 100 to 200 eggs, but even the reported maximum, about 2,500, is pitifully low. In one study, only one in twenty fingerlings made it through the first year; one in thirty-three survived to the second; one in sixty-six to the third; one in ten thousand will reach six years of age.

Despite these long odds, they require some predation in confined streams just to give the whole population enough room to grow. Many states restrict number but not size, because adult fish can measure no more than four inches long and still assault whatever you throw at them.

Today, New England's wild brook trout are in retreat, mostly backed against Maine's northern border, though a handful succeed in hiding in small spring-fed waters over the region. If any fish cries out for the angler's restraint, it is this one. Unless you know you are fishing for stocked fish, use barbless hooks to assure ease of release, and enforce your own very strict personal limits to the number, if any, that you keep.

MAINE

—— Rivers and Streams ——

Alder Stream
Allagash River
Aroostook River
Carrabassett River
Cupsuptic River
Dead River, North and South
   branches
Fish River
Kenduskeag Stream
Kennebago River
Kennebec River
Little Madawaska
Machias River
Mugalloway River
Mattawamkeag River
Millinocket Stream
Molunkus Stream

Moose River
Mousam River
Nahmakanta Stream
Nesowadnehunk Stream
Penobscot River, East Branch
Presque Isle Stream
Prestile Stream
Rapid River
St. Croix Stream
St. John River
Sandy Stream
Seboeis River
Sheepscot River
Sunkhaze Stream
Trout Brook
Union River
Wassataquoik Stream

—— Lakes and Ponds ——

Belgrade
   Chamberlain Pond
Greenville
   Moosehead Lake
Rangeley
   Rangeley Lakes

Township 9, Range 12,
   Piscataquis County
     Churchill Lake
Wallagrass
   Eagle Pond

NEW HAMPSHIRE

—— Rivers and Streams ——

Amonoosuc, Wild Amonoosuc
Androscoggin River
Connecticut River
Exeter River
Gale River
Isinglass River
Lamprey River

Mad River
Mascoma River
Pemigeswasset River
Saco River
Souhegan River
Sugar River
Swift River

VERMONT

Rivers and Streams

Barton River
Batten Kill (and West Branch)
Black River
Browns River
Castleton River
Clarendon River
Clyde River
Cold River
Connecticut River
Deerfield River
Dog River
Gihon River
Green River
Hoosic River
Huntington River
Lamoille River
Lewis Creek
Mad River
Mettawee River
Middlebury River
Mill River
Missisquoi River
Moose River
New Haven River

Nulhegan River (and the Black,
    East, North, and Yellow
    Branches)
Ompompanoosuc River
Ottauquechee River
Otter Creek
Passumpsic River (and the East and
    West Branches)
Poultney River
Saxtons River
Stevens River
Trout River
Waits River
Walloomsic River
Waterbury River
Wells River
West River
White River (and the First, Second,
    and Third Branches)
Williams River
Willoughby River
Winhall River
Winooski River (and the Kingsbury
    Branch and North Branches)

Lakes and Ponds

Barnet
    Harveys Lake

Barton
    Baker Pond
    May Pond

Brookfield
    Baker Pond

Brunswick
    Dennis Pond

Cabot
    Molly's Falls Pond

Castleton, Lake Bomoseen State
Park
    Lake Bomoseen

Charleston
    Echo Lake

Chittenden
    Chittenden Reservoir

Concord
  Shadow Lake
Eden
  Long Pond
Essex
  Indian Brook Reservoir
Ferdinand
  South America Pond
Goshen
  Sugar Hill Reservoir
Groton, Groton State Forest
  Noyes Pond
Holland
  Beaver Pond
  Holland Pond
  Turtle Pond
Lewis
  Lewis Pond
Maidstone
  West Mountain Pond
Marlboro
  South Pond
Morgan
  Seymour Lake
Newark
  Newark Pond
Newport
  Lake Memphremagog

Norton
  Halfway Pond
Peacham
  Martins Pond
Peacham, Groton State Park
  Osmore Pond
Plymouth
  Colby Pond
Pownal
  South Stream Pond
Reading, Reading Town Forest
  Knapp Brook Ponds
Sherburne
  Kent Pond
Somerset
  Somerset Reservoir
Strafford
  Miller Pond
Stratton
  Stratton Pond
Westmore
  Jobs Pond
Williamstown
  Rood Pond
Wilmington
  Harriman Reservoir (Lake Whitingham)

CONNECTICUT

Rivers and Streams

Farmington River

Salmon River

RHODE ISLAND

Lakes and Ponds

Burrillville
  Peck Pond
  Tarkiln Pond
  Wallum Lake
Charlestown
  Watchaug Pond
Exeter
  Beach Pond
  Breakheart Pond
  Dawley Pond
Glocester
  Mowry Meadow Pond
  Spring Grove Pond

Lincoln
  Olney Pond
North Kingstown
  Silver Spring Lake
Portsmouth
  Melville Pond
Richmond
  Sandy Pond
South Kingstown
  Glen Rock Reservoir
  Tucker Pond

22.
Common or White Sucker

The Suckers, *catostomi bostonienses* and *tuberculati*, Common and Horned, perhaps on an average the largest of our fishes, may be seen in shoals of a hundred or more, stemming the current in the sun, on their mysterious migrations, and sometimes sucking in the bait which the fisherman suffers to float toward them.

—Henry David Thoreau
A Week on the Concord and Merrimack Rivers, 1849

Just a word about that three-pound trout I hooked in northern New Hampshire: it was a bright spring day, and we were working a stream famed for those bright fishes. We were having no success but consoled ourselves with having sighted a half-dozen moose and quite a number of spectacular wildflowers. Over the rim of a steep hill came an osprey laboring with what at first appeared to be a pontoon attached to its legs. As the bird came nearer, this appendage proved to be a fish of considerable weight and, by its general profile, a large trout. At least someone was catching fish.

An hour later, a little below an old wooden bridge, I gave up dry flies and switched to a Black Nosed Dace. It wasn't a minute before a fish hit somewhat shyly and the line went taut. The fish was so strong I played it a good five minutes, taking care not to snap the line. The fish wouldn't quit, nor would it jump. Ever the optimist, I was already entertaining visions of a Neanderthal brook trout, the kind of legendary creature that supposedly survives today only in streams that empty into the Arctic Ocean.

I asked my companion to hurry and load the camera, to put on the wide-angle lens, and stand back. Growing impatient to see the fish, I put some pressure on it and moved toward shore. When I finally got a hand under my mega-trout and lifted it, I was surprised to find myself gazing into the baleful stare of the largest white sucker I had ever seen. A pair of great slashes across his head indicated that, as far as the osprey was concerned, this one numbered among the ones that got away.

The camera shutter snapped again and again as I posed (trying to look unabashed) with my trophy. I like to tell myself that what the angler catches is little reflection on the angler. A good cast can just as easily land a trophy trout or a trophy sucker. The sucker, though certainly no acrobat, stubbornly outlasted many of the trout I'd hooked in the Northeast.

Three species of sucker live in New England: the longnose sucker, *catsotomus catsotomus*; the creek chubsucker, *erimyzon oblongus*, and the common or white sucker, *catsotomus commersonii*. The creek chub-sucker's oblong, carplike shape makes it easily identifiable. The other two are fairly similar in appearance, though the longnose, as you might suspect, has a longer snout than the common white sucker but also a more protruding lower lip. The white sucker has an olive, brown, or dark bluish back gradually shading to a lighter, silvery ventral area. It has a long, tubular body and a forked tail. Though without an adipose fin, its conformation is similar enough to the trout's to have fooled wiser than I.

The white sucker is the one most apt to be pursued as a food fish by humans, though all three species could be grudgingly added to a list of wild edibles. If nothing else, all are important as food for other species.

The white sucker is very widely distributed in New England, thriving in cold as well as warm water, in lakes, ponds, and streams with every imaginable kind of bottom. By far the largest of the three sucker species, the average white sucker will measure about a foot in length, though an occasional fish may reach twice that length, and weigh up to four pounds. As it is a bottom feeder, its mouth faces downwards, just below the end of a homely, conical snout. That fleshy mouth functions as a suction cup with which the fish can fasten itself to rocks and vacuum the bottom for snails, algae, live and dead insects, and occasionally fish eggs.

When they head upstream in May and June to spawn in the riffles, the males acquire a rosy color and grow tubercles, also known as "pearl organs," mostly on their caudal and anal fins. Using these growths for traction, two males at a time will get a female between them and fertilize eighteen thousand to thirty-one thousand eggs as she sheds them. In lakes without tributaries, suckers spawn the same way in the shallows.

For quite a number of years, suckers have been widely regarded as "coarse" or "trash fish," unworthy of an angler's attention. "The Sucker cannot be called a sporting fish," writes Thaddeus Norris, "yet the difficulty of taking it with a hook and line, and the nicety required in fishing for it, makes the taking of it a matter of interest to those who like to accomplish something difficult in angling. As an article of food it is only esteemed when other fish are scarce."

Though I did not keep my fish, I understand that their poor reputation as food is chiefly due to their being bony rather than ill-flavored. Jordan and Evermann describe them as "firm and flaky and very sweet." Everyone seems to agree, however, that they are better eating earlier rather than later in the year, before their flesh softens and loses its spring sweetness. When the region's food gatherers were less stuffy about what they brought home for dinner, large numbers of the fish were caught in nets and salted for winter use. Nets were not the only expedient. "It is a favorite sport of country lads," wrote Jerome V. C. Smith early in the nineteenth century, "to follow a rivulet and spear them by torch light." Their roe have also been praised for their table qualities.

Because the suckers' mouths are small, one uses the same size hooks as would be used for trout. A portion of the suckers' diet consists of vegetable matter, so corn kernels will appeal to them, but bait also includes pieces of worms, freshwater mussels, dead minnows, or insect larvae like grubs. When they are found in lakes and ponds, bottom fishing is most effective. When they rise in streams to spawn, a wide variety of wet flies work, including streamers and flies representing drowned or larval insects.

New England anglers, enthusiastic trout chauvinists, view the sucker as a threat to their most esteemed prize. The errant sucker who has the misfortune to take an angler's fly often suffers an ignominious and fatal blow to the head before being returned to the water. Thus far, however, the sucker's treachery as a significant eater of trout eggs and fry has yet to be scientifically substantiated. If anything, the opposite may be the case. "When fly fishing in the month of June," wrote Norris, "I have frequently found them to collect in large numbers in some gentle current to spawn; then Trout are apt to lie at the lower end of the school to catch the ova as it drifts down stream."

In "Carp of a Parallel Universe," an amusing and enlightening essay printed in the Summer 1988 *Gray's Sporting Journal*, Greg Keeler raises the unorthodox possibility that our perspective is, after all, somewhat arbitrary: it may be that trout are spoiling perfectly good sucker streams. In any case, if one had to name one species responsible for despoiling the region's waters, I don't think the sucker would be the first creature to come to mind.

White suckers and their cousins are so widely distributed in northern New England that one can assume their presence in virtually every lake and stream, warm and cold, in Maine, New Hampshire, and Vermont. The following still-water habitat is listed for southern New England.

MASSACHUSETTS

Lakes and Ponds

Bourne
Great Herring Pond

Brewster
Long Pond

Brookfield
Quaboag Pond

Chester
Littleville Reservoir

Chicopee
Chicopee Reservoir

Concord
Warners Pond

Hinsdale
Plunket Reservoir

Hubbardston
Brigham Pond

Mashpee
Long Pond

Monterey
Buel Lake

Otis
Upper Spectacle Pond

Rowe
Sherman Reservoir

Shutesbury
Wyola Lake

Stockbridge
Stockbridge Bowl

Tyngsboro
Flint Pond

RHODE ISLAND

Lakes and Ponds

Coventry
Quidnick Reservoir
Tiogue Lake

Cranston
Meshanticut Pond
Ralph Pond

Cumberland
Howard Pond

East Providence
East Providence Reservoir

Exeter
Beach Pond
Dawley Pond

Hopkinton
Asheville Pond

North Kingstown
Pausacaco Pond
Silver Spring Lake

Providence
Upper Canada Pond
Wenscott Reservoir

Richmond
Sandy Pond

Smithfield
Georgiaville Pond

South Kingstown
>   *Barber Pond*
>   *Glen Rock Reservoir*
>   *Worden Pond*

Warwick
>   *Warwick Pond*

West Greenwich
>   *Mishnock Pond*

23.

Sunapee and
Blueback Trout

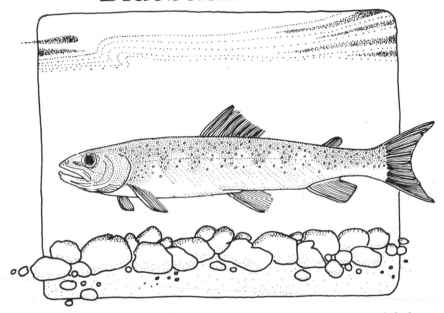

As the October pairing time approaches, the Sunapee fish becomes illuminated with the flushes of maturing passion. The steel-green mantle of the back and shoulders now seems to dissolve into a veil of amethyst, through which the daffodil spots of mid-summer gleam out in points of flame, while below the lateral line all is dazzling orange...The wedding garment nature has given to this charr is unparagoned. Those who have seen the bridal march of the glistening hordes, in all their glory of color and majesty of action, pronounce it a spectacle never to be forgotten.

—Dr. John D. Quackenbos,
quoted in *American Food and Game Fishes*,
David S. Jordan and Barton W. Evermann, 1902

Neither the sunapee nor the blueback trouts ever enjoyed wide-spread distribution in New England, but they are so rarely seen today that they have come to represent creatures akin to unicorns or basilisks: refugees from the pages of a medieval bestiary. After reading Dr. Quackenbos's vivid, almost livid, descriptions, you might half wonder if they aren't a hoax. However, the best part of an angler, and perhaps the worst part, may be credulity; do your best to accept them on faith.

Though the sunapee's description makes it sound like the more extraordinary of the two fishes (I left out the part where the doctor praises the sunapee's "diminutive aristocratic mouth" and "liquid planetary eyes"), some biologists have proposed that both fish not only have a common ancestor but may simply be color variations on the same species. They are currently believed to be dwarf, landlocked Arctic chars, *salvelinus alpinus*, isolated in fresh water after the last ice age. The sunapee or golden trout, *salvelinus aureolus*, eluded American taxonomists until 1888, probably because it seldom strayed from its preferred habitat: sixty or more feet below the surface of a handful of New England's deepest lakes. It took its name from New Hampshire's Sunapee Lake, where it was first discovered and once lived in abundance. Originally, in New Hampshire, the population is believed to have been limited to Sunapee and Big Dan Hole. In Vermont, sunapees were native to Averill Lake and in Maine, to Floods Pond.

Sunapee trout are relatively small in stature, streamlined, seldom over a foot in length, and not ordinarily able to grow to more than fifteen inches in five years. The New Hampshire record, however, caught in Sunapee Lake in 1954, weighed eleven and a half pounds.

As late as the 1950s they were still flourishing in Sunapee Lake, spawning every October and November on the same midlake reef. "Here in all the magnificence of their nuptial decoration," as the good doctor tells us, "flash schools of painted beauties, circling in proud sweeps about the submerged boulders they would select as the scenes of their loves—the poetry of an epithalamium in every motion—in one direction, uncovering to the sunbeams their golden-tinctured sides, gemmed with the fire of rubies; in another, darting in little companies, the pencilled margins of their fins seeming to trail behind them like white ribbons under the ripples."

He also notes that they are relatively prolific salmonids, the female producing twelve hundred eggs per pound. Succumbing to a less-romantic mood, Quackenbos even speculated about their potential value as a food fish.

In an attempt to extend the sunapee trout's range, they were artificially introduced into the Third Connecticut Lake in New Hampshire, but they disappeared with the subsequent introduction of lake trout. Meanwhile, the same thing happened at Sunapee Lake; the species disappeared, not from overfishing but after lake trout were introduced into the system.

No one knows whether the lake trout ate them, beat them to their meals, or crossbred them into extinction, but it is clear that the habitat of both species overlaps closely: they are both fond of deep cold lakes, feed on smelt, and tend to breed in the same places at the same times. Sunapees also compete with brook trout, though they tend to hold their own a little better. In any case, they are gone from most of New Hampshire, and the healthiest population is believed to be living in Flood's Pond, Maine.

There is one last, odd twist to this account of Adventures in Fisheries Management. A few years ago one strain of sunapee was discovered in an alpine lake in Idaho's Sawtooth Mountains, apparently stocked there sometime early in the century by an anonymous devotee of the species. It seems our desire to meddle is not only insatiable but has completely unpredictable results.

Dr. Quackenbos, who was apparently the past expert on the fish, claims they put up twice the fight of a brook trout and regales the reader with details of how he, equipped with a greenheart tarpon rod rigged with 300 feet of copper wire dangling a minnow at its end, used to troll for them from a sailboat. His statements have the hyperbolic sound one associates with "sportsmen" of the period—pompous yet also strangely appealing: "When the sailboat is running across the wind at the maximum of her speed," he assures us, "the sensation experienced by the strike of a 4 or 5-pound fish bankrupts description."

Today, sunapee trout are occasionally taken on streamer flies or on smelt in the spring when they follow those fish into the shallows. They can also be taken by Dr. Quackenbos's deep-trolling method in summer when they hold in fifty-degree water (used to be, in Sunapee Lake at least, around 60 to 100 feet) or by fishing deep with live smelt. But check local regulations, because in Flood's Pond and several others, use of live bait is forbidden.

The story of the blueback trout, *salvelinus oquassa*, is very similar to that of its cousin. Though they were prospering in Maine's Rangeley Lakes at the turn of the century, they entirely disappeared from there by 1930. Fortunately, they were planted in several other bodies of water in Maine where they continue to survive. Taking their name from their blue dorsal area, they have silver flanks, reddish fins, and a forked tail. They are even smaller than sunapees, ranging from six to twelve inches, and feed principally on plankton. They occasionally have been caught on worms or by jigging in deep water with small spoons, but, as with sunapees, the only reason I could imagine fishing for one would be out of curiosity, and I can't imagine keeping the fish. Again, carefully check local regulations on the use of live bait on particular bodies of water.

SUNAPEE TROUT
—— MAINE ——
—— Lakes and Ponds ——

Otis, Hancock County
Flood's Pond

Raymond, Cumberland County
Crescent Lake

—— NEW HAMPSHIRE ——
—— Lakes and Ponds ——

Grafton
Tewkesbury Pond

Ossipee
Conner Pond

BLUEBACK TROUT
—— MAINE ——
—— Lakes and Ponds ——

Township 2 Range 11, Piscataquis County
Rainbow Lake

Township 3 Range 4, Somerset County
Pensobscot Lake

Township 8 Range 10, Piscataquis County
Big Reed Pond

Township 8 Range 15, Piscataquis County
Wadleigh Pond

Township 15 Range 9, Aroostook County
Black Lake
Deboullie Pond
Gardner Lake
Pushineer Pond

24.
Lake Trout

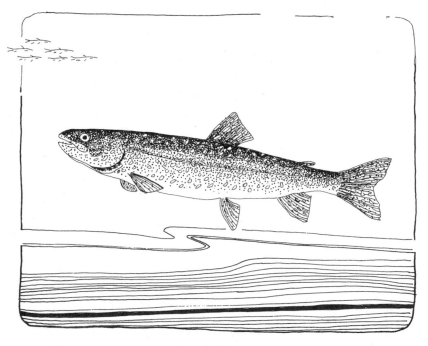

As a game-fish the lake trout is held in different degrees of esteem by different anglers. There are those who regard it with slight favor, while with others it is rated as a fish which can give the angler a great deal of sport. It is usually taken by trolling either with the spoon or live minnow, and, as it is a powerful fish, strong tackle is required. Thaddeus Norris, most delightful writer among American anglers, mentions hooking several on stout 00 Kirby hooks baited with white rag and a piece of red flannel, and the hooks in every instance but one (a small 8 pound trout) were straightened or broken and the fish lost.

—David S. Jordan and Barton W. Evermann
American Food and Game Fishes, 1902

In Vermont it's called longe; in Maine, togue; and in Massachusetts, lake trout, *salvelinus namaycush.* The national sporting press, in its passion for brevity, refers to it as a "laker."

Its detractors will tell you that it's related to the brook trout but hardly as handsome. It has a forked tail, large mouth, and wears a grayish coat dappled with pale, often yellowish spots. Unlike the romantic brook trout, it doesn't dress up in bright, mating colors but goes to love in its everyday suit. Nor is its flesh, which varies from red to pink to white, as flavorful as the rainbow's, though there is certainly more of it. Neither is it as wily or acrobatic a fighter as the brown trout. It strikes lightly and upon being hooked, sounds doggedly for the bottom until it escapes or is exhausted. The lake trout, people will tell you, is the largest of the chars, but size is its only virtue.

That it can grow large is indisputable. Ordinary specimens weigh between 3 and 6 pounds, moderately above-average specimens run between 10 and 25, and jumbos have been known to reach 65. In the nineteenth century, when they were harvested com-mercially in the Great Lakes, 100- to 125-pound individuals were reported.

Young lake trout eat insects and crustaceans. As they get older, they turn to fishes: yellow perch, smelt, lake whitefish, suckers, and eel. They thrive in large, deep, cold, well-oxygenated lakes, bodies of water that seem like small oceans: Memphremagog, Squam, Moosehead, Winnipesaukee. In New England, with notable exceptions, this is also the domain of powerboats, water skis, jet skis, sail boards, and cottages lining the shore.

The lake trout's natural range spans North America all the way from the East to Alaska. The Great Lakes and New England represent the southern margin, and the fish was originally not that widely distributed here. In New Hampshire, for example, they occurred in only seven lakes. Nevertheless, they have been successfully introduced into dozens of waters since.

In Massachusetts' Quabbin Reservoir, where lake trout were planted in 1952, they became self-sustaining in about a decade. They were so successful that sometime in the sixties they slipped from the Quabbin through an aqueduct and came to roost in the Wachusett Reservoir as well. Massachusetts has had some problems with the lake trout—low water levels in drought years, which uncovered the trout's spawning ground—and with acid rain, which curbed the number of available smelt.

Namaycush, their species name, is a Native American word signifying a creature that makes its home in the deep. Lake trout are only near the surface for a brief two weeks or so just after ice-out when they wander into shallow water in search of food. This brief period occurs sometime from mid-April to mid-May in Massachusetts but doesn't start until mid-May in the northern states. This is the only period when you can cast and reach them from shore. Likely spots to fish from include rocky points, narrows between bays, and stream mouths where lake trout wait for passing smelt.

In spring, anglers use spinning tackle with 8- to 12-pound-test line, reinforced at the end with 15-pound test leader. A slip sinker is tied above a barrel swivel and a number 2 hook baited with a four- to five-inch live or dead shiner or smelt or with cut bait. The bailer is left open allowing the baitfish to wander a little and to give the trout a head start before setting the hook.

From a boat, one can drift fish or slowly troll the same bait or a lure near the bottom. Trolling near the surface with spoons, spinners, swimming plugs, and wobblers is also productive, or, if you are flyfishing, you can troll large bucktails and streamer flies such as the Grey Ghost, smelt, and the Nine-Three.

Lake trout are most comfortable in water between forty-eight and fifty-two degrees and cannot survive long in water above sixty-five degrees. Once the water warms, the fish plunges, seldom revisiting the shallows until the fall spawn. By June they are about 60 feet down in the Quabbin; by July, 80 feet; by late August, 100 feet deep. They have been known to go as far down as 300 feet. A chart and a fishing thermometer will help—look for deeply submerged reefs that fall into the right temperature range. Early in the summer the fish may also approach shoal bars as shallow as 15 or 25 feet in the evening, but during most of the day they will be in very deep water.

In shallower lakes, this will mean fishing on or near the bottom. One alternative is still-fishing (or plugging as some call it) with live or cut bait. Another tactic is jigging with large, flashy spoons and jigs that vibrate or flutter when they are moved up and down. You can also rig a three-way swivel and troll either bait or a lure along the bottom. Tie a bell sinker on one eye of the swivel with one to two feet of light-test line, so if it gets hung up you will lose the sinker but not the lure or bait. From the second eye run four to six feet of 15-pound-test line ending in the swivel so the bait or lure won't get twisted. Depending on the bottom, and on how fast you want to troll, you can adjust the sinker's weight and the lengths of the two lines.

In deeper lakes, the fish may be neither near the bottom nor the top, and you will have to search out something in between. It was Henry David Thoreau, rowing across Walden Pond with string and thermometer, who is credited with discovering that in summer, deep lakes separate into distinct temperature zones. The top is warm, the bottom very cold, but floating between them is an intermediate layer limnologists call the thermocline.

Smelt and other bait fish tend to occupy the thermocline in the day, enjoying temperatures that range between fifty-five and sixty degrees. Lake trout often rest in schools at the lower end of the thermocline, making incursions upward to feed. This may explain why bait and lures are often struck from beneath and why lake trout may also follow a retrieved lure and strike it as it begins to depart this zone.

In 1833, before there was genuine angling for lake trout, Dr. Jerome V. C. Smith speculated wistfully about the togue of Moosehead. "Perhaps no attempt has ever been made, but could these 'monarchs of the deep' be taken by the regular angler, aided by all the devices essential to the true enjoyment of his sport, the pleasure resulting from the success of his achievement, would be proportioned to the size and strength of his captive."

Anglers have worked out ways of taking the lake trout, but whether Dr. Smith would approve of all the devices is a moot point. Needless to say, when you are doing this kind of fishing, the gentle art of casting counts for naught, and the water depths involved pretty much marry you to a boat. You embark upon a very specialized form of fishing.

Many summer anglers troll large specimens of live bait or large spoons or wobblers, using stiff baitcasting rigs loaded with wire or metal core line. Others use conventional line with downriggers. Rods are locked into their rod holders, and some anglers press electronic equipment, such as depth meters, fish finders, and other paraphernalia, into service.

There are anglers whose pleasure is not only directly proportionate to the size of the catch but also to the amount of hardware they can bring to the fray. While it's a matter of personal preference, this sort of approach numbs the human touch, turning fishing into a video game submarine hunt.

Most states have limits on taking lake trout because the fish breed in modest numbers and take a long time to grow into sizeable fish. Lake trout are particularly vulnerable when they spawn, and most states curtail fishing during that time. Spawning starts in October in the north and as late as December in the south, taking place after sunset. It is attended with something like fraternity party spirit. In relatively shallow water, from 5 to 20 feet, the males assemble over a stony bottom and sweep it clean with their tails. (In a few lakes, the fish may spawn as far down as 100 feet.) When the females arrive, a certain amount of amorous chaos ensues, though in general two males will accompany one female as she scatters eggs. No one knows if anyone respects anyone else in the morning, but spawning among the rocks assures that many of the eggs will fall into the crevices and thus be protected from predation until they hatch in the spring.

Compared with prolific, fast-growing species like perch, nature seems to have ill-favored the lake trout, at least from a human perspective. Lake trout lay only about 700 eggs per pound and, after an initial growth spurt, gain only a few inches a year over a life that may, if uninterrupted, stretch to between ten and forty years. Hence, a twenty-year-old lake trout may weigh only about ten pounds. Heavy fishing pressure can remove many large fish from a lake in a very short time.

Dissatisfaction with the lake trout's slow growth (and the brook trout's insignificant size) led fish culturist Seth Green to attempt an improvement on nature. Though it sounds a little like crossing a Great Dane with a toy collie, in 1878 Green successfully bred a lake trout female with a brook trout male. The Ontario Department of Land and Forests later dubbed the creature a splake—from *s*peckled trout and *lake* trout. The splake has daddy's squarish tail and mom's markings. It is not only fertile, but it matures quickly and seems to outdo both its parents in its growth rate and willingness to assault bait or spinners. If someone could breed more anglers that cleaned up after themselves, quit fishing when they had reached their limit, and left their radios and beer at home, I would say we really had something. In the meantime, I'm afraid I'd rather forsake the splake. Anyway, the current record splake came in at nine pounds. It presently swims in two New Hampshire waters: Crystal Lake, Eaton, and Long Pond, Lempster.

MAINE

—— Lakes and Ponds ——

Acton
Great East Lake

Allens Mills
Clearwater Pond

Attean
Wood Pond

Attean Township
Attean Pond

Auburn
Auburn Lake

Chain of Ponds Township,
Franklin County
Chain of Ponds

China
China Lake

Danforth
East Grand Lake

Dedham
Phillips Lake

Dexter
Wassookeag Lake

East Orland
Toddy Pond

East Otisfield
Thompson Lake

East Palermo
Sheepscot Pond

Ellsworth
Branch Lake
Green Lake

Embden
Embden Pond

Enfield
Cold Stream Lake

Fayette
Echo Lake

Frenchtown Township
Roach Ponds

Fryeburg
Kezar Pond

Grand Lake Stream
West Grand Lake

Greeley
Sebec Lake

Greenville
Moosehead Lake

Hobbstown Township
Spencer Lake

Jefferson
Damariscotta Lake

King and Bartlett Township
Little Jim Pond

Lakeville
Junior Lake

Magalloway Township
Richardson Lakes

Mariaville
Hopkins Pond

Millinocket
Pemadumcook Chain of Lakes

New Vineyard
Porter Lake

North Windham, Sebago Lake
State Park
Sebago Lake

Otis
Beech Hill Pond

Parkertown Township
  Lincoln Pond
Piscataquis County
  Nahmakanta Lake
Poland
  Range Ponds
Sapling Township
  Indian Pond
Shapleigh
  Mousam Lake
Sullivan Township
  Tunk Lake
Township 3 ND, Hancock County
  West Lake
Township 3, Range 4, BKP WKR, Somerset County
  Spring Lake
Township 3, Range 12, WELS, Piscataquis County
  Chesuncook Lake
Township 3, Range 14, WELS, Piscataquis County
  Lobster Lake

Township 6, Range 1, NBPP, Penobscot County
  Scraggly Lake
Township 6, Range 8, WELS, Piscataquis County
  Matagamon Lake
Township 7, Range 2, NBPP, Washington County
  Pleasant Lake
Township 7, Range 13, WELS, Piscataquis County
  Chamberlain Lake
Township 7, Range 14, Piscataquis County
  Allagash Lake
  Caucomgomoc Lake
Township 14, Range 8, WELS, Aroostook County
  Fish River Lake
Waterboro
  Little Ossipee Lake
Wilton
  Wilson Pond
Winthrop
  Maranacook Lake

NEW HAMPSHIRE

Lakes and Ponds

Bristol
  Newfound Lake
Enfield
  Crystal Lake
Harrisville
  Silver Lake
Holderness
  Little Squam Lake
  Squam Lake

Laconia
  Paugus Bay
  Winnisquam Lake
Madison
  Silver Lake
Meredith
  Lake Winnipesaukee
Nelson
  Nubanusit Lake
  Spoonwood Lake

New Durham
   Merrymeeting Lake
Ossipee
   Dan Hole Pond
   Ossipee Lake
Pittsburgh
   First Connecticut Lake
   Second Connecticut Lake
   Third Connecticut Lake
Rumney
   Stinson Lake
Stewartstown
   Diamond Ponds

Strafford
   Bow Lake
Sunapee
   Sunapee Lake
Wakefield
   Great East Lake
Warren
   Lake Tarleton
Wentworth's Location
   Greenough Ponds

VERMONT

Lakes and Ponds

Averill
   Great Averill Pond
   Little Averill Pond
Barnet
   Harveys Lake
Barton
   Crystal Lake
   Long Pond
Burlington
   Lake Champlain
Charleston
   Echo Lake
Danville
   Joes Pond
Glover
   Shadow Lake
Greensboro
   Caspian Lake
   Lake Eligo
Maidstone
   Maidstone Lake
Morgan
   Seymour Lake

Newport
   Lake Memphremagog
North Calais
   Lake Mirror
Plymouth
   Amherst Lake
Salisbury
   Lake Dunmore
South Poultney
   Lake St. Catherine
South Woodbury
   Forest Lake
Tyson
   Echo Lake
Wallace
   Wallace Pond
Westmore
   Lake Willoughby
Woodbury
   East Long Pond
   Nichols Pond

MASSACHUSETTS

Lakes and Ponds

New Salem
    Quabbin Reservoir

West Boylston
    Wachusett Reservoir

25.
Landlocked Salmon

Here let me chant thy praise, thou noblest and most high-minded fish, the cleanest feeder, the merriest liver, the loftiest leaper, and the bravest warrior of all creatures that swim!...the old salmon of the sea who begat thee long ago in these inland waters became a backslider, descending again to the ocean, and grew gross and heavy with coarse feeding. But thou, unsalted salmon of the foaming floods, not land-locked as men call thee, but choosing of thine own free will to dwell on a loftier level in the pure current of a living stream, hath grown in grace and risen to a better life.

—The Reverend Henry Van Dyke, 1898

235

The landlocked salmon, *salmo salar sebago*, is essentially an Atlantic salmon that came to live, at some obscure date back in the Ice Age, in four freshwater lake systems in Maine. The original lakes—Sebago, Green, Sebec, and Schoodic—were tied into the St. Croix, Union, Presumpscot, and Penobscot rivers. The fish also may have been native to Lake Champlain. A similar salmon, known in Canada as the *ouananiche*, came to live in the same circumstances north of the border. These groups were either isolated from the sea at some point or simply ceased to descend to salt water. Given access now, the land-locked salmon will turn its back upon the sea.

Instead of spawning upstream from the ocean, the landlocked salmon ascends its lakes' tributaries in the fall and spawns between mid-October and the end of November. It may gather at the mouths of these streams as early as September, but there is no spring run as with the Atlantic salmon. The remaining spawning details, however, are very similar: the female digs a redd in the gravel; the eggs are fertilized, pass the winter, and hatch in spring; parr stay in their natal streams for two years, then drop back into the larger body of water. Unlike the Atlantics, the adults do not winter over but return to the lake soon after the spawn.

Living apart from its seagoing relatives has brought this salmon minor physical changes—it has larger scales, fins, and eyes than its Atlantic counterpart, although it is much smaller: the average land-locked salmon weighs two or three pounds, though anglers occasionally land a specimen of ten or more pounds. The 1907 record, from Sebago Lake, still stands—twenty-two pounds. Like its seagoing progenitors it is a fish that seems to have been fashioned from beaten silver. "As Lancelot among the knights," wrote the Reverend Van Dyke, "so art thou among the fish, the plain armored hero, the sun-burnt champion of all the waterfolk." Though it may be smaller than the Atlantic salmon, fresh water hasn't dampened its enthusiasm for acrobatic jumping.

Just after the Civil War the landlocked salmon was stocked in New Hampshire's Newfound Lake, then in Squam, Sunapee, and Winni-pesaukee. In Maine the stocking program dates from 1875, and once it became obvious that it could be successfully dispersed, it was stocked all across northern New England in hundreds of lakes and is prospering as far south as the Quabbin and Wachusett reservoirs in Massachusetts. Already, the landlocked salmon may be more numerous than at any time in its history; it has even been exported to Argentina. It flourishes in oligotrophic, or relatively sterile, bodies of water that guarantee summer temperatures in the mid-fifties and a generous supply of smelt and dissolved oxygen.

For a brief period in the 1960s, the landlocked salmon demonstrated its need for clean water in unequivocal terms to the local tourist industries that were promoting its capture. In the late 1950s, heavy doses of DDT were sprayed near the water by several local camps around Sebago Lake to keep down blackflies and mosquitoes. By 1962, it was clear that something was amiss: the size and number of salmon had fallen precipitously. The DDT was not only poisoning the salmon, it attacked the smelt as well, which in turn starved the top of the food chain. It wasn't long before camps, bait shops, and restaurants felt the pinch and voted to ban the pesticide. By 1967, the fishery was on its way back.

Today, Maine considers the landlocked salmon its foremost game fish, and the salmon is supplementing and could even potentially replace the trouts as the fish that both residents and tourists will throw their dollars after. Though these salmon can live as long as a decade, most anglers land only three- and four-year-olds and, less often, five- and six-year-olds. These figures make one wonder if the whole business isn't a larger, flashier variation on the old trout put-and-take operation. Indeed, many of the salmon in these lakes are netted in the fall, artificially fertilized, and raised in hatcheries for the first two years.

But now that wild brook trout are becoming scarcer in New England, the salmon may provide a more attractive hatchery alternative that will take some of the pressure off the brookie. For the brook trout's sake one can hope that Van Dyke's rhapsodic estimation wins popular approval: "Thy cousin the trout, in his purple and gold with crimson spots, wears a more splendid armour than thy russet and silver mottled with black, but thine is the kinglier nature. His courage and skill, compared with thine,

> Are as moonlight unto sunlight,
> And as water unto wine."

Humans are tireless in their efforts to anoint one fish to the throne and insist on the abdication of another. Despite the landlocked salmon's noble nature, the season in which it makes itself available to the angler is relatively short. The life of the salmon is inextricably intertwined with that of the smelt. After the ice breaks up (in late April and early May in the north), smelt ascend the tributary streams to spawn. The salmon follow hungrily, and anglers follow the salmon. From riverbanks and bridges, anglers cast smelt hooked through the dorsal fins or use imitations like spoons, spinners, plastic minnows, or wobblers. On spinning equipment, you will need 5- or 6-pound-test and lures weighing no more than 1/4 to 5/8 ounce. A number of anglers get lucky with worms or "salmon eggs." Flyfishers can use medium-weight fly rods to cast floating line with a host of smeltlike streamers including the Black, Grey, and Green Ghost; the Nine-Three; and the Supervisor.

After the smelt return to the lake, salmon will prowl the shallows along the shorelines looking for them. Though they will also eat a variety of other bait fish, including small yellow perch, smelt remains the preferred quarry. Surface trolling is done with spinning and flyfishing tackle. Streamers are tied in tandem, which makes them look a little more like schooling smelt. Varying the motion by giving the rod a pull from time to time may occasion a strike. At this time of year the salmon may be in water as shallow as two feet. Troll and cast to shore, around islands, and over gravel bars.

Salmon loitering near tributaries and in the shallows will, just like trout, occasionally pick insects off the surface in May and June, especially in the evenings. Light and Dark Cahills, Quill Gordons, Dark Hendricksons, and others that imitate hatching aquatic insects in number 16 and 18 sizes can give someone accustomed to trout the strike of a lifetime.

Like their larger marine progenitors, landlocked salmon are admired for their beauty and their fight. They are much easier to hook than Atlantics but resort to the same energetic means of rescuing themselves—alternately jumping and dragging out line. A hooked landlock may make five or more jumps, two to three feet in the air, before being brought to the net. Once they have enough slack to hang the angler, they may decide to make a turn toward the boat. There is a fine balance: enough line to keep them from breaking off and a line tight enough to keep them from throwing the hook.

After their surface-feeding period they hover briefly in the twenty-foot range where you may successfully troll for them, reach them still-fishing, or use jigs. By June, they only sporadically and briefly break the surface in early morning, around sunset, or during a summer cold snap or a storm. For the most part the fish are sounding deep in the lakes seeking smelt and cold water.

In midsummer, salmon prefer temperatures around fifty-five degrees, but this does not necessarily mean anything simple like the bottom. At this point pursuing them resembles fishing for lake trout, though they don't go down to anywhere near those depths. Nevertheless, summer anglers absolutely set on landlocked salmon fishing must resign themselves to using metal core lines to get lures down forty to seventy feet, just below the thermocline. This means tracking across the lake like destroyers hunting midget submarines.

While fighting lake trout up from the depths challenges an angler, dragging up a salmon one-half that weight doesn't make much sense. A salmon caught by this means will arrive on the surface relatively numb and lifeless and hardly seems worth the effort. Fishing is what you make of it, and as Jordan and Evermann suggested in 1902, "the customary angling appliances on Sebago Lake...disincline the fish to prolonged antagonism."

In fall, they will return briefly to the shallows to feed for bait fish before ascending to spawn. Fishing for spawning landlocked salmon is essentially the same as fishing for Atlantics: the angler attempts to provoke a fish that is off its feed. Recommended wet flies include Parmachene Belle, Royal Coachman, Jock Scott, and Black Dose.

MAINE

—— Lakes and Ponds ——

Acton
   Great East Lake
Allens Mills
   Clearwater Pond
Attean
   Wood Pond
Attean Township
   Attean Pond
Auburn
   Auburn Lake
Belgrade
   Messalonskee Lake
Belgrade Lakes
   Long Pond
Chain of Ponds Township,
   Franklin County
   Chain of Ponds
China
   China Lake
Cooper
   Cathance Lake
Danforth
   East Grand Lake
Davis Township
   Kennebago Lake
Dedham
   Hatcase Pond
   Phillips Lake
Denmark
   Moose Pond
Dexter
   Wassookeag Lake
East Orland
   Toddy Pond
East Otisfield
   Thompson Lake

East Palermo
   Sheepscot Pond
Ellsworth
   Branch Lake
   Green Lake
Embden
   Embden Pond
Enfield
   Cold Stream Lake
Fayette
   Echo Lake
Fayette Township
   Parker Pond
Frenchtown Township
   Roach Ponds
Fryeburg
   Kezar Pond
Grand Lake Stream
   West Grand Lake
Greeley
   Sebec Lake
Greenville
   Moosehead Lake
   Wilson Ponds
Hartland Township
   Moose Pond (Great Moose Lake)
Hobbstown Township
   Spencer Lake
Island Falls Township
   Pleasant Pond
Jacksonville
   Gardner Lake
Jefferson
   Damariscotta Lake

Lakeville
  Junior Lake
Liberty
  St. George Lake
Linneus
  Drews Lake (Meduxnekeag Lake)
Magalloway Township
  Richardson Lakes
Manchester
  Cobbosseecontee Lake
Mariaville
  Hopkins Pond
Meddybemps
  Meddybemps Lake
Millinocket
  Pemadumcook Chain of Lakes
Molunkus Township
  Molunkus Lake
New Vineyard
  Porter Lake
North Windham, Sebago Lake State Park
  Sebago Lake
Orrington
  Brewer Pond
Otis
  Beech Hill Pond
  Floods Pond
Parkertown Township
  Aziscohos Lake
  Lincoln Pond
Poland
  Range Ponds
Piscataquis County
  Nahmakanta Lake
Rangeley
  Dodge Pond

Rome
  Great Pond
Sandy River Plantation
  Beaver Mountain Lake
Sapling Township
  Indian Pond
Shapleigh
  Mousam Lake
Stetsontown Township
  Little Kennebago Lake
Sullivan
  Flanders Pond
Sullivan Township
  Tunk Lake
Tauton and Raynham Academy Grant
  Brassua Lake
Township 3, ND, Hancock County
  West Lake
Township 3, Range 4, BKP WKR, Somerset County
  Spring Lake
Township 3, Range 12, WELS, Piscataquis County
  Chesuncook Lake
Township 3, Range 14, WELS, Piscataquis County
  Lobster Lake
Township 6, Range 1, NBPP, Penobscot County
  Scraggly Lake
Township 6, Range 8, WELS, Piscataquis County
  Matagamon Lake
Township 7, Range 2, NBPP, Washington County
  Pleasant Lake

Township 7, Range 9, Piscataquis County
    Millinocket Lake
Township 7, Range 14, Piscataquis County
    Caucomgomoc Lake
Township 14, Range 8, WELS, Aroostook County
    Fish River Lake
Township 16, Range 5, Aroostook County
    Cross Lake
Township 16, Range 5, WELS, Aroostook County
    Square Lake

Township 27, ED BPP
    Big Lake
Township 40 MD, Hancock County
    Nicatous Lake
Waterboro
    Little Ossipee Lake
Wilton
    Wilson Pond
Winthrop
    Maranacook Lake
Woolwich
    Nequasset Pond

NEW HAMPSHIRE

Rivers and Streams

Androscoggin River

Lakes and Ponds

Conway
    Conway Lake
Enfield
    Crystal Lake
    Mascoma Lake
Errol
    Umbagog Lake
Hebron
    Newfound Lake
Holderness
    Squam Lake
    Little Squam Lake
Laconia
    Paugus Bay
    Winnisquam Lake
Madison
    Silver Lake

Meredith
    Lake Waukewan
    Lake Winnipesaukee
Nelson
    Nubanusit Lake
New Durham
    Merrymeeting Lake
New London
    Pleasant Lake
Ossipee
    Dan Hole Ponds
    Ossipee Lake
Pittsburgh
    First Connecticut Lake
    Lake Francis
    Second Connecticut Lake

Strafford
   Bow Lake

Sunapee
   Sunapee Lake

Wakefield
   Great East Lake

Warren
   Lake Tarleton

VERMONT

Rivers and Streams

Black River
Clyde River
Lamoille River
Lewis Creek

Missisquoi River
Otter Creek
Winooski River

Lakes and Ponds

Averill
   Great Averill Pond

Burlington
   Lake Champlain

Charleston
   Echo Lake

Morgan
   Seymour Lake

Newport
   Lake Memphremagog

Salisbury, Salisbury Municipal
Forest
   Lake Dunmore

Westmore
   Lake Willoughby

Whitingham
   Sherman Reservoir

Wilmington
   Harriman Reservoir (Lake Whitingham)

Woodbury
   Nichols Pond

MASSACHUSETTS

Lakes and Ponds

New Salem
   Quabbin Reservoir

West Boylston
   Wachusett Reservoir

26.
Burbot

The moment I collected my first burbot, having been plagued with identifying hybrid pickerel and hybrid sunfish throughout the Housatonic River survey, I began wondering what species hybridized to produce this individual. It had the slender, elongated body of an eel and the head and tail of a madtom, but it also possessed brown back and sides, plus a yellowish belly and a single chin barbel.

—Joseph Bergin
"Those Weird Little Fishes," *Massachusetts Wildlife,*
July–August 1974

The burbot, *lota lota*, a homely creature with an almost unbelievable affection for dark and cold, is one of the northern hemisphere's strangest rangers. Burbot once enjoyed a wide distribution that included Europe, Asia, and North America; and though that distribution is much narrower today, quite a few may still be found in New England.

The only member of the codfish family that lives in fresh water, the burbot looks like something a saltwater angler might reel in miles offshore—from Stellwagen Bank or Jeffrey's Ledge. It has an elongated brown body, with two barbels extending from its snout and one more from under its chin, like the goatee of the ocean cod. Because of its resemblance to its saltwater relatives, it is also known as ling and cusk; and someone with less than great regard for the legal profession dubbed the slippery fish (supposedly because it is hard to pin down) the "lake lawyer."

In stark contrast to the rest of nature in New England, the burbot feels the heat of the reproductive urge in February, in the dead of night, under a mantle of ice. At that time, when the water is but a few degrees above freezing, the tribe ventures into the shallows where they roll in an orgiastic ball with other members of their cold-loving species, scattering and abandoning their fertilized eggs on the gravel. In summer, reversing the usual habits of hibernation, the burbot retires to the deepest, coldest part of our north country lakes. It seems to have little or no tolerance for water above seventy-four degrees.

In rare cases it is found in rivers and streams—in Massachusetts, for example, its range is limited to the Housatonic River. Otherwise, the burbot is found in deep, cold-water lakes in Maine, New Hampshire, and Vermont.

Burbot are principally nocturnal feeders, but like the bullhead, they occasionally can be caught on overcast days. They feed almost exclusively on fish: smelt, walleye, whitefish, and yellow perch. Because they often compete with lake trout, anglers fishing for lake trout often find a surprise at the end of their lines. An average burbot grows to about twenty inches, though it may occasionally reach three feet in length and weigh ten pounds. One specimen pulled from Moosehead Lake in Maine in 1979 tipped the scales at seventeen pounds. Depending on the size of the fish you expect to catch, you can go from a number 4 hook all the way on up to a 1/0. Because nature equipped the burbot with a good set of teeth, some anglers add six inches to a foot of heavier leader to the end of their lines.

During the warmer months burbot are inactive; at other times they can be caught by bottom fishing with minnows or cut portions of other fish. On rare occasions they have been taken on spinners or streamer flies. A few anglers report success using dough balls or cheese. Whatever the bait, it is slowly drifted along the bottom or within a foot of the bottom. During the winter, when ice fishing, anglers use large yellow perch for bait.

Like its saltwater relatives, the burbot has earned a reputation as a hearty meal, an excellent candidate for chowders, tasting, perhaps not surprisingly, like cod.

MAINE

Lakes and Ponds

Allens Mills
  Clearwater Pond
Aroostook
  Eagle Lake
  Long Lake
  St. Froid
Attean
  Wood Pond
Attean Township
  Attean Pond
  Clearwater Pond
  Holeb Pond
Bridgton
  Long Lake
Cumberland
  Crescent Lake
  Long Lake
  Panther Pond
  Raymond Pond
Dexter
  Wassookeag Lake
Eagle Lake
  Eagle Lake
East Otisfield
  Thompson Lake
Elliotsville Township
  Onawa Lake
Embden
  Embden Pond
Enfield
  Cold Stream Lake
Fayette
  Echo Lake

Fayette Township
  Parker Pond
Frenchtown Township
  Roach Ponds (Third, Fourth, Sixth)
Greeley
  Sebec Lake
Greenville
  Moosehead Lake
Hartland Township
  Moose Pond (Great Moose Lake)
Hobbstown Township
  Spencer Lake
Island Falls Township
  Pleasant Pond
Kennebec
  Flying Pond
  Minnehonk Lake
Lakeview Plantation
  Schoodic Lake
Little Squaw Township
  Big Indian Pond
Long Pond Township
  Long Lake
Millinocket
  Pemadumcook Lake
Mt. Vernon Township
  Minnehonk Lake
North Windham, Sebago Lake
State Park
  Sebago Lake

Orono
  Pushaw Lake
Piscataquis County
  Nahmakanta Lake
  Onawa Lake
Raymond
  Panther Pond
Raymond Township
  Crescent Lake
  Raymond Pond
St. Agatha
  Long Lake
Sapling Township
  Indian Pond
Shawtown Township
  Trout Pond
Somerset
  Clearwater Pond
  Holeb Pond
Tauton and Raynham Academy Grant
  Brassua Lake
Township A, Range 12, WELS, (Shawtown Township) Piscataquis County
  Beaver Pond
Township A, Range 11, WELS, Piscataquis County
  Crawford Pond
Township 1, Range 3, NBKP, Somerset County
  Tomhegan Lake
Township 1, Range 4, NBKP, Somerset County
  Seboomook Lake
Township 1, Range 10, WELS, Piscataquis County
  Lower Jo-Mary Lake
Township 2, Range 10, WELS, Piscataquis County
  Debsconeag Lakes (Third)

Township 3, Range 5, BKP EKR, Piscataquis County
  Big Indian Pond
Township 3, Range 5, NBKP, Somerset County
  Dole Pond
Township 3, Range 11, WELS, Piscataquis County
  Harrington Lake
Township 3, Range 12, WELS, Piscataquis County
  Chesuncook Lake
Township 5, Range 1, NBKP, Somerset County
  Long Pond
Township 6, Range 8, WELS, Piscataquis County
  Matagamon Lake
Township 6, Range 11, WELS, Piscataquis County
  Telos Lake
Township 7, Range 11, WELS Piscataquis County
  Haymock Lake
Township 7, Range 13, WELS, Piscataquis County
  Chamberlain Lake
Township 7, Range 14, Piscataquis County
  Allagash Lake
Township 8, Range 9, WELS, Piscataquis County
  Munsungan Lake
Township 8, Range 13, WELS, Piscataquis County
  Eagle Lake
Township 9, Range 4, Washington County
  Spednick Lake

Township 9, Range 11-12, Piscataquis County
Spider Lake

Township 9, Range 12, WELS Piscataquis County
Churchill Lake

Township 9, Range 15, WELS, Piscataquis County
Crescent Pond

Township 10, Range 11, WELS Piscataquis County
Clear Lake

Township 10, Range 4, WELS, Aroostook
Squa Pan Lake

Township 11, Range 13, WELS, Aroostook
Umsaskis Lake

Townships 11-12, Range 11, Aroostook County
Musquacook Lakes

Township 15, Range 9, WELS, Aroostook
Togue Pond

Township 16, Range 5, WELS, Aroostook County
Square Lake

Township 17, Range 5, Aroostook County
Cross Lake

Township 18, Range 10, WELS, Piscataquis County
Galzier Lake

Township 19, Range 11, WELS, Piscataquis County
Beau Lake

Vanceboro
Spednick Lake

Vienna
Flying Pond

Wayne
Androscoggin Lake

West Middlesex Canal Grant
Tomhegan Lake

Winterville Plantation
St. Froid

NEW HAMPSHIRE

Lakes and Ponds

Hebron
Newfound Lake

Holderness
Little Squam Lake
Squam Lake

Madison
Silver Lake

Meredith
Lake Winnipesaukee

Ossipee
Dan Hole Pond
Ossipee Lake

Pittsburgh
First, Second, and Third Connecticut Lakes
Lake Francis

Rumney
Stinson Lake

Stewartstown
Diamond Ponds

VERMONT

Lakes and Ponds

Burlington

Lake Champlain

MASSACHUSETTS

Rivers and Streams

Housatonic River

27.
Lake and Round Whitefish

T he whitefishes are by far the most important group of freshwater fishes of North America, and probably of the world.
The common whitefish is the best of the tribe, but some of the
others nearly equal it in merit, and all are more or less esteemed
as food. [It]...ranks next in value to the lake herring, lake trout,
and wall-eyed pike. In 1897 the catch in the United States
amounted to 8,000,000 pounds, having a value of nearly
$300,000.

—David S. Jordan and Barton W. Evermann
American Food and Game Fishes, 1902

251

Alas, the whitefish. In the nineteenth century, it was probably as wellknown on some dinner tables as halibut or cod. In the Great Lakes it fell victim to sea-lamprey infestation, pollution, and the gill net. In New England too, it commanded a high price until overfishing destroyed the market, nearly taking the native population with it. Today, most of the smoked whitefish one finds for sale in the local delicatessen are imported from the Arctic wilds of Canada. Fortunately, with commercial exploitation no longer a threat in New England, it continues to survive here as a prize for anglers—provided they don't abuse the remaining fish.

There are two species of whitefish in New England—the lake whitefish and the round whitefish. Though somewhat nondescript, both species are distinguished by their narrow, conical heads, small mouths, and deeply forked tails. The back of the adult lake whitefish arches slightly. It also has a double flap of skin between its nostrils, while the round whitefish has a single flap. They both travel in schools and are often found in the same waters that hold lake trout.

Because of their herringlike shape and large silvery scales, whitefish were popularly confused with the largest member of the herring family—the shad. But both species of whitefish are, in fact, closely related to the salmonids. By one theory, whitefish are refugees from ice-age streams and rivers; cold-loving creatures that hid in the deep lakes as the glaciers slouched back northward.

The round whitefish, *prosopium cylindraceum*, as its name suggests, is cylindrical in shape while the lake whitefish is somewhat flatter. When the round whitefish was commercially fished it was known as the pilotfish or frostfish in Lake Champlain, as the chivey in Maine, and as the shadwaiter in Lake Winnipesaukee. An excellent table fish, the round whitefish is mostly a nocturnal feeder and far more interested in plankton, crustaceans, and lake trout eggs than anything an angler would generally put on the end of a hook. Nevertheless, it is occasionally taken, usually by anglers using small hooks and fishing for something else. Unlike its cousin, the round whitefish prefers the shallows to the depths and may also be found in some rivers. It grows to about a foot and seldom reaches a pound. Overall, it's a fish whose life is not welldocumented or even known—an excellent subject for someone's doctoral thesis.

Although lake whitefish specimens, *coregonus clupeaformis*, were once known to reach twenty pounds, most whitefish caught today weigh between one and five pounds. The fish's diet consists principally of insect larvae, freshwater plankton, and snails, though when available, smelt make up a good part of its winter diet. Lake whitefish spawn in November and December on rocky bottoms near shore, and their eggs hatch late in the winter. They are creatures with steep odds against them: they grow very slowly, reaching maturity in their third or fourth year, and although the female lays between ten thousand and one hundred and fifty thousand eggs, most of them end up food for yellow perch and other predators even before they hatch.

In some places, anglers on a campaign for lake whitefish chum a fifty-foot-deep area for a few days with chopped fish, then gently jig with cut minnows on number 8 hooks.

For a brief period after ice-out—especially during an early mayfly or caddis fly hatch—lake whitefish can also be taken on the surface with small dry flies. These feeding sprees usually occur on calm days, early in the morning or at dusk. Under these conditions, whitefish feed very actively over a large area. Part of the trick to taking one near the surface is anticipating where the fish will rise next: keep in mind that they feed while swimming in a straight line. As they have weak mouths like the shad, the angler must take care not to pull the hook out, and because they take a fly more slowly than other fish, you need to wait a split second longer when setting the hook than you would when fishing for trout. Despite the flashy fight they put up—sometimes leaping clear of the water—at present most fishing for the species is done in winter through the ice.

ROUND WHITEFISH

MAINE

Lakes and Ponds

Danforth
East Grand Lake

Farmington
Clearwater Pond

Frenchtown and Shawtown
Townships, Piscataquis County
Roach Ponds

Greenville
Moosehead Lake

Hobbstown Township, Somerset
County
Spencer Lake

Township 1, Range 6, BKP EKR,
Somerset County
Indian Pond

Township 6, Range 11,
Piscataquis County
Chamberlain Lake

Township 7, Range 14,
Piscataquis County
Allagash Lake
Caucomgomoc Lake

Township 11, Range 11, WELS,
Aroostook County
Musquacook Lake

Township 13, Range 8, Aroostook
County
Fish Lake

NEW HAMPSHIRE

Lakes and Ponds

Bristol
Newfound Lake

VERMONT

Lakes and Ponds

Burlington
Lake Champlain

LAKE WHITEFISH

MAINE

Lakes and Ponds

Acton
Great East Lake

Danforth
East Grand Lake

Frenchtown Township
Roach Ponds

Grand Lake Stream
West Grand Lake

Greenville
Moosehead Lake
Lakeview Plantation
Schoodic Lake
Lakeville
Junior Lake
Little Squaw Township
Big Indian Pond
Locke Mills
South Pond
Millinocket
Pemadumcook Lake
Newfield, Somerset County
Turner Pond
North Windham, Sebago Lake
State Park
Sebago Lake
Sapling Township
Indian Pond
Shawtown Township
Trout Pond
Somerset County
Fish Pond
Taunton, Somerset County
Long Pond
Thorndike Township
Fish Pond
Township A, Range 10, WELS
Piscataquis County
Upper Jo-Mary Lake
Township 1, Range 4, NBKP,
Somerset County
Seboomook Lake
Township 1, Range 5, (Jim Pond
Township) Piscataquis County
Jim Pond
Township 1, Range 1,0 WELS
Piscataquis County
Lower Jo-Mary Lake

Township 2, Range 3, NBKP,
Somerset County
Canada Falls Lake
Township 2, Range 10, WELS
Piscataquis County
Debsconeag Lakes
Township 3, Range 5, BKP EKR
Piscataquis County
Big Indian Pond
Township 3, Range 5, NBKP,
Somerset County
Dole Pond
Long Pond
Township 3, Range 11, WELS,
Piscataquis County
Harrington Lake
Township 3, Range 14, WELS,
Piscataquis County
Lobster Lake
Township 5, Range 17, WELS,
Somerset County
Fourth St. Johns Pond
Township 6, Range 8, WELS,
Piscataquis County
Matagamon Lake
Township 6, Range 11, WELS,
Piscataquis County
Telos Lake
Township 7, Range 2, NBPP,
Washington County
Pleasant Lake
Township 7, Range 11, WELS
Piscataquis County
Haymock Lake
Township 7, Range 13, WELS,
Piscataquis County
Chamberlain Lake
Township 7, Range 14, Piscata-
quis County
Allagash Lake
Caucomgomoc Lake

Township 8, Range 9, WELS, Piscataquis County
  Munsungan Lake
Township 8, Range 12, WELS, Piscataquis County
  Cliff Lake
Township 8, Range 13, WELS, Piscataquis County
  Eagle Lake
Township 8, Range 14, WELS, Piscataquis County
  Johnson Pond
Township 9, Range 11-12, Piscataquis County
  Spider Lake
Township 9, Range 12, WELS, Piscataquis County
  Churchill Lake
Township 10, Range 1,1 WELS, Piscataquis County
  Clear Lake

Township 10, Range 15, WELS, Piscataquis County
  Chemquasabamticook (Ross) Lake
Township 11-12, Range 11, Aroostook County
  Musquacook Lakes
Township 13, Range 8, WELS, Piscataquis County
  Carr Pond
Township 14, Range 8, WELS, Aroostook County
  Fish River Lake
Township 18, Range 10, WELS, Piscataquis County
  Galzier Lake
Township 19, Range 11, WELS, Piscataquis County
  Beau Lake
Willimantic
  Big Greenwood Pond

NEW HAMPSHIRE

Lakes and Ponds

Holderness
  Squam Lake
Meredith
  Lake Winnipesaukee

Wolfeboro
  Wentworth Lake

VERMONT

Lakes and Ponds

Burlington
  Lake Champlain

Part IV

Ice Fishing

28.
Ice Fishing

Early in the morning, while all things are crisp with frost, men come with fishing rods and slender lunch and let down their fine lines through the snowy field to take pickerel and perch; wild men, who instinctively follow other fashions and trust other authorities than their townsmen, and by their goings and comings stitch towns together in parts where else they would be ripped. They sit and eat their luncheon in stout fear-naughts on the dry oak leaves on the shore, as wise in natural lore as the citizen is in artifical.

—Henry David Thoreau
Walden, 1854

Ice fishing, then as now, is an endeavor for the strong and restless in spirit, for those souls willing to abandon their warm burrows for chill acres of frozen water. Today we can don warmer, lighter clothing and cart along a host of paraphernalia unknown to our forebears. In place of the messy job of hacking a hole in the pond's shield with an axe, we have razor sharp, even gasoline-powered augers. Where Thoreau's contemporaries arrived armed with alder branches and a knife to probe rotten logs for grubs, we have diminutive, store-bought fishing rods, or "jigglers," not to mention bait and tackle shops that maintain a stock of live bait all winter. There are portable plastic ice houses, Styrofoam bait buckets, aluminum and plastic tip-ups with Day-Glo flags, chemical hand warmers, electric socks, kerosene lanterns, and eventually, if we pursue our equipment fetish far enough, a sled or even a four-wheel drive pickup to cart all this hardware out onto the ice.

However, as an antidote to cabin fever, nothing beats ice fishing, and the flavor of New England's fish is greatly improved by the decrease in the water's algae. It adds a fresh dimension to winter camping, cross-country skiing (frozen lakes are great places to ski), and snowshoeing. If you are lucky enough to have a pond that froze quickly and evenly, ice skates can be a great asset in checking your tip-ups.

Though winter allows you to walk to the place you want to fish in a lake or pond, if the fish are not biting there's a lot more to trying another place than casting again a little to the left. Winter concentrates fish, so hitting a school ends up being an all or nothing proposition. Keep in mind, especially with the creatures occupying the top of the food chain, that one lucky angler with no self-restraint can probably decimate the bass or large pickerel in a small pond. Except for panfish—the perch, smaller pickerel, calicos, and pumpkinseeds—you need to be conscious that what you take out in winter will not magically reappear in summer. You will need to read the rules of the state in which you're fishing regarding regulating the catch, number of tip-ups allowed, and seasonal limits on fish like smelt.

If you leave your catch on the ice it will freeze and need to be thawed before you clean it, so either store it in an insulated container or wrap it in cloth or newspaper and bury it in snow if there is any.

The ice should be at least four inches thick to be safe to venture out upon, and you need to keep in mind that underwater springs make the ice thinner in spots. When the ice is thick but clear enough to see the fish, you may end up spooking your quarry. You may either have to keep at a distance from your tip-ups or return after a snow masks your presence.

Some of the most enjoyable fishing is on the local lakes and ponds in your neighborhood, seeing a familiar place in utterly unfamiliar conditions. If you don't know the lake you're fishing, a good strategy is to work out in a straight line perpendicular from the shore, so you can sample the fish population at a variety of depths. In lakes with irregular shorelines, parts of the lake that pinch together are good places to investigate, because you have a better chance of intercepting schooling fish on their way from one part of the lake to another. Because schools roam a winter lake in pursuit of food, it pays to drill a lot of holes: sitting tight waiting for the school to come to you makes for a long day, while drilling an additional hole every once in a while goes a long way toward increasing the odds, not to mention keeping you warm. Remember to mark your holes with branches when leaving so skaters and other anglers won't trip on them on their way across the ice.

The only difference between tip-ups for small fish and large fish is the line weight and how much of it you need. Tip-ups in shallow water will probably need only a few feet of 2- to 4-pound-test while line suitable for walleye will run longer, and that for lake trout may run to more than 200 feet.

Yellow perch are probably the single most sought-after fish in winter and one of the most easily caught. Because they tolerate a relatively low oxygen content, they are active all year and will tend to thrive in the deeper lakes and ponds. Unlike the other panfish, perch are usually found in the deeper parts of the lake within a foot or two of the bottom. Small minnows make the best bait, and productive fishing is mostly limited to daylight hours. Once you have a school's attention, you can switch to a lure or jig. Leaving the first few fish to move around on the hook a moment will often attract the others into the area and stimulate their interest. White perch are increasingly a quarry of ice anglers. The best bait is angle worm, which some people put aside in the autumn.

Black crappies occupy shallower water than perch in winter and are seldom found in water deeper than ten feet. They favor minnows, just like they do in summer, and are mostly caught late in the day or at night.

Bluegills and pumpkinseeds are interested in a variety of insect larvae in the winter, including cornborers and grubs. Mousees or mousies, the larvae of the syrphus flies, are stocked in many bait shops and make excellent bait for the sunfish family. They will also take small minnows, scraps of worm, and salmon eggs. Putting the bait on very small, colorful spoons will help the fish find it. They prefer relatively shallow water. If you don't find them at the bottom, bring your line up at one-foot intervals and try jigging all the way to the top.

Chain pickerel are one of the commonest winter prizes in New England's southern waters, and the number of unexpected large ones pulled out of local ponds are frequently a source of wonder. Where were they hiding in summer?

Northern pike will concentrate in shallower bays and coves, and laying out holes in a circle can help locate them faster. You will want line of 10- to 20-pound-test, and if you really expect large specimens, you may also want to drill a hole up to ten inches in diameter. Use large shiner or sucker minnows for bait.

Muskellunge, solitary and difficult to catch in summer, are even more so in winter. Generally, one uses the same bait and tackle as for northern pike—only at the extreme end in size. Remember that muskellunge carry their bait some distance, mauling it in their mouths before turning it head first and swallowing it, so wait until the fish runs a ways before striking. You will definitely want a gaff for this one.

Largemouth bass are interested in scraps of worm and the same larval insects you would use to catch other members of the sunfish family like the bluegills. The best fishing is usually early in the winter in relatively shallow water, though overall ice fishing for largemouth is no where near as productive as after ice out. Smallmouth bass hold in deeper water in the winter, but like largemouth, they are not much sought after through the ice. They are occasionally taken on insect larvae and jigs.

In freshwater lakes, smelt can go fairly deep at times, as far down as 100 or more feet. Fortunately, they can be taken between 15 and 50 feet. Scraps of shrimp make good bait as do clams.

Trout attract a lot of attention in the winter, especially when a lake is stocked in the fall. Anglers out after panfish secretly hope they can hit into one of the holdovers. In deep water jigging lures near the bottom, especially shiny spoons, account for the most success. In shallower water, trout will often station themselves near the mouths of feeder streams.

Lake trout in winter are found in deep water, usually between 100 and 150 feet down. The ideal bait is large specimens of live smelt. Shiners and chubs are good substitutes when smelt are unavailable. You jig either bait or lures, and if you are lucky, you may need a gaff to land your fish.

Burbot, or cusk, which actually spawn under the ice, are more in season in winter than any other time of the year. Bait includes small yellow perch, minnows, suckers, and smelt. Because the burbot is chiefly a nocturnal feeder, tip-ups are usually left overnight. Note that New Hampshire allows only six tip-ups to be set for burbot, and they may not be left unattended for more than twenty-four hours. Jigging to attract cusk is prohibited.

In contrast to burbot, the horned pout thrive in the dog days of summer. They are almost completely inactive in winter, burying themselves in the mud and hibernating until spring.

Walleye can be found in deep water near the edges of weed beds in winter and in the channels where a river enters a lake. Shiners and sucker minnows make good bait. They are most active early and late—just after freezing and just before ice-out.

Whitefish, though formerly more plentiful, today are limited to only a few deep, cold-water lakes. They are bottom feeders who are fond of small minnows or cut bait on a small hook and are most often caught at depths of around fifty feet. Chumming with cut fish, rice, and offal is commonly practiced to attract whitefish to a particular location.

To find likely locations for the above species, check the previous chapters.

Bibliography

The Atlas of Vermont Trout Ponds, Second Edition. Burlington, Vermont: Northern Cartographic, 1987.

Allen, Farrow, Edward, Antczak, and Peter Shea. *Vermont Trout Stream*. Burlington, Vermont: Northern Cartographic, 1985.

Amos, William H. *The Life of the Pond*, Our Living World of Nature series. New York: McGraw Hill Book Company, 1967.

Arnosky, Jim. *Flies in the Water, Fish in the Air*. New York: Lothrop, Lee and Shepard Books, 1986.

Bates, Jr., Joseph D. *Fishing; An encyclopedic guide to tackle and tactics for fresh and salt water*, 2nd edition. New York: E. P. Dutton and Company.

Attributed to Berners, Dame Juliana. *A Treatise on Fishing with an Hook*, 1946, Rendered in Modern English by William Van Wyck. North River Press, Inc., 1979.

Blaisdell, Harold F. *Trout Fishing in New England*. Lexington, Massachusetts: Stone Wall Press, 1973.

Chauvin, Bill and Carl Apperson. *Bassin' in New England*. Thorndike Press, 1985.

Chiapetta, Jerry *Modern ABC's of Ice Fishing*. Stackpole Books, 1966.

Cronon, William. *Changes in the Land; Indians, Colonists, and the Ecology of New England*. New York: Hill and Wang, 1983.

Downes, Stephen. *The New Compleat Angler*. Stackpole Books, 1983.

Elliot, Robert. O. E. *Bass Fishing in New England*. Lexington, Massachusetts: Stone Wall Press, 1973.

Fellegy, Joe. *Walleyes and Walleye Fishing*. Minneapolis: Dillon Press, 1973.

Gibbons, Euell. *Stalking the Wild Asparagus*. New York: David McKay Company, 1962.

Gingrich, Arnold. *The Fishing in Print*. New York: Winchester, 1974.

Goodspeed, Charles Eliot. *Angling in America*. Boston: Houghton Mifflin Company, 1939.

Guthrie, Richard C. and John A. Stolgitis. *Fisheries and Managment in Rhode Island Lakes and Ponds*. Fisheries Report No. 3, Rhode Island Division of Fish and Wildlife, 1977.

Henshall, James A. *Bass, Pike, Perch and Other Game Fishes of North America*. Cincinnati: Robert Clarke, 1919.

Henshall, James A. *The Book of the Black Bass*. Cincinnati: Robert Clarke, 1881.

McClane, A. J. *McClane's New Standard Fishing Encyclopedia and International Angling Guide*, Enlarged and Revised Edition. New York: Holt Rinehart Winston, 1974.

Norris, Thaddeus. *The American Angler's Book*. Philadelphia: Porter and Coates, 1864.

Janes, Edward C. *Salmon Fishing in the Northeast*. Stone Wall Press, 1973.

Jordan, David Starr and barton W. Evermann. *American Food and Game Fishes*. New York: Doubleday, Page & Co., 1902.

Orvis, Charles F. and A. Nelson Cheney. *Fishing with the Fly*. Boston: Charles E. Tuttle (Houghton Mifflin), 1886.

Parsons, P. Allen. *Outdoor Life Complete Book of Fresh Water Fishing*. New York: Harper and Row, 1963.]

Profumo, David and Graham Swift (eds.). *The Magis Wheel, An Anthology of Fishing Literature*. London: Picador, 1985.

Raychard, Al. *Fly Fishing in Maine*. North Country Press, 1990.

Rosenthall, Mike. *North America's Freshwater Fishing Book*. New York: Charles Scribner's Sons, 1982.

Scarola, John F. *Freshwater Fishes of New Hampshire*. New Hampshire Fish & Game Department, 1987.

Schullery, Paul. *American Fly Fishing; A History*. Nick Lyons Books, 1987.

Smith, Jerome V. C. *A Practical Essay on Angling with a Natural History of the Fishes of Massachusetts*. Boston: Allen & Ticknor, 1833.

Swainbank, Todd and Eric Seidler. *Taking Freshwater Game Fish, A Treasury of Expert Advice*. Woodstock, Vermont: Countrymen Press, 1988.

Swasey, Charlton J. and Donald A. Wilson. *New Hampshire Fishing Maps*. Freeport, Maine: DeLorme Publishing Company, 1984.

Tarr, Yvonne Young. *The Great East Coast Seafood Book*. New York: Vintage, 1982.

Thompson, Leslie P. *Fishing in New England*. New York: D. Van Nortrand Company, 1955.

Thoreau, Henry David. *The Annotated Walden: Walden; or Life in the Woods*. New York: C. N. Potter, 1970.

____. *The Maine Woods*. New York: Perennial Library, 1987, 1864.

____. *A Week on the Concord and Merrimack Rivers*, 1849. New York: Harper and Row, 1961.

Tryckare, Tre and E. Cagner. *The Lore of Sportsfishing*. New York: Crown Publishers, 1976.

Vanderweide, Harry. *Maine Fishing Maps*, volumes 1 and 2. Freeport, Maine: DeLorme Publishing Company, 1986.

Walton, Izaak, *The Compleat Angler*, 1676, Fifth edition. London: Harrap, Ltd, 1984.

Waterman, Charles, *Fishing in America*. New York: Holt, Rinehart and Winston, 1975.

Whitlock, Dave, *L.L. Bean Fly-Fishing Handbook*. Piscataway, New Jersey: Winchester Press, 1984.

New England Departments of Fisheries and Wildlife

Maine Department of Inland Fisheries and Wildlife
284 State Street, Station #41
Augusta, ME 04333
(207) 289–2766

New Hampshire Fish and Game Department
2 Hazen Drive
Concord, NH 03301
(603) 271–3421

State of Vermont Department of Fish and Wildlife
103 South Main Street
Waterbury, VT 05676
(802) 244–7331

Massachusetts Division of Fisheries and Wildlife
Information and Education Section
Fish and WIldlife Headquarters
Westboro, MA 01581
(508) 366–4479

Connecticut Department of Environmental Protection
165 Capitol Avenue
Hartford, CT 06106
Inland Fisheries (203) 566–2287, 566–4477
Marine Fisheries (203) 443–0166

Rhode Island Division of Fish and Wildlife
Oliver Stedman Goverment Center
4804 Tower Hill Road
Wakefield, RI 02879-2207
(401) 277–3075

About the AMC

The Appalachian Mountain Club is where recreation and conservation meet. Our 40,000 members have joined the AMC to pursue their interests in hiking, canoeing, skiing, walking, rock climbing, bicycling, camping, kayaking, and backpacking, and—at the same time—to help safeguard the environment in which these activities are possible.

We invite you to join the Appalachian Mountain Club and share the benefits of membership. Every member receives *Appalachia Bulletin*, the membership magazine that, ten times a year, brings you news about environmental issues and AMC projects, plus listings of outdoor activities, workshops, excursions, and volunteer opportunities. Members also enjoy discounts on AMC books, maps, educational workshops, and guided hikes, as well as reduced fees at all AMC huts and lodges in Massachusetts and New Hampshire. To join today, call 617-523-0636; or write to: AMC, 5 Joy Street, Boston, Massachusetts 02108.

Since it was founded in 1876, the Club has been at the forefront of the environmental protection movement. By cofounding several of New England's leading environmental organizations, and working in coalition with these and many more groups, the AMC has influenced legislation and public opinion.

Volunteers in each chapter lead hundreds of outdoor activities and excursions and offer introductory instruction in back-country sports. The AMC Education Department offers members and the public a wide range of workshops, from introductory camping to the intensive Mountain Leadership School taught on the trails of the White Mountains.

The most recent efforts in the AMC conservation program include river protection, Northern Forest Lands policy, support for the American Heritage Trust, Sterling Forest (NY) preservation, and support for the Clean Air Act.

The AMC's research department focuses on the forces affecting the ecosystem, including ozone levels, acid rain and fog, climate change, rare flora and habitat protection, and air quality and visibility.

The AMC Volunteer Trails Program is active throughout the AMC's twelve chapters and maintains over 1,200 miles of trails, including 350 miles of the Appalachian Trail. Under the supervision of experienced leaders, hundreds of volunteers spend from one afternoon to two weeks working on trail projects.

The Club operates eight alpine huts in the White Mountains that provide shelter, bunks and blankets, and hearty meals for hikers. Pinkham Notch Camp, at the foot of Mount Washington, is base camp to the adventurous and the ideal location for individuals and families new to outdoor recreation. Comfortable bunkrooms, mountain hospitality, and home-cooked, family-style meals make Pinkham Notch Camp a fun and affordable choice for lodging.

At the AMC headquarters in Boston, the bookstore and information center stock the entire line of AMC publications, as well as other trail and river guides, maps, reference materials, and the latest articles on conservation issues. Also available from the bookstore or by subscription is APPALACHIA, the country's oldest mountaineering and conservation journal.

Begin a new adventure— Join the AMC

AMC membership is a great way to start a life-long adventure in the outdoors— and your membership helps protect our open spaces and natural resources for the future.

Join the AMC Today!

The Adventure Begins Here

YES! I want to join the Appalachian Mountain Club!

Name

Address

City   *State*   *ZIP*

Home Phone   *Work*

MEMBERSHIP CATEGORIES

❑ ADULT $40
❑ FAMILY $65

METHOD OF PAYMENT

I enclose $_____   ❑ Check ❑ VISA ❑ MC

CREDIT CARD ACCNT. NUMBER   *EXP. DATE*

Signature

AMC CHAPTERS

The AMC has an active network of regional chapters, from Maine to Washington, D.C. Please indicate your preference:

❑ Please sign me up with my local chapter.
❑ I prefer to be a Member-At-Large.

MAIL YOUR MEMBERSHIP APPLICATION TODAY

Send this form and payment to:

**AMC Membership Office
5 Joy Street, Boston MA 02108
617-523-0636
or use our FAX 617-523-0722**